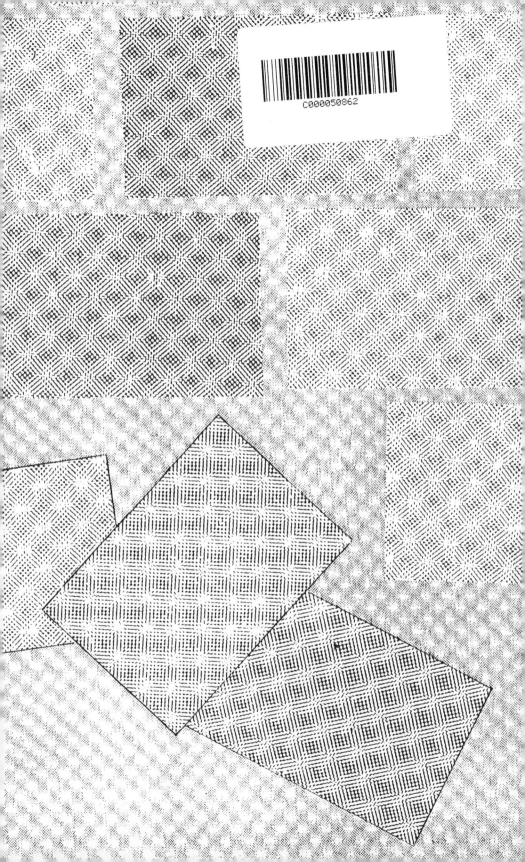

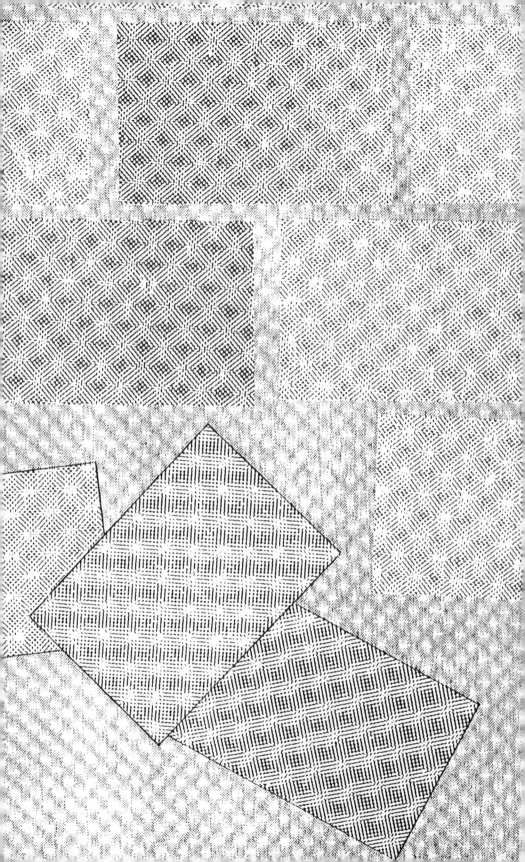

Outside analytic circles one often hears it said that psycho-analysis is only concerned with the individual. The work of the noted Kleinian analyst, Isabel Menzies Lyth, is a powerful answer to that claim. Continuing the themes of *Containing Anxiety in Institutions: Selected Essays* (Volume 1), she reflects here on a variety of social situations: the dynamics of the Fire Brigade, conflicts between psychiatric hospitals and the communities they serve, family patterns of consumption and the unconscious meaning of ice cream. Drawn from work done over the last three decades at London's Tavistock Institute of Human Relations, the collection concludes with a wide-ranging survey of the psychological aftermath of disaster, which makes new links between a Kleinian model of the earliest mental states and both the immediate and longer-term needs of disaster survivors – be it an earthquake or a plane crash. The work is a reminder of the need for a sophisticated psychoanalytic perspective on the social. Its publication confirms that Isabel Menzies Lyth's writings constitute the most important body of psy-choanalytic work on the social bearings of the psyche.

Isabel Menzies Lyth is a Member of the British Psycho-Analytical Society and has combined part-time private practice with consultancy work and many research projects. She lives in Oxford.

The Dynamics
of the Social

Selected Essays

Volume II

By Isabel Menzies Lyth

'*an association in which the free development of each
is the condition of the free development of all*'

Free Association Books / London / 1989

First published in Great Britain 1989 by
Free Association Books
26 Freegrove Road
London N7 9RQ

British Library Cataloguing in Publication Data
Dynamics of the social: selected essays (Volume II)
    1. Social psychology. Applications of psychoanalysis
    302

    ISBN 1-85343-051-X
    ISBN 1-85343-052-8 pbk

Typeset by MC Typeset Ltd, Gillingham, Kent
Printed and bound in Great Britain by
Short Run Press Ltd, Exeter

This first edition of
The Dynamics of the Social
was finished in June 1989

It was typeset in 10/14½ Ehrhardt
on a Linotron 202
and printed on a Miller TP41,
on to 80g/m² vol. 18 book wove.

This book was commissioned by
Robert M. Young, edited by Ann Scott,
copy-edited by Gillian Beaumont,
indexed by Peter Rea,
designed by Carlos Sapochnik with Wendy Millichap and
produced by Martin Klopstock and
Selina O'Grady for Free Association Books.

Contents

Preface and acknowledgements

Choosing and preparing material for this second volume of my selected papers has proved a more formidable task in many ways than choosing for Volume 1*. Selection was made from a large number of papers – most of them, unlike those in Volume 1, not previously published. In a sense, rejection rather than selection was the problem. In selecting for Volume 1, I knew that it was possible that a rejected paper could still appear in Volume 2. Non-selection for Volume 2 means that rejection is final. A few of the rejected papers have appeared elsewhere and are referred to in the complete list of writings in this volume. Many, however, being confidential reports to clients, were never published and now never will be. They are mainly in the archives of the Tavistock Institute of Human Relations, a few in my own files only; some of them could be made available to be read at the Tavistock Institute with the permission of the Tavistock Institute and the author.

I found some of those papers exciting and evocative and would have liked to share them. They include a large number of reports on attitude research surveys of which the ice-cream, chocolate and road-safety papers in this volume are representative. I selected those papers for this volume because of their theoretical interest and also because they are still topical. There are one or two psychoanalytic papers such as 'Pathological aspects of introjection', given originally at the Brazilian Psycho-Analytic Congress in 1982. Many of the papers did not even get

*All references to vol. 1 are to *Containing Anxiety in Institutions: Selected Essays*, Volume 1, by Isabel Menzies Lyth, Free Association Books, 1988.

into typescript, since it is my habit when giving papers to speak from manuscript notes. So I am left to regret not sharing these papers more widely and to mourn their committal to eternal silence.

However, in spite of the missing papers, I think that the two volumes together do exemplify the wide range of areas in which I have worked. I hope they also show that there has been a consistent theoretical and technical orientation throughout the work. This reflects psychoanalytic theory and certain aspects of social science theory, notably field theory and open systems theory. In particular, in all situations where I have worked, anxiety has been a central issue: how anxiety, its experience and expression and the related defences, adaptations and sublimations are a major factor in determining personal and institutional behaviour; anxiety both personal and communal in members of institutions, and anxiety in apparently more isolated individuals such as consumers, individuals, however deeply affected by their immersion in the networks of society and their internalization of that society.

What I think has emerged for me in all this is how often emphasis on the good or exhortations to behave in 'better' ways fail to achieve much positive change, either in institutions or in individuals. Real movement often takes place only when attention is given to dealing with the 'bad', particularly the anxieties and defences that inhibit positive movement.

I hope that evolution in both theory and practice is evident, as my work was influenced by later theoretical developments, notably by Bion's work and by shifts in practice particularly fostered by Tavistock colleagues. I hope also that I have learned from my own experience. I have felt growing assurance in my theoretical background. I can see how these developments enter into my later work and how some earlier elements in theory and practice have declined. Comparing 'The functioning of social systems as a defence against anxiety' (vol. 1, pp. 43–85) with 'The development of the self in children in institutions' (vol. 1, pp. 236–58) shows some greater use of management theory. Similarly, I think my practice became more confident and assured as it became less influenced by orthodox social science methods and more by psychoanalysis. Compare, for example, the initial approach to the work in the general hospital as described in 'The functioning of social systems as a defence against anxiety' (vol. 1, pp. 43–85) and the initial approach to the Royal National Orthopaedic Hospital as described in 'Action research in a long-stay hospital' (vol. 1, pp. 133–52). There the team worked collaboratively and 'therapeutically' with the hospital from the beginning and data was collected gradually in the course of that work.

However, although it is true in a sense that my practice became more confident and assured, there is another sense in which it did not, at least in terms of my subjective experience. Working in the field remained marked by anxiety and uncertainty, living with and tolerating ignorance and submersion in the unknown. If anything, these experiences became more intense and acute as there was an increase in my capacity to bear them and in my awareness of their importance to understanding what was going on in the field. Working in the field continued to be a painful experience which one never felt one fully mastered, but the rewards of trying continued to be great. Some idea of this development may be seen by comparing 'Some methodological notes on a hospital study' in Volume 1 (pp. 115–29) with 'A psychoanalytic perspective on social institutions' in this volume.

As regards the preparation of the papers for Volume 2, much more writing and rewriting has had to be done than for Volume 1, since so many of the papers were originally reports prepared for clients who had sought consultant help and financed the work. These reports were confidential and orientated towards helping clients to deal more effectively with the problems they presented, their own or others', as in the case of the road-safety research. Thus they were not entirely suitable for direct publication and had to be rewritten in whole or in part. This meant some changes in my writing style, which I hope has improved over the years. It has made it possible in some cases to add postscripts giving a more up-to-date commentary on the situations described. With the chronic aversion to writing that I mentioned in Volume 1, it goes without saying that I have not particularly enjoyed doing so much writing. However, I have enjoyed reviewing the work and sometimes thinking how I might set about it differently now. I hope the results are worthwhile. Some repetition of material discussed in Volume 1 has been unavoidable, but I have tried to keep it to a minimum.

To come now more specifically to the papers in Volume 2. The two papers on groups are very personal: 'A personal review of group experiences' was a statement of personal experiences at the time given to a group of students who were just entering the group field. The second, 'Bion's contribution to thinking about groups', was both an attempt to explore Bion's contribution to groups and a personal expression of what I owed to him as consultant to a group of which I was a student member, as my analyst and later as a trusted colleague and friend. 'A psycho-analytic perspective on social institutions' is a condensed though comprehensive statement of my theoretical and practical position at the point where I am preparing to leave 'active service'. Further developments must now be left to successors. This paper shows a great deal of where I came from as well as where I arrived. It has much in common in this sense with 'The aftermath of disaster: survival and loss', which reflects my professional experience in dealing with the mini-disasters in society: hospitalized children, patients in general and mental hospitals, children in day and residential care, often the precipitates of tragic family disturbance. It draws attention to the danger that society turns a blind eye to these mini-disasters while concentrating attention and resources on dramatically devastating disasters. If I could be tempted back to the field, it would be to help deal with persistent mini-disasters and support the services that cope with them and suffer great stress in doing so, among others the police, fire and ambulance services. (A small part of my professional heart remains with the London Fire Brigade.)

The papers included under 'Safety on the roads' and 'Pleasure foods' show something of the way in which the Tavistock Institute approached research in the 1950s. The 'eating' papers, one of which was written with E.L. Trist, were in the commercial field although they contributed to the theoretical paper 'Psychosocial aspects of eating'. The road-safety papers addressed problems in society which were of concern to the government and voluntary bodies who funded the research. The approach to these problems was the same: to get people talking freely, individually or in groups, and to make observations in the field; to try to understand the deeper psychological meaning of this data within the context of relationships in society; then to try to set out the findings in such a way as to expand the client's understanding and help orientate him towards finding a more appropriate way of tackling his problems. Quite a lot of change resulted from these studies. 'Family breakdown in urban communities' has much in common with these papers. The study attempted to find out more about the causes of the increasing rate of family breakdown. The project of which this was a part led ultimately to the setting up of the Family Discussion Bureau within the Tavistock Institute, now the Institute of Marital Studies.

Finally, 'Recruitment into the London Fire Brigade', 'The interaction between Epsom and the five mental hospitals adjoining it', and 'Day care of children under five: an action research study' complete the account of my work in large institutions. In each case, these studies were initiated and funded by the institutions themselves or the authorities concerned, but not a great deal happened directly as a result of them. This highlights a difficulty which I, at least, have not solved: that of bringing about change in a large organization composed of individual smaller units. While one may change one small unit by working in it, how does one affect the others? How does one spread the model?

In preparing Volume 2, I have continued to enjoy the support, encouragement and active help of my editor, Ann Scott of Free Association Books, which I very much appreciate. Margaret Walker of the Tavistock Joint Library and Jill Duncan of the Institute of Psycho-Analysis Library have continued to be extremely helpful in putting the services of their libraries at our disposal. To Margaret Walker my particular thanks for providing most of the information needed to compile the complete list of my writings. Annie Gamble has coped patiently and very efficiently with complicated and often messy manuscripts. Her interest in the work has been a pleasure.

Acknowledgement is due to the following organizations for permission to publish what were originally confidential reports: to the London Fire and Civil Defence Authority for permission to publish 'Recruitment into the London Fire Brigade'; to the South West Thames Regional Hospital Board for permission to publish 'A study of the interaction between Epsom and the five mental hospitals adjoining it'. My thanks are due to A. J. Kember, Regional General Manager, both for arranging for permission to publish this paper and for his postscript to the paper commenting on the present situation in Epsom. Acknowledgement is due to the Tavistock Institute of Human Relations for permission to publish the revised versions of the papers on ice cream, chocolate and safety on the roads. Acknowledgement is due also to the following publishers: to Tavistock Publications for 'A psychoanalytic perspective on social institutions' and 'Family breakdown in urban communities'; to Pergamon Press for permission to publish 'Psychosocial aspects of eating'.

I A personal review of group experiences*

INTRODUCTION

I T SEEMED that perhaps the most useful thing I could do in this paper would be to discuss with you some of my own preoccupations in the hope that these might interest you and perhaps extend your perspectives a little. I should perhaps begin by explaining briefly the background from which I approach groups. The clinical aspect of my approach stems from psychoanalysis and I agree with Bion and Foulkes, who strongly emphasize the importance of psychoanalysis as a background for work with groups (Bion, 1961; Foulkes, 1964). I also agree with their view that it is inappropriate to transfer psychoanalytic models directly to group therapy and that one has to develop different theories and techniques relevant to the group itself. And a long, slow and difficult struggle that is.

Although I have this clinical background, my main work with groups has not been with therapy groups but with the so-called 'training' groups we run at the Tavistock Institute. The difference between the two kinds of group, as far as I am concerned, is more apparent than real. The 'training' I am talking about is, at least in theory, solely the growth of insight and understanding about the self and group processes, leading to personal development. The learning/therapy boundary is ill-defined. My aims and related technique would be the same in both types of group, although the content supplied by members for work would be different.

*This paper was prepared as an introduction to a seminar given to a course in Group Analysis at the Group Analytic Society in London in 1974.

Lastly, I have done much work with groups embedded in institutions and interacting continuously and intimately with each other. This has aroused my interest in the interplay between small groups and the effect of this on the internal dynamics of the groups. These influences are probably least in the group of strangers who come privately for group psycho-therapy to a single doctor in his own consulting room. They are probably most vivid, powerful and explicit at group training conferences of the kind run by the Tavistock Institute and others, temporary institutions which have as their task the study of such processes as they happen (Rice, 1965).

SMALL GROUP THEORY

I shall begin by discussing small groups and return later to intergroup processes and institutions. In preparing this paper I reread the now classic books of Bion and Foulkes, and was very much struck by the considerable degree of agreement between them about the basic approach to understanding and working with groups, even if they had formulated their views in different ways. I will stick to Bion's formulations, with which I am more familiar and have worked over many years, even if my theories and techniques have developed since he wrote his original papers (Bion, 1961).

Technically, the crucial point for me is that one works with group processes and the individual as related to them, and not with the individual separately. Every member is always engaged in the group dynamic, even if he is absent. This is linked with the point made above: that models imported from psycho-analysis directly are not relevant since they are based on a two-person relationship, with group membership held only in the minds of patient and analyst. One should not, therefore, get into the position a colleague described to me once in an early therapeutic group, which evoked in her the fantasy of a circle of analytical couches with the patients being attended to in turn by a psychoanalyst.

My own preferred mode of working with these group pro-cesses would be by interpretation aimed at helping group members to acquire insights and understanding, confront painful truths, extend their knowledge of themselves and their relationships, and so gradually achieve change, ideally development. My interpretations would be focused on what is going on in the here and now, not concerned with the historical, nor the meaning of accounts of outside events except in so far as they help me to understand what is going on now. Finally, my concern would be with the transference, not to be understood, however, in the narrower psychoanalytical sense – that is, the transference to the therapist only – but as including a multiplicity of transference processes between group members. Also I have found, as Bion did, that countertransference can be the crucial clue to what is going on. My own experience, at least, in groups is that I generally undergo more violent and intensive changes in my own feelings and self-perception than I do in individual psychoanalysis and that these feelings, used with caution, are a useful guide. Bion, indeed, states that sometimes they are the only guide.

This rather brief description of one particular style of group psychotherapy impresses me with the enormous difficulty of the task it imposes on the therapist, really far beyond anything that is called for in individual therapy. The complexity of the data one has to handle is obvious. What is perhaps not so immediately obvious is the nature of the data, since groups are inherently so skilled in covering it up – that is, how primitive and disturbing the phenomena exposed in such non-structured groups can be. I will not expand that point here, but will return to it later. It is a very major task, then, for the therapist to keep himself in a state where he is receptive to the phenomena he must work with.

Here I would like to introduce a concept that Bion has developed over the years, mainly from his psychoanalytical work, which I think is, if anything, more important for groups and more difficult to achieve there: what he calls negative capability (Bion, 1970). He takes this concept from a letter of the poet Keats, who says: 'Negative capability – that is, when a man is capable of being in uncertainties, mysteries, doubts, without any irritable reaching after fact and reason.' In the same book Bion makes another related point: the need for the psychoanalyst to rid himself of memory and desire – for example the memory of what patients have previously said or the desire for their welfare. The rationale for this view is again to free the analyst's mind to be receptive to the here and now and in this way to allow the evolution of understanding.

My own experience of working with groups over the years is that it is enormously difficult to sustain such states of mind, since the data is not always welcome, being too great in quantity and too disturbing in quality to be easily comprehended. In so far as I have been able to sustain negative capability and dispense with memory and desire, I have indeed spent long periods in sessions and afterwards in a painful state of not knowing at all what is going on. Since – I hope – my training has helped me to be better at doing this than the ordinary group member, I am frequently the only person present who does not think I know what is going on. Group members tend to produce theories, backed not by evidence but only by false certainty, whose main purpose is to protect members against the pain of uncertainty.

I would now like to return to the theme of the disturbing and primitive phenomena in the groups I am discussing. These phenomena are always present in groups but their operation is usually obscured by structure, by traditions, by various formalities. In the groups of which I speak, structure is minimal though it can never be nonexistent. It consists of the formal role allocation of consultant and group members, the room and seating arrangements, times of meetings, and so on. The purpose of the removal of structure, indeed, is exactly that of exposing the usually hidden and primitive processes for study.

Bion's formulation of the situation is more novel, perhaps, than any other and less directly derivative from psychoanalysis (Bion, 1961). A group is an agglomeration of individuals, and as you know, the argument had gone on for centuries about whether it is more than the sum of the individuals or not. I have never myself understood how it could be more, yet Bion in a way shows how it seems to be more: he shows that the group consists of two distinct sets of aspects of the individual. The first set comprises those aspects of the individual which he is aware of and acknowledges; the second the unacknowledged aspects which are implicitly contributed to a pool which Bion calls group mentality and Foulkes, I think meaning much the same thing, the 'social and interpersonal unconscious'. So the group is more than the acknowledged aspects of individual members, but not more than their totality. This is an important distinction and all of us who work with groups are only too aware of the power of the primitive group mentality unacknowledged by individuals.

THE WORK GROUP

Clearly linked with the acknowledged aspects of individual members – though not, I think, coincidental – is the aspect of a group that Bion calls the work group. The group meets to perform a task: to get therapy, or to learn. In the 'work group' individual members support that task and contribute to it. The consultant has an especial and usually formal responsibility for pursuing the task. The work group has certain important and necessary characteristics. There is, for example, the idea of development in contrast to the idea of 'full equipment by instinct'. There is the idea of a scientific and rational approach. There is belief in the validity of learning by experience. This in turn is linked with belief in things happening over time. The work group also makes use of verbal communication linked with the sophisticated use of symbolism. Thus it is analogous to the concept of the ego in psychoanalytic theory. Individuals appear in the work group in distinctively individual ways, their contributions being idiosyncratic and interactive, sometimes in conflict. The individual may also feel very isolated as he tries to struggle with the task and further its achievement in co-operation with others. The leader of the work group is predominantly, but by no means exclusively, the consultant.

BASIC ASSUMPTION GROUPS

In marked contrast to the work group and linked closely to the group mentality are what Bion called the basic assumption groups. These again are only special aspects of the total agglomeration of individuals. Their characteristics are in general the opposite of the work group's. They have, for example, no real recognition of time and of the activities that require an awareness of time – for example, there is no awareness of a process of development. There is hostility to a rational approach and the use of evidence. There is no learning from experience. Bion also states that what seems to be verbal communication may really be just sound or noise, and that sophisticated use of symbolism is absent. There is loss of individual distinctiveness akin to depersonalization, with the possible exception of the leader of the basic assumption group, who may become only too distinctive in a way that may be very uncomfortable for him. This is linked with a great sense of group cohesiveness, in marked contrast to the struggle in the work group to establish co-operation. This cohesiveness is closely linked to the fact that the group holds the basic assumption in common.

The basic assumption groups, too, have their leaders, who may or may not be actual members of the group and, if members, may or may not be actually present. In theory, the consultant of the group should never be the leader of a basic assumption group, since that is inconsistent with his responsibility for work and could have disastrous consequences. In practice, it is exceedingly difficult for the consultant not to succumb on occasion to what can be enormous group pressure and to take on, at least temporarily, basic assumption leadership. The process of 'election' for basic assumption leadership is a fascinating one and demonstrates the operation of primitive group processes. It demolishes any idea that leaders are leaders, for example, because of their competence, their popularity, or anything like that. In the basic assumption group the leader is often 'elected' by a process of splitting off the unacknowledged facets of other individuals and projecting them into the leader or an idea, agreement being reached rapidly and collusively as to which member or idea it should be. If an individual is 'elected' he is likely to find the natural characteristics which suited him for the job vastly exaggerated by the involuntary acquisition of similar aspects of other members, until his own identity is almost obliterated – a most alarming experience. Such leadership is no honour and no sinecure. He may also find that the group, for a time, makes it impossible for him to 'resign' and he can be 'rescued' only by active interpretation by the consultant leading the work group and trying to gain understanding.

Basic Assumption Dependency

Bion describes three types of basic assumptions, which I shall discuss only briefly since they are already well known. First, basic assumption dependency: that is, a group based on the idea that the group is met to be dependent on their consultant, who will give them material and spiritual nourishment and protection, an assumption particularly prone to develop in both therapy and learning situations where the idea that therapy or learning involves the individual in work and suffering is not necessarily popular. The 'dependent' leader may well be the most ill or the least intelligent or intuitive member of the group, who is pushed forward for the special attention of the consultant. I can remember still the force with which the first group I ever took on my own, a group of university students who had come for training, consistently pushed its most ill member forward for my individual care and attention, and the anger and outrage when I refused to give it. Sometimes the attempt may be to elect the consultant himself to the role; if he accedes, this can be disastrous. Bion quotes the example of the disastrous effects on Egypt of the expensive means used by the Egyptians to protect the 'leader', the pharaoh, and therefore themselves against anxiety about the pharaoh's death.

Basic Assumption Pairing

The second basic assumption groups may make is 'pairing'. In group dynamic terms the group seems to be in agreement that all other members will allow a pair of members to monopolize the conversation while the others form an audience. As Bion says, this situation is characterized by hopefulness and expectation, connected with the idea that all will be well in the future even if not now. A person or an idea to come in the future will resolve all problems. Bion relates this feeling to a Messiah or a messianic hope which must never come to fruition because then it cannot in reality meet the hope or expectation. Again there may well be attempts to entice or control the consultant into being one of the pair, God with the Virgin Mary to produce Christ yet again, a group situation that may not be too easy to distinguish in practice from basic assumption dependency, with God looking after the Virgin. The difference would be in atmosphere. If basic assumption dependency were in operation the group would be characterized by anxiety and feelings of need; if basic assumption pairing were in operation, by hope and expectation.

Basic Assumption Fight or Flight

The third basic assumption is basic assumption fight or flight. Bion states that the group assumes that it is met to fight something or to run away from something, and is quite prepared to do either indiscriminately. The consultant and the work group, trying to understand what is going on if basic assumption fight or flight is in operation, are constantly attacked by such things as anti-psychological views, hatred of psychological difficulties and attempts to evade problems. Such a situation may only too easily involve the consultant himself in fight or flight. As he sees things and people he cares for attacked, he may be trapped in fighting to defend them. That is 'fight' also, although it is defensive, or it is flight, too, that is a desertion of the work and understanding which it is his responsibility to support.

This brings me to a point which has long fascinated me and which I think is of great importance for the group therapist and others who work with groups: one's own personal preference for basic assumption as an essential feature of one's personality, which affects one's work whether one is analysed or not. This means that groups may be influenced not only by the membership but also by their consultant towards particular basic assumptions rather than others. It is important to try to assess one's own particular 'favourite' and to be wary of being trapped in that with the members of one's groups.

Over the years I have learned to know and be prepared for the particular preferences of close colleagues with whom I have worked. Some have groups that show predominately fight or flight, with the consultant fighting back to defend what is precious to him and describing his group to staff meetings in terms of hatred and disregard for work. Others favour dependency. They have quiet, peaceful groups which attend assiduously to what the consultant says and are usually described in staff meetings as 'working very well'. I have learned to be suspicious of that comment. Others favour pairing, establishing a strong relationship with a particular group member. They talk in staff meetings of what a good person that member is, how insightful, how hardworking, how he supports the consultant with his work.

Like all other consultants I have had my private struggles with this problem. In my less experienced days it was only too easy for me to be drawn into basic assumption fight or flight, being distracted from work to fight in defence of what I thought I stood for: work towards understanding. My behaviour in fighting was also anti-work. I rarely get trapped in that one now. I am tempted by the apparently helpful member who pairs with me. But I think now my basic problem would be much more in being enticed into dependency, not only because I am feminine and a psychoanalyst, which might predispose me to that position, but for another reason more related to groups themselves. Bion makes a point about all basic assumption groups: they do not really listen – that is, understand. I agree with this point; but would add another: there is also the question as to whether they hear.

The dependent group is quiet and all agog for the words of wisdom it expects from the consultant. Therefore, the work group coexistent with it has the opportunity to listen and interpretations are more effective. By contrast, when a group is in basic assumption fight/flight, the group is likely to be very noisy and the coexistent work group is frequently unable to hear the consultant's or anyone else's contributions to work, or to be influenced by them. I well remember a rather large group I had in an intergroup exercise, where I would be prepared to swear that not a single interpretation I made was ever heard, let alone listened to! The temptation to try and fight back by shouting myself against the din was, as you may imagine, not always resistible. Anyway, nowadays my groups are much quieter and, on the whole, show much less of the disarray that goes with fight/flight.

RELATION OF WORK GROUP TO BASIC ASSUMPTION GROUP
Now, ideally at least, in the group that persists the work group

9

function is always to some extent sustained, but the basic assumption groups that always function alongside the work group tend to present a kaleidoscopic picture. They are by nature unstable and always changing, so that one has to be perpetually on the alert for the changes and the particular way in which they are interfering with or sometimes supporting the work group. The reasons for the changes are manifold. For me, a major factor in these changes is that they are an unreal or even magical attempt at achieving objectives or solving problems, and are therefore doomed to failure. They inevitably generate frustration. In general, the basic assumption groups are so linked to early intense primitive anxiety situations and distinctly psychotic phenomena that the group is compelled to take defensive action, by escape into another assumption or even back to the work group. The loss of individual distinctiveness, for example, becomes threatening to the identity of the individual, and he seeks to escape from this situation. Each basic assumption also generates its own special problems that individuals find irksome. The fight/flight group is characterized by a lack of care and concern for the individual, which may become intolerable. The dependent group is likely to release intolerable envy, jealousy, deprivation and rivalry with the dependent leader who is getting all the attention. Pairing is too uncomfortably close to early oedipal anxieties.

Bion stresses very forcefully in his descriptions the psychotic quality of the basic assumption phenomena in groups and the need to give them careful interpretative attention if the work group is to be sustained, and insight and development to take place.

THE INSTITUTIONAL CONTEXT

I would like now to change my frame of reference somewhat to give more attention to other aspects of the small group: the institutional context in which it exists, the effect of this on what goes on within the small group itself, the use the group makes of its environment, and how the group is used by it.

The Permeability of Group Boundaries

The first topic I would like to discuss is the permeability of group boundaries and the relation of that to the here and now as developed and interpreted in the group. I commented above about the importation, into any group, of the other group memberships of the individual members, and indeed of the consultant. However, I think that the quality of importation differs between group members who are strangers and import private other memberships, and between members who mutually belong to the same other groups or belong jointly to an institution within which a variety of other group memberships is sustained. This gives rise to an enormous intensity and complexity in the 'other-group-membership' importation to a group – even more so when the consultant is also perceived to be a member of the institution and of other groups of his own within the institution: for example, the staff or management group.

The most vivid experiences I have had of the phenomena arising in a group embedded in an institution have been at the Tavistock–Leicester conferences, where the fact that the work task is to study group processes highlights this dynamic (Rice, 1965). But these are also everyday features of all institutions, and are of great importance if one is doing group psychotherapy within a psychiatric institution.

In such circumstances, how does one define the 'here and now' in one's own small group? How does one work with the shared experiences members have of other groups and the institution, and the consultant's other roles? This is, I think, to some extent an unresolved issue between myself and immediate colleagues working in this field. Some take a very narrow view and tend to regard these groups as being engaged in work in the 'here and now' only when they are engaged in discussion of their own internal group processes, narrowly interpreted. They tend to interpret comments on other situations as within the flight basic assumption. I myself have moved a long way from that position, taking a much wider and more liberal view of the 'here and now'. Initially I regard everything that is brought into the group in the minds of members as in the 'here and now', and in the institutional setting a great deal of what is in the minds of members, and sometimes shared between them, stems from their joint membership of the institution, and from joint and separate membership of other groups within it.

While I regard it as possible that a group talking of an outside-the-group experience is in flight from its immediate problems, I certainly do not regard this as inevitable. Important intra-group dynamics may be expressed in such communications. Relationships in other situations affect relationships in the small groups, are active there, and are therefore part of the 'here and now' and need to be worked with there if development is to continue. For example, multigroup membership in an institution raises questions of primary belongingness and loyalty. Members who have achieved some feeling of intimacy and togetherness in a small group may find themselves estranged and in conflict elsewhere, and the effect of this on the small group needs to be worked out there. This is particularly evident in the Leicester conferences, where small-group members who find themselves belonging to different groups, and are often in active conflict with each other carry the scars of that conflict back into the small group with them.

Likewise the transference to the group consultant may be greatly complicated by the fact that he is known to have relationships with other staff as well as with other members. The behaviour of the other staff, either alone or directly in relation to the consultant, and fantasies about these relationships, then become an active ingredient of the transference. For example, a conference director behaved in a plenary session in an aggressive way that greatly upset conference members. Privately, it upset me too, although I did not disclose this to my group and hope I was able to keep it out of the work with them. The group's fairly well-developed confidence in my performance as a consultant was greatly disrupted by this event. How could I participate in this institution with such an aggressive director was a summary of the problem. I considered it necessary and enlightening for the group to do a great deal of work with this problem. It is of the essence of institutional life.

On another occasion I was seen by some members of my group to depart before some free time with another small-group consultant – male. The following session was opened by a zoologist in the group giving an account of the sex life of beetles, listened to and encouraged with unusual interest by the other members. Again it seemed to me important to work with both the sexual fantasies about staff and the denigration of staff thus expressed – important to the learning both about the sexual aspects of life in mixed-sex institutions and about envious and denigrating attacks on figures in authority. In other words, I regarded the group boundary in that situation as extremely permeable, and considered it definitely a part of the group's work to study the repercussions within the group of this permeability: to study what came through the boundary from total institutional membership and from membership of other groups within the institution.

There is another reason why I regard this as important. In the institutional setting, the small group concerned with the task of studying itself, whether for psychotherapy or training, is very often the situation which represents the best – or even the only – opportunity for really quiet, reflective group thinking because of its comparative peace and encapsulation. At the Leicester conferences certainly, the other group situations are generally more characterized by action and less by thought, and by a great deal of 'noise' in the system, which is disruptive to thought. The same, I think, is true of other institutions. The small group, therefore, is needed to work through still active and unresolved input from other situations which, because it is not resolved there, is dynamically present in the small group itself.

Intergroup Processes

Another important aspect of small groups within institutions is the interactions between them and their use of each other. I think there was a time when we (my colleagues and I) might have regarded small groups in an institution as more or less encapsulated within their own boundaries. I would certainly no longer do so. The members of the small groups interact with each other between sessions and enter into all kinds of collusions, often unconsciously and in basic assumption ways, that are then fed back into the small-group meetings and affect the dynamics of the small groups themselves.

For example, small groups develop very distinctive characteristics, not wholly consistent with the individual characteristics of their members, by splitting off and projecting into other groups characteristics of their own that they do not want to have to deal with in their small groups. They also receive and act on projections from other groups. One group may acquire a reputation for quiet and constructive work, while another is notoriously aggressive and difficult, its consultant in despair about getting any work done. Careful investigation will show that the first group is projecting its anti-task attitudes and hostility to staff as represented by its consultant into the second group, thus freeing itself for work but greatly increasing the difficulties of the members and consultant in the second group. It is obviously important for both groups to track down and undo these projections and their resulting introjections.

What may also be important here are the preferences of the consultants themselves for basic assumptions which are often intuitively recognized and used by members. I have already stated my own preference for groups which are predominantly characterized by basic assumption dependency. I have had repeated experiences at Leicester conferences when my group was of the quiet, constructive variety while the group of a particular colleague was always noisy, aggressive and hostile to him, and he was in despair. I can only conclude that he preferred fight/flight, and that our groups were perfectly well aware of our preferences and used them in mutual collusive interaction with each other and with us.

Part of the task, therefore, seems to be to work out such mutually collusive intergroup processes as one sees them reflected in one's small group, since real work cannot be done in one's group if important aspects of it are being split off and lodged elsewhere in another group where in reality they cannot be effectively worked through. One may, therefore, have to engage actively in searching for and retrieving projected aspects of one's group, as well as dealing with the imports from outside made by other groups' projections into one's own group, if one is to make the most of learning or therapy situations.

THE SIGNIFICANCE OF THESE PHENOMENA
IN INSTITUTIONS

The Leicester conferences, where I have learned so much about these processes, are of course, so far as the members are concerned, a temporary institution. However, similar processes are at work in permanent institutions where they may become reified as integral features of institutional life: for example, in the hierarchical structure, the culture and traditions, and the mode of operating of the institution itself. Such devices are a part of what Jaques has called the 'socially structured defence system' of the institution (Jaques, 1955). They can be seen as defences built by members into the institution as a means of dealing with their anxieties, especially those stemming from deep psychotic levels in the personality and evoked by group and institutional membership itself.

These socially structured defences are in operation in all institutions but I think they are perhaps most obvious in certain kinds of institutions: those whose function – that is, primary or work task – is in reality closely related to Bion's basic assumptions. The community at large splits off and projects, or delegates to specialized institutions, the task of dealing with dependency needs, fighting or pairing. Bion quotes the Church as an example of a specialist institution to deal with dependency, the army with fighting, and the aristocracy with pairing and the messianic hope. The point about such institutions is that they are in consequence particularly liable to suffer in their functioning from the operation of basic assumption phenomena, and find it particularly difficult to mobilize as a work group for the performance of the specialist task.

The institutions that deal with split-off dependency with which I am personally most familiar are hospitals, and I imagine they are also those with which many people are most familiar. In my experience, hospitals' structure, traditions and mode of functioning are pervaded by the kinds of phenomena that one finds in basic assumption groups, and in particular those of basic assumption dependency. Primitive psychological phenomena are rife, and the socially structured defence system is based on the most primitive psychological defences.

This became very clear to me when I engaged in consultancy with the nursing service of a large general teaching hospital, helping to improve the functioning of the nursing service (Menzies, 1960; vol. 1, pp. 43–85 gives a full discussion of this work). Very striking, for example, was a phenomenon described as typical of basic assumption groups: loss of individuality or depersonalization, affecting both nurses and patients. There was a marked tendency, for example, to refer to patients not by their names, which contained their individuality, but by a bed number, an illness or a damaged part of the body. This implied that the patient was no longer a whole person who needed care but a part-object only, the retreat into part-objects being another feature Bion attributes to basic assumption group phenomena. The dynamic seemed a massive protection for the nurses against the pain, anxiety and responsibility of confronting the totality of the patient, his emotional distress as well as his physical condition. An interesting fact here is that when one talked to the nurses as individuals away from their nursing groups they deplored this practice, but in their basic-assumption-laden working groups they were trapped by it and relatively powerless against it.

The nurses also were stripped of their individuality. Each main grade of nurse had an absolutely standard uniform which increased the difficulty of telling them apart. The nurses used to argue that they needed protective clothing. We agreed, but challenged the view that this meant uniformity. The 'protection' afforded by the uniform was more psychological than physical. The 'uniformity' was extended by the practice of assigning responsibilities and tasks uniformly to whole grades of nurses rather than to individual nurses according to individual capacities and skills. This again had a protective function in that decisions about allocation of work could be avoided. It was totally prescribed and consequently doubts and uncertainties about decisions and the possibility of mistakes could be avoided.

Very interesting basic assumption phenomena were also apparent between groups, the main mechanisms employed being denial, splitting and projective identification. We became interested in the way different grades of nurses talked about themselves and each other. Each grade talked of all of her own grade as responsible, of grades below that as irresponsible, and of grades above them as unnecessarily harsh disciplinarians. Note again that there was no differentiation of individuals within grades. It was 'all nurses in that grade'. Such talking rarely produced any evidence for these views – again typical of basic assumption phenomena. What we felt we had exposed here was a massive social defence system designed to protect the nurses against each individual's painful conflicts about the heavy responsibility of her task, often regarded exaggeratedly as life or death; the conflict between her own genuine sense of responsibility for her tasks and her wishes to escape or evade these tasks when they became too burdensome. So each grade split off and projected into lower grades its own unacknowledged irresponsibility, and honestly but incorrectly described them as irresponsible. Each grade retained and acknowledged a high sense of responsibility and felt responsible. Each grade projected upwards in the hierarchy the harsh, primitive superego stemming from primitive basic assumption levels in order to be rid of its persecution, and genuinely felt supervisors to be too harsh.

There was a tendency, of course, for people to act according to the projected images they introjected. The pressures on them to do so were very great – pressures with which one is indeed very familiar as a group consultant. We were interested to hear the lowest grade of nurses 'confess' that they were irresponsible, adding: 'Everyone expects it of us.'

Another interesting example of basic assumption phenomena in nursing is considerable disbelief in development through training, combined with belief in being born like that. Statements are made such as 'Good nurses are born, not made' or 'Nursing is a vocation'. These imply that nurses are born with something which makes them good nurses almost by instinct and that all that has to be done to train them, therefore, is to give them the necessary skills and practice. The idea of personal development into a professional role is largely missing. Nurse training contains little provision for this kind of personal maturation.

A final example illustrates a lack in the nursing service of a scientific or rational approach to problems based on the collection and use of evidence. We had been asked to help the nursing service deal with a particular problem (the details are not important). One of the first things we discovered was that although all the necessary facts were indeed available in the hospital, no one had actually collected them together and assessed them as a basis for action. The nursing staff concerned struggled on with the problem in a persecuted, confused and hopeless state, and in a rapidly deteriorating work situation.

CONCLUSION

I feel I should end by apologizing – this paper has turned out to be something of a series of disconnected themes around the small group rather than necessarily about it. But I hope that it has given some entry into the thinking of one group consultant, and that it will prove useful to you in developing your own work.

2 Bion's contribution to thinking about groups*

I HAVE FOUND it unexpectedly difficult to separate Bion's work in groups from his work in psychoanalysis. The consistency is more striking than the difference: the development is continuous, not disparate. His relationship with psychoanalysis began in the 1930s and continued throughout his work with groups in the army and later. The two areas of his work seemed to grow closer and to have an even more creative interaction when he went into analysis with Melanie Klein and found her theory and practice so enlightening. Still, it was through his work in groups that his thinking first began to have an impact on a wider audience with his papers in *Human Relations* (Bion, 1948–51), later republished in *Experiences in Groups* (Bion, 1961). These made clear his extraordinary clinical acumen. Many people have remarked on his superb powers of observation, but in some ways that seems an understatement. His observation was backed by an equally striking capacity to make sense of his observations. As we know, it is almost impossible to make 'pure' observations, a fact of which Bion himself was only too well aware. It was the 'mix' in Bion that was so extraordinary.

A companion point about his work is perhaps less familiar and would be most obvious to a member of one of his groups: his remarkable capacity to be observed. His papers show that he was aware of being under constant scrutiny and that he experienced considerable turmoil, the effect of massive projection by the

*Read at a memorial meeting for Dr Wilfred Bion held by the British Psycho-Analytical Society, 20 February 1980.

group, his own doubts and uncertainties, the pain of waiting for insight to evolve, the frequent unwelcomeness of his interpretations. He remained apparently unmoved and imperturbable. His colleague and friend A. K. Rice said of him: 'Bion can sit farther behind his own face than any other man I know.' This was an invaluable asset to the clinician in groups, giving the group freedom to pursue its own course uncontaminated by inappropriate messages from the leader. Those of us who have tried to emulate him know how difficult this is.

I will now discuss some points about Bion's work with groups which, for me, are definitive. First, his insistence on the use of the group *per se*, the dynamics of the group in the here and now, as the instrument of therapy and learning. Group therapy, he said, should not be a debased form of psychoanalysis. It is essentially different. Reflections of this can be seen in his group papers, where he uses language and concepts specific to groups, although acknowledging his debt to Kleinian theory. And the reader can himself make the links – noting, for example, the constant operation of projective identification. It is only in 'Group dynamics: a re-view' (Bion, 1952) that he makes explicit the close connection between his group theories and Kleinian theory.

His insistence on the use of the group *per se* was critical at a time when other workers were either not of the same opinion or were less skilled or determined in practising it. There was a good deal of debased psychoanalysis, as I know from experience. But the use of the group *per se* is the true derivative of psychoanalysis. I suspect that this view has not yet been fully accepted in group work or in therapeutic communities, which only too often fail to make appropriate use of the group or community as the therapeutic instrument, viewing the individual and his disturbance in isolation rather than as a nodal point in a group dynamic, both contributing to and reflecting group tensions. One may compare Bion's own use of the community in the Northfield Experiment (Bion, 1961).

My second point concerns his elucidation of the psychotic elements in groups. Previous references to psychotic group behaviour had almost exclusively described gross phenomena, akin to diagnostically psychotic disorders. The subtlety of Bion's intuition was in pinpointing the less obvious but immensely powerful psychotic phenomena that appear in groups that are apparently behaving sanely, if a little strangely – groups that are working more or less effectively and whose members are clinically normal or neurotic. He described clusters of these psychotic phenomena as the three basic assumptions in groups about how to achieve their objectives: the basic assumptions of dependency, fight/flight and pairing. They have in common massive splitting and projective identification, loss of individual distinctiveness or depersonalization, diminution of effective contact with reality, lack of belief in progress and development through work and suffering. Once one's eyes have been opened, one cannot but be impressed by those aspects of groups and institutions whose individual members are sophisticated, intelligent and capable of learning from experience. They are reminiscent of Melanie Klein's descriptions of the infantile psychotic positions. Bion himself compares them, saying:

> The adult must establish contact with the emotional life of the group in which he lives; this task would appear to be as formidable to the adult as the relationship to the breast appears to be to the infant, and the failure to meet the demands of this task is revealed in his regression. (Bion, 1952)

Thirdly, Bion regards the human being as essentially a group or political animal. He says that the human being is a group animal, at war both with the group and with those aspects of his own personality that constitute his 'groupishness'. Yet he cannot exist without groups, even if it be only the group he asserts he does not belong to or the internal group with which the solitary individual is in a dynamic relationship. Bion regards individual and group psychology as different ways of looking at the same phenomenon, group psychology illuminating aspects of the individual that may seem alien to individual psychology. He makes many references to this duality and the dilemma it creates for the individual. These clearly demonstrate his humanity, his sympathy, tolerance and compassion for the human being in his dilemma.

The last point in my list is more general. It concerns the quality of the man, his wisdom and erudition combined with his capacity for speculative and creative thinking and his perception of the relevance of findings in one situation for others. He carries his insights from groups and psychoanalysis into an incredible variety of other areas: many in which he was well read and knowledgeable, others in which he capitalized on personal experiences. These include religion, the army, the Church, the aristocracy and economics. His remarks about monetary systems now seem prophetic in our society, dominated as it is by primitive group phenomena, the anti-work basic assumptions of dependency, fighting and pairing – a society whose monetary system seems to be going mad.

This picks up another quality shown in Bion's writing and in personal contact. His work on groups has often been described as seminal. It is evocative and inspiring, albeit also often shocking and hard to assimilate. Bion's work has been carried farther and into many other areas by other creative thinkers and men of action. One discovers and rediscovers his findings in one's own work. This seems to stem partly from the generous way he shared his pioneering struggles with groups. He knew what we would experience because he experienced it himself, even if he made more of his experience than we can, thus helping us, however, to make more of ours. If one tries to follow him, there is no let-up. Like Freud, he knew that the task of being a psychoanalyst or a group leader is no easy one. It demands constant training and vigilance and the ability to stay with ignorance and uncertainty 'without any irritable reaching after fact and reason' (Keats, cited by Bion, 1970). Every fresh discovery leads to further awareness of ignorance and the need to continue the painful search. We follow him at our peril. But if one *can* be in touch with his thinking, one also fails to follow him at one's peril.

People often ask why Bion gave up working with groups to concentrate on psychoanalysis. He replies in *The Dawn of Oblivion* (1979): 'I had more pressing problems which could be adequately dealt with only by psychoanalysis – or something better' – that is, pushing further and further into the primitive in the individual. He seemed compelled by these problems and his work on them has certainly contributed to making psychoanalysis 'something better'.

But Bion did not entirely give up groups. He followed up in psychoanalysis some of his group findings, notably the importance in normal and neurotic individuals of the psychotic elements and the need to deal with them in psychoanalysis or in the group. There are many references to groups in his psychoanalytical writings that imply there is more work to be done. When he writes about groups again at length and in depth much later in *Attention and Interpretation* (1970) the continuing development of his theories is clear. His presentation of group theory here is not, however, intended for use basically as such but as a 'fable, constructed in terms of the group' to be regarded as 'a dramatized, personified, socialized, and pictorialized representation of the human personality'. He brings psychoanalysis and group theory close indeed here. He is concerned with the processes of change, the way the creative idea is handled and what may happen to it, our need for it if vitality and growth are to be sustained, and our fear of disruption by it, change being experienced as catastrophic.

I will conclude by discussing what he says about groups in this context, because it demonstrates the development in his thinking, because it seems to stem from his personal experiences – at times it seems almost autobiographical – and because it now relates to his future. I select only one aspect: his exploration in various contexts of the relationship between three entities – the genius, mystic or Messiah, the group and the Establishment. The mystic produces the creative idea, scientific, artistic or religious. The group needs the mystic, 'a continued supply of genius' (Bion, 1970) if it is to remain vital and grow. The mystic needs the group to provide conditions in which his genius can flourish and be propagated. But the relation between them is fraught with hazards; the mystic is always potentially disruptive to the group, whether he is a declared revolutionary or not. Inevitably his contribution challenges the existing state of the group and its coherence and seems to threaten catastrophe. This arouses tensions and emotional drives appropriate to the primitive group which are directed to destroying the mystic and preserving group coherence at all costs, even at the cost of growth and vitality.

The resolution of this dilemma is crucial for the mystic *and* the group and brings in the Establishment, the subgroup that exercises power, responsibility and containment on behalf of the group. Ideally, the Establishment should manage the situation in a way Bion describes as 'symbiotic'. This implies both hostility and benevolence: the mystic's ideas are subjected to a critical scrutiny which benefits both mystic and group. The Establishment can then develop laws or techniques that help the ordinary member to use the mystic's ideas. The alternative relationship Bion calls 'parasitic': mystic and group destroy each other – 'Even friendliness is deadly.' The Establishment may promote the mystic to a position which deflects him from his creative and destructive role and absorbs him in administration. Bion writes him an epitaph: 'He was loaded with honours and sank without a trace' (Bion, 1970). Or the Establishment may try to deny the mystic a place in society where he can deploy his powers.

This configuration is universal and Bion gives convincing examples of its appearance in groups and in the psychoanalysis of the individual. We need look no further than our own society to find repeated occurrences of the pattern. The hazards are daunting, but Bion is hopeful. Truth will ultimately triumph, and though truth may not give much consolation, it makes for growth. The forces in the group orientated to growth and development will also ultimately triumph through work, despite the hindrance of basic assumption phenomena, and although it may take a long time.

Bion experienced this personally. After six weeks of exciting work in the Northfield Experiment, he was removed from his post. The creative idea did not die. He continued his work in War Office Selection Boards and at the Tavistock Clinic and Institute, and it was taken up by many others. Speculating, I have wondered how far the danger of being made 'respectable' influenced his decision to leave London. He had been successively the Director of the London Clinic of Psycho-Analysis, the President of the British Psycho-Analytical Society and a member of its Training Committee. The hazards were perhaps greater for Bion than for some mystics, since his understanding of group processes contributed to his flair for that kind of role.

What of the future? The tasks and the problems remain with us. The death of the mystic does not necessarily end his creative and destructive influence, as Bion vividly describes in relation to both the religious mystic and the scientist. The need continues for the symbiotic relationship to facilitate critical scrutiny of his work, to develop ways in which it can be used by more ordinary workers, and to foster conditions for the 'continued supply of genius' in psychoanalysis and group work.

3 A psychoanalytic perspective on social institutions*

PSYCHOANALYSTS have been interested in society and its institutions ever since there were psychoanalysts. Freud himself set the pattern, as appears in a number of papers, notably *Totem and Taboo* (Freud, 1913). However, these early contributions were mainly by armchair scientists and not yet by practitioners. Fenichel wrote that social institutions arise through the efforts of human beings to satisfy their needs, but then become external realities comparatively independent of individuals that nevertheless affect the structure of the individual (Fenichel, 1946). This is a profound remark and stresses two elements that have been amply demonstrated in institutional practice. Institutions, once established, may be extremely difficult to change in their essentials and they do actually modify the personality structure of their members, temporarily or permanently. Indeed, to change the members one may first need to change the institution.

Later the situation changed, much stimulated by the Second World War when new institutions were needed to support the war effort. Significant developments came from two converging directions – from psychoanalysts and psychiatrists of a similar dynamic orientation who ventured into the field of institution-building and extended their skills, and from social scientists who became increasingly aware of the value of psychoanalytic insights in their work. This was a powerful partnership. It has continued, involving in particular psychoanalysts with a social

*Revised version of a paper read in the Freud Memorial Lectureship series, University College, London, 20 October 1986.

science background and social scientists who have added a psychoanalytic element to their practice by long personal analysis and extensive study. So the psychoanalytic perspective implies psychoanalysis *per se* and not only psychoanalysts.

The psychoanalytic view of groups and institutions owes much to early pioneers in group work like Bion and Foulkes (Bion, 1961; Foulkes, 1948). They began the important task of bridge-building between psychoanalysis and groups and institutions. Other notable contributors are psychoanalysts like Elliott Jaques and social scientists like E.L. Trist, A.K. Rice, E.J. Miller and A. Bain. It is invidious to mention names, but these people have most influenced my own theory and practice.

Bion emphasizes how difficult it is for human beings to relate to each other in a realistic way in a joint task (Bion, 1961). He describes the human being as a group animal: as such he cannot get on *without* other human beings. Unfortunately, he cannot get on very well *with* them either. Yet he must establish effective co-operation in life's tasks. This is his dilemma. Understanding his attempts at solving this dilemma, at evading it or defending himself against the anxieties it arouses, are central to the understanding of groups and institutions, since these attempts become permanent features of institutions. Such understanding is central also to practice orientated to helping institutions and their members to solve the dilemma more effectively and function better.

My title covers a vast topic. I have decided, therefore, to limit myself mainly to the contribution of psychoanalysis to institutional practice, usually called consultancy: to practice – as in psychoanalytic practice – orientated to facilitating change for the benefit, ideally, of the client. I will now try to set out the main ways in which derivatives from or parallels to psychoanalytic practice appear in psychoanalytically orientated institutional consultancy.

Most important is a deep conviction about the existence of the unconscious, of a kind that most easily comes through having an analysis oneself. This was how it came to Freud as he pursued the difficult course of his self-analysis. A useful alternative experience is an intensive and lengthy membership of a group where the work is based on psychoanalytic principles as applied to group phenomena and directed towards increasing insight into group processes. There is no harm in having both. They are different and complementary, the latter leading more directly into work with institutions.

Such experience develops the capacity to recognize and understand the manifestations of the unconscious mind, both content and dynamics, in the conscious thoughts, feelings, speech and behaviour of the people one is working with – and in oneself. One also learns to recognize its presence in the institution itself. In institutions, significant elements of both content and dynamics are likely to be held in common by members, derived from a shared external situation and possibly common internal situations, through conscious and unconscious collusive interaction between them. I have described elsewhere how the external realities of nursing stimulate powerful anxieties in all nurses to do with unconscious phantasies of ill, injured, dying and dead people (Menzies, 1970a; vol. 1, pp. 43–85).

In institutional practice such understanding is extremely useful in orientating oneself to the nature of the situation. It is fairly unlikely, however, that one would interpret it directly to the client, as a psychoanalyst might to a patient. I cannot imagine that Trist and Bamforth took up with the coal-miners they worked with some of the cruder interpretations one hears about what the miners are doing, such as tearing out the contents of their mothers' insides (Trist and Bamforth, 1951). True or not, such interpretations are irrelevant, an insult or assault. Perhaps more important than content in any case are the dynamic processes that go on in institutions at both conscious and unconscious levels. Of particular significance are the defences developed to deal with anxiety-provoking content and the difficulties in collaborating to accomplish the common task. These defences appear in the structure of the institution itself and permeate its whole way of functioning.

It is obvious that people do not say what they really mean even when they honestly and sincerely say what they consciously think, let alone when they do not. Neither patients nor clients are likely to be absolutely sincere and honest, although they become increasingly so if work is going well and trust in the analyst or consultant is growing. In the institutional setting it is not always unconscious thoughts and feelings one needs to understand, but also the implicit: what is not being said. Thoughts conscious in some people, or even shared in twos and threes, are not openly shared with everyone in a work situation where they could be realistically and constructively used. A manager said of a meeting with others at the same level that they had been able to say things to each other that previously they had been able to say only to friends in private. He commented on how valuable that had been.

Bain (1982) gives a good example of this kind of thing. In the initial stages of his work in Baric, a computer processing company, he heard a great deal about what operators felt was wrong with their life at work and the action necessary to put it right: for example, more flexible hours, being allowed to chat as they might in an office job, free tea and coffee, and so on. Little was said at first about experiences in the job itself. Bain was not convinced that these complaints were really the substance of the matter. He felt there must be something more basic and significant concerning the job and job-centred experiences. It seemed this had somehow got out of focus, so that while the workers felt intuitively that there was something wrong with the job, they could not at first formulate it.

With Bain's help they became increasingly able to focus on the job itself and their experience of it. A rather terrible picture emerged: loss of the sense of self or fears of this, loss of awareness of what was going on although they continued to function, feeling like an automaton or like the machine they worked on, irritation, boredom, alienation, depersonalization. This account was more convincing and suggested that action to ameliorate matters needed to be directed at the work situation itself and not – or not only – at the fringe benefits. It is, unfortunately, only too common for situations of the kind Bain describes to develop in institutions, large and small, with a failure to diagnose the real nature of the problem. Remedies of the kind at first requested by the Baric operators are then instituted. Their beneficial effect is quite likely to be slight and disappointment considerable. Sadly, this process may be repetitive. The ineffectual remedies may be tried time and time again with only minor modifications, leaving the core problem virtually untouched.

I think what may be happening is something like this. There is within the job situation a focus of deep anxiety and distress. Associated with this there is despair about being able to improve matters. The defensive system collusively set up against these feelings consists, first, in fragmentation of the core problem so that it no longer exists in an integrated and recognizable form consciously and openly among those concerned. Secondly, the fragments are projected on to aspects of the ambience of the job situation which are then consciously and honestly, but mistakenly, experienced as the problem about which something needs to be done, usually by someone else. Responsibility has also been fragmented and often projected into unknown others – 'Them', the authorities. One meets this same process frequently in psychoanalysis when a patient feels himself to be up against an intractable problem and believes he cannot manage the feelings associated with it. Such defensive reactions to institutional problems often mean the institution cannot really learn. The solutions tried before had failed, but they will work this time – as though there is a kind of magic about them. Effective resolution can come only when the institution, with or without the help of a consultant, can address itself to the heart of the matter and not only to its ambience, and introduce relevant changes there.

The relation of the consultant to the client institution that facilitates the elucidation of such situations strikingly resembles Freud's recommendations about the way the psychoanalyst may best gain access to his patient's mind (Freud, 1911–15). I recently found the following statement which puts forward a view very close to my own. It is from a review by Almansi of a book by Wallace, *Freud and Anthropology* (Almansi, 1986) and it says: 'All in all, Wallace believes that Freud's most valuable gift to anthropology was the clinical method of psychoanalysis itself and the unequalled insights it provides.'

Freud recommends 'evenly suspended attention', not directing one's attention to anything in particular, not making a premature selection or prejudgement about what is significant, which might distract one's attention from whatever *might turn out to be* the most significant feature. If one can hold to this attitude, something will – one hopes – evolve that begins to clarify the meaning of what the patient is showing the analyst. Bion takes Freud's advice seriously and has developed the point further (Bion, 1970). He recommends eschewing memory and desire, not consciously summoning up memories about the patient or what has previously happened; or previous understanding about the patient, desires for him or for the progress of the analysis; or for that matter for oneself. These would also interfere with the evenly suspended attention needed to be in touch with the patient and the evolution of meaning.

Bain also stresses the value of ignorance and adds that even if one is not ignorant, a 'cultivated ignorance' is essential to the role of the social consultant (Bain, 1982). In my paper on work done in the Royal National Orthopaedic Hospital, I talk of the need to take a fresh look at the situation, to set aside habitual ways of looking at things, to blind oneself to the obvious, to think again (Menzies Lyth, 1982; vol. 1, pp. 153–207). This statement suggests that it is beneficial if the client too can foster these attitudes so that consultant and client together can work towards the emergence of new meanings and appropriate action. In other words the consultant may – indeed, should – encourage the members of his client institution to speak as freely and widely as they can about their work situation, relationships and experiences: something akin to psychoanalytic free association. In the initial exploratory survey of the nursing situation we invited nurses to talk about the presenting problem – difficulties in the deployment of student nurses in practical training – but invited them also to talk about anything at all that seemed to them significant in their experience of nursing (Menzies, 1970a; vol. 1, pp. 43–85). It was this invitation that evoked much of the material that led to our deeper understanding of the work and training situation, particularly the anxiety situations and the socially structured defences developed to cope with them.

The strain of this way of working is considerable for the consultant, as it is for the analyst. One does not have many props since one has at least temporarily abandoned such conveniently useful things as memory, consciously set objectives and theory; they are in the background only and not to be used for guidance in the field. One exists most of the time in a state of partially self-imposed ignorance which may feel profound, frightening and painful. One needs faith that there is light at the end of the tunnel, even when one does not have much hope. Bion writes movingly of this experience, elaborating on Keats' quotation describing 'negative capability' (Bion, 1970; see above, pp. 3, 22).

What compounds this experience is its repetitiveness. If we can hold on to our ignorance with evenly suspended attention, meaning will probably emerge and we will experience the reward of at least one mystery or part of a mystery solved, uncertainty and doubt dispersed. But it will not last, especially if one communicates one's understanding to the client who accepts one's interpretation and is prepared and able to proceed again into the unknown. One is thrown back again on ignorance, uncertainty and doubt and must experience the process all over again. One may need to give a good deal of support to the client to go along with the process, especially a client who is accustomed to using the 'expert' and expects him to produce a definitive answer quickly. If one resists this pressure, one may be bitterly attacked as though one is delinquently withholding goodies to which the client is entitled – or, failing that, the client clutches at straws and magical unrealistic answers. I have often had the experience, while consulting to a group, that I was the only person in the room who did not know what was going on. The group members 'knew' – that is, they had abandoned ignorance. Fortunately, people can identify with the model presented by the consultant and learn to work in this way, so that collaboration in the process becomes progressively easier and more rewarding to both parties. Patients are similar. A new patient may ask an analyst to tell him what to do about a problem or how to use an interpretation; an experienced patient knows, even if he may not like it, that he has to take responsibility and work out for himself what to do.

This brings me to another way that psychoanalytically orientated consultancy runs in parallel with psychoanalysis: the initiative for taking appropriate action as insights and meaning evolve lies with the client. Just as the patient makes his own life decisions without advice or suggestion, so the client makes his own decisions about change and is responsible for implementing them. Ultimately he has to take the consequences – not that it always feels like that, especially if the action is unwelcome to some people. At the Royal National Orthopaedic Hospital (RNOH) the ward sister, caring for the welfare of her child patients and acting properly within her management authority, ruled that no hospital staff from outside the ward should visit the children in the Cot Unit unless they had a task to perform for them. The sister and her staff did not think that casual visitors were good for the children. This rule distressed and angered many well-disposed hospital staff who had visited the children to cheer them up and encourage them. In fact the rule became known by hospital staff as the 'Tavistock rule' – the anger about it was diverted on to the Tavistock and away from the ward sister, who was liked and respected by her colleagues.

The analyst's or consultant's responsibility lies in helping insights to develop, freeing thinking about problems, helping the client to get away from unhelpful methods of thinking and behaving, facilitating the evolution of ideas for change, and then helping him to bear the anxiety and uncertainty of the change process. This feature is notable in psychoanalytically orientated consultants and others whose work has been influenced by them. They stay around. Other consultants without that orientation are more likely to do their investigations and send their report to their client – a blueprint of what he should do about his problems. They then leave the client to do what he can about it on his own. This seems to happen surprisingly often, for example in the repetitive attempts to reorganize the British health and social services. It is unlikely to work: the client is left on his own with what may well be the most difficult part of the task. It would be unthinkable to give a patient a detailed report on his psychopathology, instruct him as to what he should do about it and send him away to do it.

I find it equally unthinkable to leave a client institution in a similar situation. Serious change in a social institution inevitably involves restructuring the social defence system and, as Jaques has described, this implies freeing underlying anxieties until new defences – or, better – adaptations and sublimations are developed (Jaques, 1955). There is a sense in which all change is felt as catastrophic even when it is rationally recognized as for the better, since it threatens the established and familiar order and requires new attitudes and behaviour, changes in relationships, a move into a comparatively unknown future (Bion, 1970). At this point, the problem of containment seems central: the presence of someone who can give strength and support, continue the process of developing insight and help to define the exact nature of desirable changes.

Some of the changes that institutions make actually bring their members into more direct and overt contact with difficult tasks and stressful situations than before. I am postulating that this is a good thing, not a bad thing, since it allows workers to deploy their capacities more fully. This happened in the RNOH when the Cot Unit changed from multiple indiscriminate caretaking[1] to case-assignment. This removed a traditional defence against anxiety. Nursery nurses were more intimately and intensely in contact with patients and families. This in fact strengthened them and fostered maturation, but while the change was going on they needed help, support and training to develop and sustain new ways of coping with stress in themselves as well as patients and families: for example, by confronting it and working through its meaning.

I am indebted to Bain for helping me to formulate my ideas on the function of the consultant who follows a dynamic approach to institutional practice (Bain, 1982). He states that the institutional consultant must concern himself with three kinds of analysis: role analysis, structure analysis and work-culture analysis. Of these, work-culture analysis appears the most closely related to psychoanalysis. It considers such things as attitudes and beliefs, patterns of relationships, traditions, the psychosocial context in which work is done and people collaborate in doing it. However, a second look may show that both roles and structure are infiltrated and partially determined by dynamics familiar to psychoanalysis. For example, the content of roles is partially determined by projection systems which contribute to the view taken, by themselves and others, of the incumbents of different roles and of the roles themselves.

Anxieties about one's capacity to do one's job are projected downwards into subordinates and their roles. This is linked with a tendency to filch their capacities so that subordinates' capacities are underestimated and their roles diminished. Projection of one's capacities upwards also takes place, along with an expectation that one's superiors will take over one's responsibilities as well, so that anxiety about one's capacity to do one's job properly is relieved. Anxieties about whether one's subordinates are capable and trustworthy – partly arising from one's own projections – may lead to unduly narrow and rigid prescription of their roles and to unnecessarily close supervision. This is not a magical process – messages are conveyed through attitudes and action: little interchanges like '*I* will do that *for* you', the tone of voice conveying that 'you' are not really capable of doing it and 'I' am. The effects of such attributions can sometimes be seen in roles at all levels in a structure, as the author found in studying the nursing service of the general teaching hospital (Menzies, 1970a; vol. 1, pp. 43–85), but they are probably most obvious in the lowest rung of the hierarchy, where the role content may be well below the capacity of the workers. Bain found this strikingly in Baric, as we did among student nurses in the general teaching hospital. Similar factors influence structure: diminution of the content of roles may lead to too many levels in the hierarchy, with people doing jobs that people below them could easily do, and to too many supervisors.

This three-pronged analysis may seem very different from what goes on in a psychoanalysis which, as I said above, may appear to be more analogous to work-culture analysis. I do not think this is so, however. Psychoanalysis is directly concerned with the patient's internal world as he shows it to the analyst. This internal world consists of images and phantasies, conscious and unconscious, of other people, the self and interpersonal relationships, of roles and role relationships, all of which exist within a structure. It is a social system, an imaginary institution.

Psychoanalytic exploration of this internal world changes it – that is, the patient's personality. The internal changes are reflected in changed relationships with the external world. For example, analysis of internal role systems leads to changes in the roles the patient operates, how he operates them, or both. Membership of a psychoanalysis, like membership of other social institutions, changes the structure of the personality (Fenichel, 1946).

One difference between psychoanalytic practice and psychoanalytically orientated consultancy lies in real differences between the two situations. The patient takes action in the external world himself and copes with the way he and the changes in him affect and are affected by real people and situations that facilitate or inhibit his efforts. If and when an institution uses a consultant to facilitate institutional change, individuals or even small groups with whom he is working cannot usually take decisions or initiate action on their own. Other people and groups need to be involved if understanding and insights are to grow and relevant action take place. Role and structure analysis need to be explicit and related to each other and to work-culture analysis; they go hand in hand. Further, the work must usually range fairly widely throughout the institution. People who affect and are affected by change need to be overtly involved. The work cannot be too narrowly restricted to the group or unit where the problem is said to exist. Significant changes in the so-called problem area require counterbalancing changes in surrounding areas if they are to be effective and lasting.

Bain found in Baric that the level of the operators' role could be raised only if other roles and the structure were also changed, with less supervision, fewer supervisory roles, and so on. Similarly in the RNOH a significant change in the nursery nurses' role had to be balanced by change in the roles of the staff nurse and ward sister. They delegated more patient and family care to the nursery nurses and themselves became more involved in management, technical nursing, support and training. The nursery nurses also took over certain aspects of the social worker's role in family care while she trained and supported them. Similarly, work was done with other wards and departments both to help develop attitudes consistent with those in the Cot Unit itself and to assist in desirable role and structure modification. The health service being what it is, results were somewhat limited: unnecessary supervisors could not be removed, for example, since the health service decreed they should be there.

Rather frequently in institutional consultancy one or two types of analysis are neglected and the consultant concentrates on the other two or one. Psychoanalytically orientated workers may and often do concentrate exclusively or almost so on some form of work-culture analysis orientated to achieving significant attitude change. This can make their work inadequate, useless or even harmful. This happens only too often, for example, in sensitivity or support groups aimed at helping care-takers to be more understanding and sensitive both to themselves and to clients. Such attitude change is not hard to achieve: care-takers basically want to be like that. The problem is that the existing roles and structure may make it virtually impossible to deploy their changed attitudes. For years student nurses have been exhorted to 'nurse the whole patient as a person'. This is usually what the student wants to do, but the role system and the institutional structure in nursing, especially multiple indiscriminate care-taking, too often make it impossible. The danger is that people become disappointed, frustrated and disillusioned. Attitudes change back in defence against these feelings and in line with the demands of the institutional system, or people cannot tolerate the system and leave. The consultants and what they stand for may be discredited.

The author's job title and role in two therapeutic communities caring for delinquent and deprived children illustrate the point. I was a management consultant. My task was continuously to explore with the staff the therapeutic impact of the roles and structure in the institution and help modify them so that the institution as a whole became more therapeutic. In other words, therapy was understood by the staff and by me as the impact of the whole institution on the children – not only activities more usually regarded as therapeutic or developmental, such as counselling or education; staff sensitivity was not enough. Work-culture analysis was not neglected but was carried out mainly by another consultant[2] who particularly handled staff attitudes to children, their own reactions, and so on. The division was not rigid and, perhaps strangely, it worked. Too many therapeutic communities appear to lack sufficient awareness of role and structural factors and therefore their therapeutic impact is diminished because these are inadequate (Menzies Lyth, 1985; vol. 1, pp. 236–58).

By contrast, the consultant who lacks a psychoanalytic orientation may well confine himself to role and structure without having sufficient understanding of the contribution of unconscious content and dynamics to them. He may well suggest changes in role and structure without the backing of the requisite changes in work culture. Indeed, attention to work culture might not support his ideas about role and structure. This is likely to prevent anything effective happening. There seems to be a crying need for work-culture analysis if real improvement is to be effected in the health and social services.

Psychoanalytic practice and consultancy differ in ways that mean the consultant may not be able to follow Freud's wise precepts fully. The psychoanalyst refrains as far as possible from contact with the patient outside the analysis and with his relatives and friends. He is to be as much as possible a mirror that reflects the patient back to himself and shows nothing about the analyst. This is recommended for the protection of the patient and the analysis, to give freedom for fantasy and to help the patient follow his own direction. Desirable as this is in institutional consultancy, it is possible only to a limited extent. One usually has to function in the client's territory so that one shares activities and places in a perfectly ordinary way: coffees, drinks, meals, canteen, lavatories. It is inevitably more sociable and it may be difficult to fend off ordinary human curiosity about oneself without seeming or even being offensive. One can hardly avoid contact with spouses or relatives, especially when staff and families as well as their clients are resident.[3]

A.K. Rice said his clients became his friends – fair comment; yet one has to try to keep one's distance, not to get too drawn in and, of course, not to let one's own or one's clients' social feelings interfere with the work. Holding the balance of one's social and work relationships is often a problem. One may be perceived by some as being too much in the pockets of others. With whom does one eat in the canteen, and why? Does one mix enough socially with the lowest-level workers? It is conventional for higher managers to entertain outside consultants – dinner in the matron's flat, not the student nurses' canteen. One has to wend one's way carefully through these intricacies, noting that they are likely to have an effect on the transference and counter-transference and on one's own transference to the client. It is important to understand what that effect is.

Transference is still an important concept, even if it gets a bit cluttered by the greater real presentation of oneself to one's clients. To further the work, it may be essential to draw such transference phenomena into work-culture analysis, especially when they lead to suspicion of bias. This will not necessarily be easy or welcome. Careful attention to the countertransference is also necessary; one's own bias may make careful observation and deduction more difficult.

Here another difference between psychoanalysis and consultancy is helpful. One need not work alone. An institutional consultancy may, in any case, be too big an undertaking for one person. The advantages of having at least one colleague are inestimable. Indeed, it may not be really advisable to work alone. It is an old Tavistock Institute principle that it takes a group to study a group: or, at least, a person working alone needs his own consultant 'to come home to'. As regards transference and countertransference, two people can be very useful in helping each other to sort them out, check and recheck them and disentangle each other from relationships that interfere with work or from attitudes inconsistent with consultancy.

Several times after I had done a long continuous spell of work in the RNOH I would begin to get too possessive of the children and too identified with the hospital. I would begin to talk about 'our children'. My colleague, Tim Dartington, would say: 'They are not our children, you know.' That was all that was needed to remind me of my place. Two or more people give added richness to interpretation of the data. Their perspectives are different, their field experiences are different, since they do not always work alongside each other. Their relationships with different members of the client institution are different. Two people are much more than twice one, in my experience. I have done a great deal of useful work in cars, buses and trains going to and from the field with colleagues, and am grateful to these colleagues for the insights they have helped me develop.

Note-taking and keeping of records are another example of differences. Freud discouraged the analyst from making notes during sessions since it would involve selection of data and would interfere with evenly suspended attention. Having a colleague in the field allows other possibilities. One can split the roles, one person conducting the discussion with evenly suspended attention while the other takes notes, inevitably selectively. But these selective notes may be useful afterwards, in conjunction with memory from evenly suspended attention, in recording significant aspects of what went on and keeping track of the vast amount of data one collects in the field.

Lastly, the question of reports. As remarked earlier, one does not give written reports to patients. I have also criticized the practice of sending the blueprint type of report to clients (additionally discussed in conversation. See vol. 1, p. 11). However, reports do have their usefulness in certain forms and in certain settings. A written report may be a useful mnemonic. It would never, however, be my first report. First, its contents would have been reported verbally in a face-to-face situation where one can work with their effect on the client, tackle resistance to their acceptance as a means to further understanding, stand corrected and amend conclusions if one is wrong, and so on. The final document is likely to be a distillation of joint work between the client and oneself. This was what I did regularly in one of the children's communities.[4] I worked there two consecutive days a month and sent a 'field note' outlining where I thought we had got to and giving them something to work on by themselves until my next visit. I had sufficient trust and respect for that particular client to feel this was a safe and helpful way of working.

A complication is that one may be obliged to write reports, for example, if one is being financed by a research grant. In the RNOH we had to submit annual and final reports to the Department of Health and Social Security, who financed the work. The same principle applied. The reports crystallized discussions with the Project Steering Committee and other people in the hospital and were approved by them before being sent. The question of confidentiality is implicit in this and affects wider publication. One cannot, as a rule, disguise an institution effectively. One's clients are literate and interested in themselves and are entitled to be told where the work will be published. This means that results can be professionally and ethically published only when contents have been agreed and consent given for publication. Sometimes one cannot publish.

The end of a consultancy is rather like the end of an analysis. One needs to work through termination to try to ensure that the patient or client will be able to carry on by himself. This means more than simply sustaining the gains that have been made or the fact that the person has solved the problem he originally brought. It means that the patient or client can continue to make progress on his own through having 'learned' a method of tackling problems which will survive the departure of the analyst or consultant and facilitate creative developments in the future. Bain was rewarded by a follow-up study in Baric which showed that this method of tackling problems had been sustained and creative solutions to other problems were found. Similarly in the RNOH: after we left, Mavis Young Remmen, the ward sister, and her staff reorganized the care of latency children in a unit separate from the Cot Unit where we had worked together. The exciting thing was that this was not a slavish copy of the model we had developed together but a different model realistically related to the needs of latency children and taking into account the differences in resources – notably that all Cot Unit staff were permanent whereas the latency unit was mainly staffed by transitory student nurses.

CONCLUSION
I want to return briefly to Fenichel's view that the membership of an institution affects the personality structure of its members.

They introject and identify with the institution, the more so the more malleable the members. This is why the design of children's institutions is so important (Menzies Lyth, 1985; vol. 1, pp. 236–58). Members become like the institution in significant ways – by introjecting and operating its characteristic defence mechanisms, sharing common attitudes, carrying on traditional types of relationships. If an individual cannot achieve this identification, he is unlikely to remain a member. If he remains too different, he is likely to be rejected by the institution because he does not 'fit'. If he tries to conform to something which is too foreign to him, he may find it too stressful and leave. Over 30 per cent of student nurses give up training, mostly of their own volition, because they cannot follow the institutional model, which is regressive. Labour turnover was over 400 per cent per annum in the day nursery where Bain and Barnett worked (Bain and Barnett, 1986). Note the plight of children who usually cannot opt to leave if they are placed in an institution which is a bad model.

Unfortunately, I have come to a depressing conclusion: that institutions have a natural tendency to become bad models for identification; and the bigger the institution, the more likely this is. I have already suggested reasons why this should be so, the basic difficulties human beings have in co-operating effectively together, the anxieties these arouse and the defences against these anxieties. (This part of the paper is amplified in conversation. See vol. 1, p. 12.) The defences are only too likely to be powerful and primitive and to provide bad models for identification. As psychoanalysts we know that a person's mental health is intimately linked with the conscious and unconscious anxieties he experiences and the methods he uses to deal with them. Illness is linked with excessive use of defences, usually primitive, as against other methods like sublimation, development of skills and engagement in constructive anxiety-related activities. Excessive use of regressed defences is the model many institutions offer. The risk tends to be greater where situations of real danger occur, such as in coal-mining, or where there is shared impact of great human suffering, as in the humane institutions.

However, all is not lost. Some institutions manage quite well in spite of everything and establish healthy functioning by their own efforts. Trist and Bamforth's work in coal-mining demonstrates this, a natural experiment. Two neighbouring coal-mines had the same kind of coal seams and used the same technology. By chance they had developed very different social systems. There were dramatic differences in the human experiences in the two systems – for example, in labour turnover, absenteeism and sickness rates as well as in more subtle social indicators. There was also a dramatic difference in coal production, one mine producing nearly twice as much per man-shift as the other.

Work in consultancy has shown that other institutions can be helped to change so that they become better places to be in and better models which help their members to become more mature people, more able to act effectively and constructively and reap the rewards of that, and to have a richer experience of life in general. People of all ages have developed and expanded their horizons: work in children's institutions aimed at providing better developmental situations for the children had a considerable spin-off in the development and maturation of the adults who cared for them. Another by-product is that the institution itself becomes more effective – productive, if it is that kind of institution – as in the coal-mine. It is as though the institution's 'ego' strengthens as defences are modified and it copes more effectively with its real-life tasks.

One can also begin to establish principles – or theories – about what constitutes a healthy institution: principles, not blueprints; just as one has theories about what constitutes a healthy personality: the avoidance of overuse of regressed defences, more adaptation and sublimation, the ability to confront and work through problems, opportunities for people to deploy their full capacities – neither more nor less than they can manage – opportunity to have realistic control over their own life in the institution although taking the needs of others duly into account, independence without undue supervision, visible relation between work and rewards. The principles are not so new – it is implementing them that is the problem.

NOTES

1. A care system in which all the nurses care 'indiscriminately' for all the patients in a ward.

2. Mrs Barbara Dockar-Drysdale, formerly of the Mulberry Bush School, Standlake, Oxfordshire.

3. For example, in hospitals and other residential institutions.

4. The Cotswold Community: Principal, Richard Balbernie.

4 Family breakdown in urban communities*

This is a brief report on the early developmental stages of a project, the aim of which is to contribute to studies of the nature of family maladjustments and to consider methods by which family caseworkers may contribute to their solution.

THE ORIGIN OF THE PROJECT

The PROJECT was initiated by the Family Welfare Association, a family casework agency established about eighty years ago to serve the metropolitan boroughs of London, and was a response to changes in the demands placed on the Association by its clients and the community. The Association operates through a number of local offices, with a central co-ordinating office responsible for such things as selection of staff and general development of policy. Each local office is run by a secretary, who is a trained social worker, and a small staff, for the most part also trained social workers.

The secretary in each office is responsible for the day-to-day conduct of the casework and is supported by a voluntary committee drawn from the leaders of the local community. Members of these committees form the largest group from which the Council of the Association and various central committees are recruited. They are therefore largely responsible for the govern-

*This paper (full original title: 'Factors affecting family breakdown in urban communities'), originally published in *Human Relations*, vol. 2, no. 4 (1949), describes a preliminary study which led to the establishment of two pilot Family Discussion Bureaux.

ment and policy of the Association, though the paid professional workers are also members of these central bodies.

At first, the work of the Association was mainly among the very poor, and was related to the giving of material relief. This was reflected in its original title, The Charity Organization Society. At that time its purpose was to prevent the indiscriminate giving of relief, and to help applicants to overcome their difficulties and become more capable of leading independent, responsible lives. The giving of relief, therefore, was only part of a plan whose aim was what would now be called rehabilitation. However, the pressure of material needs was commonly so great that the workers tended to become preoccupied with temporary relief measures at the expense of the other aims. In more recent years, a gradual change in the material situation has made it possible for the workers to give more of their time and energy to the Association's original objective. There has been a long period of full employment with reasonably adequate wage levels, rationing, food subsidies, and price control. To these have been added the provisions made by the state since 5 July 1948 for sickness and unemployment. In view of the basic statutory welfare provisions, such material need as now exists can largely be regarded as one symptom of a more general inability to deal adequately with the demands of life. Requests for material relief very frequently expose the need for help with personal problems of an entirely different kind.

The Association was also affected by the alarm of the community about the increasing incidence of divorce and family breakdown, and was anxious to make a contribution to the solution of this type of community problem. The Association, therefore, determined to further the skills of its workers in the handling of these personal problems, and to begin this programme decided to concentrate on problems of marital relationships.

For this purpose a special subcommittee was set up to plan the project. This subcommittee decided to seek outside technical help in planning the project and in developing the new kinds of skills involved, particularly in relationship and interpretative therapy. Accordingly, two staff members from the Peckham Pioneer Health Centre and two from the Tavistock Institute of Human Relations joined the subcommittee.

The project has since been carried out by a staff of from three to five social workers employed by the Association, with the collaboration in planning, training, and field work of a psychologist from the Tavistock Institute of Human Relations. A psychiatrist and an anthropologist from the Tavistock Institute and the two Peckham Pioneer Health Centre staff members have acted as consultants. Two offices were opened as a first step, from which a study could be made of the problems and the effects of different methods of therapy. These offices, which came in the course of the investigation to be known as Family Discussion Bureaux, were located in districts chosen because they presented distinct contrasts with each other. Other factors which affected the location of the bureaux were the availability of psychiatric backing for them and the relation between the existing offices of the Association and the community, which had to be good enough not to interfere with the effective rooting of the new bureaux.

Borough A lies in north-west London. It has a population of 170,000–180,000 and covers an area of about sixteen square miles. The population has been increasing rapidly; the census figures for the area show it as 40,000 in 1911, 57,000 in 1921 and 116,000 in 1931 – that is, the population has more than quadrupled in less than forty years. Despite the large amount of building which has necessarily taken place, the district is exceptionally well supplied with open spaces and there is still an almost rural feeling in some parts. Other amenities and community services, such as schools, clubs, and recreational facilities, also reach a standard above the average for London boroughs, and one has the general impression of a young, expanding, progressive and socially conscious community. Accurate details of the socioeconomic distribution of the population are not available, but it is clear that the general pleasantness of the borough has attracted to it a considerably higher proportion of middle and upper classes than is to be found in the population as a whole.

Borough B is in south-west London. It has a population at

present of about 120,000–130,000 and covers an area of eleven to twelve square miles. The present population is 20,000–30,000 lower than the pre-war population, since the borough was very badly bombed. Overcrowding is gross, and in addition many families have had to be moved to other areas. Even before the war, however, the population was beginning to decrease. It fell from about 158,000 in 1911 and 1921 to 151,000 in 1931, as families were moved into better accommodation in other districts. There is very little land available for new building, except, at present, bombed sites, and there is a marked absence of open spaces. The general standard of amenities is a good deal lower than in Borough A. This is partly due to the age of the borough, which meant that the comparatively recent development of any social services was inhibited by the lack of building sites and difficulties about converting old buildings to the new purposes. Also there is in this older community less general feeling of development and progress than in Borough A. The socioeconomic distribution of the population in Borough B is much nearer to that of the population as a whole than is that of Borough A.

DEVELOPMENT OF THE COMMUNITY RELATIONS OF THE PROJECT STAFF

For the first few months, the work of the two pilot bureaux was confined to a type of 'consumer research' and almost no therapeutic work was undertaken. This plan was adopted for a number of reasons:

1. Very little information was available about the patterns of family and community living in the communities in which the work was to be done. Pilot surveys were therefore initiated to find out something about their culture patterns, and about the particular satisfactions and difficulties of family life in them, in order to achieve a perspective on norms of behaviour and divergencies from the norm. Further, if, as the workers supposed, the norm itself represented an unsatisfactory level of community and family living, it would be necessary to consider whether there was a role for caseworkers

operating at the family level in trying to raise it.

2. It was thought desirable to find out more about what the members of the community themselves thought about the problems with which the project was concerned; whether there was an awareness of such problems, a general dissatisfaction with family and community living, or a feeling of a high incidence of more acute family problems. In other words it was desirable to estimate the felt need for help, in particular the kind of help the workers could offer.

3. A by-product of the workers' growing knowledge about the community was that the community would get to know more about the workers. The existing office of the Association was known only to a limited section of the community, mainly to those members of the lowest socioeconomic levels who had gone to it for help in a state of crisis, and to other agencies who might refer such clients. But the services which were to be offered were applicable to a wider range of consumer, and had to be made more widely known: for example, many problems arise in ordinary families which are not felt to be severe enough for outside help to be sought and are resolved somehow, but could be brought to a more rapid and effective solution if only contact could be made. The best way of doing this was felt to be by personal contact, first of all by the workers themselves, and later through the recommendations of satisfied clients.

4. The avoidance of therapeutic work and concentration on consumer research also arose from the fact that at present comparatively few marital problems reach agencies until they are at an acute stage, when the stabilization of the relationship is very difficult. It was felt that if the project once became associated by the community with that kind of work, then the chance of getting earlier problems and of developing effective family-life education and preventive work would be reduced. It was hoped that in time a case-load might be built up from contact with the more healthy part of the community, which would contain a large number of sub-acute problems with a good prognosis. Thus the ultimate aim was to try to prevent acute

crises by educative, preventive, and early therapeutic work. It was thought possible that consumer research might indicate certain 'danger points' in marriages, where things may start to go wrong and where immediate help might stabilize the marriages, and if so, methods of making contact with couples at these points may be devised for prophylactic purposes. For example, it was thought that the major change in the relationship of the husband and wife resulting from the first pregnancy and the birth of the child might be one such point, in which case work with agencies such as antenatal and infant welfare clinics might prove valuable. By the time a marital problem has reached an acute stage it is usually too late to trace its beginnings.

The consumer research was carried out through extensive contact with existing community organizations. In order to facilitate two-way communication and establish as wide contacts as possible, group discussions rather than individual interviews were arranged; individual interviews being mainly confined to various officials. A request to meet a group of members of such a community organization was sent through its leader, and where the request was granted, two or three of the workers went to meet the group. They then told the group about the background of the project and suggested some of the family problems which are probably easier to talk about, such as questions of disciplining children. They asked the group members to talk about these problems as they saw them in the community around them, and to consider whether help might be given of the kind the workers could offer. It was indicated that the group members were free to discuss whatever else they wished. From then on, the workers usually took little active part in the discussion.

An attempt was made to contact as wide a range of groups as possible, in order to get a fair cross-section of the community. Contact was made with such organizations as community centres, infant welfare clinics, schools, ex-servicemen's clubs. It was recognized that one of the great difficulties at this stage in the work would be that of making contact with the fairly large proportion of the population which was thought not to participate actively in any organized community group, and who might well be feeling the disturbing effect of community disintegration even more than those who did participate. Some such people have been met in places like infant welfare clinics, and attempts have been made to establish contact with others in industry – where, however, it has not proved easy to effect an entry.

In all, some 450 people were met in rather more than fifty groups. Of these about 400 were working-class, and the remainder middle- and upper-class; these were more difficult to contact. Women and younger age groups were more easily contacted than men and older age groups. All-male groups were met only at the local fire stations and ex-servicemen's clubs, and this covered only fifty to sixty men. About 100 more men and boys were seen in mixed groups. Approximately 100–120 people seen were in the 15–25 age group, 250–300 in the 25–45 group, and the remainder over 45. Accurate records of ages are not available.

SOME PRELIMINARY FINDINGS AND HYPOTHESES

These findings and hypotheses apply, at this stage, mainly to working-class families, which have been easier to contact than middle- and upper-class families.

Hypothesis 1. Difficulties are frequently created in families by the multiplicity of culture patterns in modern communities with respect to family living; for example the roles and functions of husband and wife, the training and disciplining of children.

The workers found that husbands and wives frequently begin marriage with very different notions, conscious or unconscious, of their respective roles, their privileges, their duties towards each other, and their share in common family and domestic tasks. When the husband and wife are mature, adaptable people these differences can generally be resolved, and a new pattern of family living worked out which is acceptable and satisfactory to both, but with the majority of less mature, more rigid personalities the mutual creation of a new pattern takes place less easily; dissatisfaction tends to remain, and in extreme cases may become so great that the total breakdown of the relationship results.

51

Such was the case, for example, with a husband and wife whose difficulties were principally in financial matters. The attitudes and behaviour patterns in their parent families were very different. The wife came from a family of seven, brought up on a very low income by a mother who, however, provided a secure environment and planned family expenditure very carefully; she regarded some saving for irregular large expenditures like holidays and clothing and for emergencies like illness as an essential and 'right' part of her budgeting. Her daughter grew up to regard careful budgeting and saving as an essential part of her duty as a wife and mother. The husband, on the other hand, came from a family which had had recurrent crises of one sort or another since he was a baby. His mother died when he was two; his father remarried and died when he was four. The client had a spell in a home with his sister before his father's remarriage and again as an adolescent, this time for delinquency. During the greater part of his childhood he was looked after by his stepmother, whose attitude in financial matters was somewhat carefree. She did not plan her budget at all carefully, did not regard saving on a small income as possible or even desirable, and was inclined to let emergencies take care of themselves. The husband and wife entered marriage without any idea that their own family attitudes and behaviour patterns were not the only right and proper ones, and each was surprised to find that the other had different ideas. Each thought the other 'wrong', and attempted to follow out the old family pattern and make the other adjust to it. The wife plans her expenditure and savings carefully and thinks money not devoted to 'useful' family expenditure like food, clothing, and holidays is wasted. The husband spends his share of the income carelessly and sometimes on things like gambling, which she considers useless. He quite frequently overspends and gets into debt and has to be rescued by her carefully planned savings. In his case the family patterns are accentuated by the deprivations and insecurity of his early years, and he needs this continual reassurance of her affection. She, on the other hand, finds this disturbance of her careful planning and attack on her security intolerable. Very little spontaneous change in attitude or behaviour patterns had been possible for this couple and the wife was threatening to leave the husband when they were referred to the bureau.

Similar phenomena can be observed in relation to child-rearing. In a closely knit community, such as a village, there tends to be a single accepted method of child-rearing. The mother has been reared that way herself, she has watched many other children being reared that way, and when she comes to rear her own children she is confident that she knows the 'right' and the 'wrong' things to do with them and is capable to a great extent of doing the 'right' thing. Not so the young mother in a modern urban community. She has been brought up one way, not always consistently; she has watched other children, perhaps even her own brothers and sisters, being brought up in different ways with different results; she may have read a good deal of literature recommending all kinds of contradictory things; and by the time she has to bring up her own children she is likely to be assailed by many doubts, both about her ultimate objectives for her children and about the best methods of reaching them. A series of discussions with a group of young working-class mothers showed clearly the conflicts about such things as whether or not a child should be smacked; about cleanliness training; about the nature and timing of sex education. These mothers felt strongly the need for someone to tell them the 'right' things to do and the way to do them, and so to resolve their doubts and anxieties.

Fathers and mothers also frequently come into conflict because of different ideas about child-rearing. The result is again inconsistency and often entirely different methods with siblings, so that the situation is likely to repeat itself. This situation may well be an inevitable consequence of the high mobility of the modern urban population, but it appears to be a very unsatisfactory one from the point of view of the individual, the family, and the community.

Hypothesis 2. The various patterns of family living in the two communities are generally unsatisfactory and lead to difficulties for the individuals concerned.

There was a marked lack in many families of 'family' life in

53

any real sense; that is, families were frequently little more than a collection of individuals, usually sharing the same home and to some extent the same meals, but not a real group with a coherent and satisfying life of its own and with real, deep and enduring ties between its members.

The low degree of participation of the husband in family life was in many cases particularly striking, and his lack of real responsibility for his family (apart from providing for their material needs) – for example in budgeting, directing the children's education, and even frequently in buying his own clothes. What appeared to be a patriarchal family structure from the outside looked matriarchal from the inside. The wives had a very ambivalent attitude to this. On the one hand they expressed resentment at being left with all the responsibility, but on the other they would have objected strongly if their husbands had tried to take a greater share. Again, husbands and wives frequently do not regard each other as the natural person to go to with important problems, but when the burden becomes too great to be borne alone, it is shared instead with a complete outsider.

An extreme case of this sort, but one which could be matched with many others, was that of a woman who complained that she had no idea what her husband earned. He gave her a weekly fixed amount with which she had to meet all family expenditure including such items as rent, family presents, holidays and outings, and clothes, even her husband's clothes. She had no idea how her husband spent the undisclosed amount of his income, which he kept to himself. He showed little interest in the children's school or career planning, merely stating that the children were her business, and he took almost no part in the domestic work of the family except for carrying in fuel.

This attitude was less marked in younger than in older people, but it was impossible to tell whether this was the beginning of a change in the situation or whether the drifting apart would repeat itself later. It was also much less marked in middle-class families, where husbands take considerable responsibility for planning family affairs and frequently share largely in household tasks now that domestic help is scarce and expensive.

Contact with groups of young people and with their parents suggests that they are being brought up in a way which is likely to perpetuate the pattern, the boys especially having no real role in their home, and often spending almost none of their spare time there.

Boys and girls also feel difficulty in making effective relationships with their parents, according to their statements, because of their own superior education and experience. Some even go so far as to claim superior knowledge in sexual matters, in spite of all the evidence to the contrary. They feel need of help and guidance in such things as choice of careers and expect to be able to depend on their parents for it, but generally say their parents are not experienced enough to give it. On the other hand they show anxiety about such things as their own sexual development, their lack of real knowledge in sexual matters and about life in general, and blame their parents for not helping them more. On the parents' side similar difficulties exist. Many parents, for example, feel strongly that they should give their children sexual information but are unable either to create or to use opportunities to do so; this, they feel, inhibits the development of a satisfactory relationship.

Hypothesis 3. The 'normal' family is relatively isolated, and is not related as a unit to other similar units. There is a lack of strong, positive links between the families in the same community and of constructive concern for people outside the immediate family.

The normal family appeared to lead a fairly isolated life, and this was particularly hard on those members of the family who have no extrafamilial role in the community – particularly, of course, the wife with no job other than running the home. As a result the family was not enriched and strengthened by the feeding back into it of mutual experience and shared extrafamilial relationships, but was rather weakened and impoverished by the high libidinal involvement of each member in people and activities in which the other members had no share.

The important work done in the family area by the Peckham Pioneer Health Centre has shown that one of the effects of providing a common interest and centre of activity for the family outside the home has been to strengthen the bonds between family members, increase their satisfactions inside the family, and lead to an increased use of the home.

One husband and wife, for example, who had joined the Centre merely because their children wanted it and because only complete family membership is permitted, remarked after a time on the change in their family life which had taken place: before they joined the Centre, they had found it almost impossible to spend an evening at home because they got so bored and discontented with themselves, and felt that they had nothing to talk about. As the husband put it, his wife had been in the home all day and had nothing to talk to him about when he came home from work; he had been at work and she did not know the people there, so he could not talk about that; his children had other interests outside the home, such as their youth clubs, but he knew nothing about them or the people there and did not want to hear about them, so he said he got tired of all their talk and went off to spend the evening in the public house. Afterwards, they found they could thoroughly enjoy two evenings a week at home together, for they had so many interesting things to talk about with each other arising out of their common experiences of activities and people at the Centre.

The isolation of families has been intensified by the changing structure of the family. In communities of relatively low mobility the parent–child family group is generally supported by a number of surrounding groups with close libidinal ties, such as the grandparents and the families of the parents' siblings. The real family unit is in fact a multiple one. In modern urban communities, however, the parent–child unit frequently has none of these groups of close relatives within its day-to-day life space and is impoverished by the lack of that intimacy and ease of contact, which is more difficult to establish with non-related families.

THE COMMUNITY'S AWARENESS OF FAMILY PROBLEMS

The people in the two communities studied appeared to be

aware to a varying extent of a vague feeling of malaise about their lives – a feeling that life was difficult and gave them too little satisfaction. Blame for the unsatisfactory nature of life was variously attributed to budgeting difficulties, housing shortage, the effect which the war had on people. There is, of course, no doubt that these factors have had a very real effect on people's lives and have often been major contributory elements in present difficulties, but the feeling was common enough among people with no particular material difficulties to make it probable that the basic causes of the feeling were not these, but some of the other factors mentioned above.

This vague feeling of malaise was accompanied by a feeling of hopelessness and apathy. People were dissatisfied but had little hope that anything could be done about it, or idea of how to improve things. Many people had been frustrated in their attempts to make effective relationships in their community, had given up trying, and found the ability to do so likely to become atrophied through disuse. It appeared to the workers that despite the comparative lack of integration of the communities, numerous opportunities remained for building up relationships, but many people were not able to grasp them. For example, one woman, herself at a very low socioeconomic level, when asked if she did not find that she made friends through her children with the parents of their school friends, said she would never think of being friendly with people like that. But she complained bitterly of loneliness. Other more mature and determined personalities had, on the other hand, managed to build up a satisfactory set of relationships in spite of the difficulties.

It was possible also to observe people at various phases of the transition from hope, through frustration, to apathy – people who, for example, had come into the communities from other more stable, more integrated communities in which it was still possible to establish satisfactory relationships, and had set about building up such relationships again.

There was despair about the possibility that anything could be done about family maladjustments; this was to be found not only in the people themselves but also in many of the existing therapeutic agencies who could see no possibility of making an effective contribution to the solution of this problem. In a few of them, this had reached such a pitch that they were forced to deny the existence of problems of relationship in the families with whom they came in contact in the ordinary course of their work.

As well as despair, however, there was evidence of resistance to attempts to deal with the problem. Not much has so far been learned about the nature of that resistance, but it appears to be related to difficulties in discussing intimate matters with strangers before an acute problem makes it necessary; a feeling of loyalty to the other people concerned; a feeling of shame about failure to cope with life adequately; a feeling that coming to discuss problems implies a serious breakdown in relationships which people do not want to admit.

Both the need for help and the resistance to it were shown by groups in their reactions to the workers. Their first approach was met with great enthusiasm and a willingness to talk about problems, which contradicted the expressed views of most groups that no one would talk to strangers about the kind of problems the workers were interested in. Frequently, the first meeting ended in a strong request for the workers to come again so that the group could go on talking, or in individuals coming at the end with their own problems. Where these requests were taken up later the enthusiasm appeared to have died away in the interval and resistance to have increased; attendance was poor, or the group entirely disintegrated. Individuals failed to make use of the worker's address and telephone number, which were given at the first approach. In fact, the building of permanent discussion groups has proved a slower, more painstaking business than early contacts suggested, and many resistances are encountered to the serious discussion of such problems as have been mentioned above.

INITIATION OF SOME TENTATIVE SERVICES
Following approximately three months of consumer research, it was decided that enough preliminary material had been collected and that it was necessary to try to establish a more intensive relationship with particular sections of the community. A start

was accordingly made in two areas of work: in setting up therapeutic relationships with individuals or families seeking help with problems, and in offering educative or preventive services to groups of people drawn from what are felt to be key areas in the community.

So far, comparatively few cases are being worked and it is too soon to say very much about them. Up to the present, the majority of the cases have been in fairly acute stages and considerable difficulty is being met, as was anticipated, in making contact with earlier problems. A few of these have appeared, however, including some requests for premarital consultation, and contact work is continuing, with one of its main objectives that of making the work known in the 'healthy' part of the community.

In casework at the moment an attempt is being made to use a kind of interpretative method which cannot be described in detail as yet; but generally the worker tries to help the clients clarify for themselves the issues involved in their problem and work out solutions based on a deeper understanding, including particularly the effects of their own attitudes and behaviour on other people, and some of the underlying reasons for them, so that some of these attitudes and behaviour patterns can be tackled, and possibly changed. At present the treatment consists entirely of individual interviews, but it is hoped that as the caseload increases a start may be made to help some clients through interpretative group discussions. The social workers are at present being trained in the use of group methods and consideration is being given to criteria for the selection of clients for group instead of, or in addition to, individual treatment, and also for the passing of clients from individual to group treatment, or group to individual, as the problems may require.

In educative group work, a group of mothers has been under way for some months in a maternity and child welfare clinic; another has been started in the top form of a girls' school (for girls aged seventeen to eighteen) and a group of girl factory workers has met several times. Here also the technique may be described as primarily clarificatory and interpretative. In the mothers' group the mothers choose each week a problem for discussion the following week. They are then free to raise such aspects of the problem as are important to them. The workers try to help the mothers to understand their own attitudes to the problems raised, the source of these attitudes, and the effect of their attitudes on the other members of their families. After a start, where the discussion kept closely to the very 'safe' topics of housing and budgeting difficulties, they have now gone on to a variety of problems about children, including disciplinary problems and the question of sex education. More recently the group has been concerned with the problem of one mother with an adopted child of three who is in difficulty about whether the child should be told of her relationship to the family, and about how she should be told.

The schoolgirl group is at an early stage of development, but it is clear that the girls are already preoccupied with the question of marriage, the role of woman in society, her 'privilege' of becoming a wife and mother, and the problem of the women who must inevitably be denied these things.

These groups are being regarded as trial runs, and with later groups, when the workers feel more sure of their techniques, an attempt will be made to make a study of the behaviour patterns and attitudes of members, before the group begins and again later, to find out whether modifications can be effected by this type of group discussion.

5 Pleasure foods

Two papers

INTRODUCTION: Psychosocial aspects of eating

THIS PAPER was given in 1969 at the Thirteenth Annual Conference of the Society for Psychosomatic Research, London, whose theme was 'Appetite and Disease'. The paper collates some of the field experiences and their theoretical derivatives that are described in the papers that follow.

The concept of the internal world, in particular the internal society, links the psychological with the social in this paper. An important element in the psyche is the internal society composed of images, concepts, memories and fantasies about people, in a great complexity of roles, functions and relationships. I concentrate on this concept for two reasons: because the internal world and society *alone* influence behaviour – to become a significant influence, an external stimulus must first be taken in and experienced inside – and because the internal society is a particularly significant influence in determining behaviour about food and eating (Klein, 1957, 1963).

In the earliest experiences that form the matrix of the internal society, feeding, the relationship with the mother and emotional experiences are inextricably linked. The baby's feelings about the mother and what she does or does not do for him are intense and extreme. Food given by a loving and skilled mother helps the baby to feel safe, understood, loved and loving, sane and well rooted in life. Hunger or the absence of a loving, comforting mother can lead to wild rage, desperate anxiety or despair, the baby feeling that security, sanity or even life itself are threatened. Primitive causal connections are established between food, feeding, interpersonal relationships and feelings. Eating becomes and remains a significant social and emotional activity. I should perhaps makes it clear that I am talking of the mother as the baby takes her in and experiences her as an *internal* mother, not the mother as she really is. The baby's own feelings can turn a good real mother into an experienced bad one, and vice versa. In particular, the mother–child relationship is complicated by feelings of greed, envy and jealousy which predispose the baby to internalize a bad feeding mother, even when the real mother is a good one.

The end result of this mother–child interaction is that every baby establishes both good and bad images of the mother and the feeding relationship. From those he 'learns' in a primitive way that taking in good food in a relationship with a good mother evokes good emotional experiences and mitigates bad ones, and that lacking food or taking in food in a bad relationship with the mother evokes bad emotional experiences and lessens good ones. These primitive causal connections remain with us as we grow up, although the memories are unconscious and are reinforced and modified by later experiences so that the connections become very complex. One may truly say that people never eat alone or uninfluenced by others, since they always eat in the context of the internal society.

The internal society never accurately reflects the external society. This implies that all our internal societies are different. However, since we live in the same external society there tend to be significant areas of similarity in our internal societies arising from our being subjected to similar external influences. There are, for example, acceptable or unacceptable ways in our society of dealing with the continuing influence of early feeding experiences. These are widely reflected in customs and conventions, meal content and patterning, the rewards and sanctions applied to feeding. We cannot avoid the influence of the external society, whether or not we conform (Pyke, 1969).

To focus attention on one main aspect of this topic, the connections between food, interpersonal relationships, pleasure and pain: these connections create a situation where the realistic nutritional use of food may be submerged by its use to increase pleasure and reduce pain within relationships. Food is used to mediate and to symbolize relationships. Many common practices in our society reflect this. A widespread practice among mothers is to try to comfort children in distress by giving them something to eat (Brosin, 1955; Bruch, 1961). When the distress arises from hunger, this is an appropriate response. When it arises for other reasons – like injury, wet nappies, boredom or loneliness – it is not. In pathological cases an inadequate mother may respond to almost every distress by giving food, which may lead to severe personality disorder as well as obesity (Bruch, 1961).

The mother who reacts to non-nutritional distress by giving food may be internalized. The child, later the adult, identifies with her, often unconsciously, and treats himself and others in the same way. For example, one obese young married woman whose husband was frequently absent on business said: 'I can't help it. When he is away I just nibble biscuits all the time. I feel so lonely.' A dramatic example of food as a relationship-substitute is to be seen in the film 'John' by James and Joyce Robertson (Robertson, 1969). In the residential nursery shown food is plentiful, but the children aggressively steal it from each other as though it were scarce. What is really scarce is the opportunity for a close, stable and intimate relationship with one or a few familiar and loving adults, the effect of the real scarcity being reinforced by the circumstances of institutionalization which had prevented the children from developing such a loving mother figure internally. They had learned that it was no good fighting for a mother-substitute, so they fought for food.

Many mothers consciously or unconsciously fear what they describe as the onslaught of tired, greedy, irritable children coming home from school and try to divert this onslaught from themselves by giving the children food in anticipation of the 'proper meal' that will come later when father comes home. A visit to the sweet shop on the way home from school is only too common. Similarly, mothers try to deal with separation problems when children go off to school by giving the children food to take with them, and with their own separation anxieties, loneliness and boredom at home by feeding themselves.

The ritual of the bedtime drink is often linked with the

63

longing for a good internal mother–baby relationship through the emphasis on milk, on the feeding properties of the drink and on its sweetness. The drink establishes the symbol of a good mother inside who will give or protect the good experiences of sleep or even life itself, since many people seem to fear that sleep will deepen into death. Night starvation is a very apt concept. The bedtime ritual is often associated with reconciliation. When people take their drink together they draw closer together, become more intimate and sort out any difficulties of the day, thus gaining reassurance about the goodness of the internal society into which they will retire in sleep.

Commercial advertising often picks up these widespread patterns in our society and exploits them with great sensitivity and sophistication. This reinforces the patterns as well as giving commercial success. I quote only one outstanding success from many: 'Bridge that gap with a Cadbury's Snack'. The gap is not only or even primarily a hunger gap; it is a relationship gap. The advertisement and product offer a temporary resolution of the gap in a way that excellently matches common modes of dealing with separation in our external and internal societies – that is, by food.

The hazards of this situation from the nutritional point of view are obvious. First, it tends to divorce food and eating habits from nutritional needs in the short and long term. Meal content and the patterning of meals and other food consumption are heavily infiltrated with non-nutritional needs and satisfactions. Eating is not closely related to hunger and physiological need. We often eat when we do not need food. This threatens the control systems that relate nutritional signals to nutritional needs (Brosin, 1953).

Secondly, and perhaps more important, the foods that best satisfy emotional rather than nutritional needs are essentially the high-carbohydrate foods, particularly those that contain a large amount of refined sugar (Pennington, 1953). This stems from both the influence of internal figures who have used those foods in such ways and from inherent qualities in the foods themselves. These foods are freely available with little trouble or expense. They are usually significantly cheaper than alcohol, tobacco or drugs, are less subject to social disapproval and threaten less dire consequences if taken in excess. It is easy to deny the consequences. They can be bought prepared and stored ready to eat, often for long periods without deterioration. Thus they can be always available. Many people experience a rapid improvement, both physically and emotionally, when they eat them, a result widely attributed to their causing a rapid increase in blood sugar. They can be sucked, nibbled or chewed in considerable quantities over quite long periods without satiation. However, these very characteristics may lead to addiction in some people.

According to Randolph and others, an addiction to such foods may exist of which the sufferer himself is unaware (Bernton, 1952; Randolph, 1947, 1948, 1956; Rowe, 1928). They ascribe this addiction to the sufferer's successfully masking what they describe as a chronic food allergy or sensitization, by frequent repeated doses of the food in question. The sufferer, in fact, experiences rapid improvement after eating these frequent repeated doses. This subjective experience is more probably a function of the allergic/addictive qualities than of the rapid increase in blood sugar mentioned above. By contrast, if the dose is not repeated often enough the sufferer will have disturbing symptoms such as fatigue, restlessness, nervousness, headaches or depression. This undoubtedly encourages frequent and repeated eating.

One may also trace the psychosocial correlates of such addiction. In an unpublished study of the food habits of a provincial community where carbohydrate consumption was unusually high and the consumption of proteins, fruit and vegetables low, one could trace common patterns in the internal societies linked with carbohydrate-addictive traits. The internal mother linked with the carbohydrates was felt to be depriving and frustrating, but this was denied and an attempt was made to assert that she was capable of giving good food and to force her to give what she could not or would not give.

It appeared that the people concerned had a mild compulsion to go on working out this pattern with carbohydrate foods, to try to get from carbohydrates nutrients that they could not get – or not, at least, in sufficient quantities. One felt that these people had an intuitive awareness of a deficiency but their internal societies militated against a realistic method of putting it right. Their eating habits closely resembled the pattern described by Randolph: that is, they ate at very frequent intervals and the food always contained carbohydrates. People often carried food with them to ensure that their next intake would be easily available, and considerable anxiety was experienced by people likely to miss meals or have them late – an anxiety reminiscent of the addict uncertain of when he will get his next fix.

So significant do the high-sugar carbohydrate foods appear in this context that my colleagues and I at the Tavistock Institute came to call them generically 'the pleasure foods' – that is, foods that are used not primarily for nutrition but for increase of pleasure and reduction of pain, particularly in internal interpersonal relationship systems. The hazard for the consumer of such foods is obesity or malnutrition, or both together.

In conclusion, I will comment briefly on the task of changing eating habits. Unlike manufacturers of carbohydrate products who achieve their objectives by accepting and exploiting existing internal patterns, the nutritionist or doctor who wants to change eating habits for the better is too often faced with the task of challenging the internal society in order to change people inside, their relationships and the direction of their influence – not always an acceptable activity. Crash diets tend to be both popular and unsuccessful because they neither require nor facilitate any permanent restructuring of the internal society. Unfortunately, facts about nutrition and the people who convey them are likely to be less powerful influences when internalized than the long-established and highly emotionally toned mother and other related internal figures.

Necessary changes involve a number of features: for example, increased ability to distinguish between nutritional and non-nutritional uses of food; the ability to deal more effectively and directly with emotional needs; a revision of self and other images in the internal society and their reflection outwards. The internal mother who pops a sweet into a child's mouth every time he cries must be replaced by one who responds more adequately to emotional needs by understanding, cuddling or playing or by appropriate adult derivatives. An obese office worker may have to be rescued from identification with an internal father who is a coal-miner, while his wife may have to stop identifying with her mother feeding her father, who is also a coal-miner, before they can jointly develop a meal system realistically appropriate for an office worker.

Sorting these things out is not usually easy. Success will depend on having the opportunity to work through with the individual or community, implicitly or explicitly, the relevant aspects of the internal society and help to effect the appropriate changes. For encouragement one may note that there have been some dramatic successes. For example, to go back to the 1940s, group discussion methods were used effectively to help American women change the content of family meals so as to make better use of available foods during wartime (Lewin, 1943). Both group and individual psychotherapy have been effective in the treatment of obesity.

1 The development of ice cream as a food* (with Eric Trist)

This study was undertaken at the request of an advertising agency and their client, a food manufacturer whose products included ice cream. The background to the request was that the sales of ice cream in 1950, when the study was done, were highly seasonal, which was awkward from the manufacturing and marketing point of view. The manufacturer and his advertisers were therefore anxious to even out seasonal fluctuations. This would mean a considerable increase in winter sales.[1] The attempt to increase winter sales had been based on an advertising campaign directed to increasing the use of ice cream in the meal system in the home. The first attempts to do this had met with little success and it was then that the help of the Tavistock Institute of Human Relations was sought. We were to provide a social-psychological critique of the advertising approach. We would find out what had gone wrong and, if possible, suggest a more effective approach.

Surveying the situation as we started work, we gathered that the approach had been based on three interlocking assumptions:

1. The ordinary private home would be the most likely market in which to realize a substantial increase in winter sales in the short term. Accordingly the central objective was to secure for ice cream an accepted and permanent place in the meal system of the family.

*Revised version of a paper originally entitled 'Changing the perspective on the psychological position of ice cream in society'.

2. The product as then marketed, without modification or development, would be capable of freely entering this chosen market and securing the desired place within a reasonable time.

3. The degree and type of social change in national food habits involved in attaining this objective was within the competence of the advertising skills available.

However, ice cream did not enter the family meal system in any sizeable amount, so we tested the validity of these assumptions by a survey of attitudes and behaviour in a sample of the population of Greater London. The survey was conducted through individual and group interviews with consumers, potential consumers and gatekeepers – that is, people who control or influence the flow of the product to potential consumers. Observational studies were carried out at key points in the marketing system. And, as always in our market-research projects, the team conducted an in-depth study of its own attitudes, habits and reactions to the product. This survey enabled us to draw a kind of psychodynamic and social map of the territory in which the product existed, of the patterning of the psychosocial context – what we sometimes called depth anthropology. As the work progressed we also explored the economic dimension that interacted with the psychosocial in affecting consumer behaviour.

The findings of the survey supported our initial doubts about whether the home was necessarily the best place to seek to establish new habits of consumption. Other research confirmed those doubts in showing that intimate aspects of family life may be particularly hard to change rapidly and this notably affects eating habits, which are – or were then – at the core of family life (Lewin, 1943). We would have expected, therefore, that the home would have been a particularly difficult, not an easy, place to introduce a significant new food, and ice cream, as we found and as I shall describe below, was a particularly significant food.

This stemmed from its symbolic closeness to the breast and the mother–child relationship. Some genius thought of the name 'ice cream', thus making a link with the breast, but better than that, a breast that gives cream. (The fact that there never was much cream in ice cream, nor necessarily even a lot of milk, is neither here nor there.) The breast theme is sustained in the little round blobs in which ice cream is served in dishes and in the cones or cornets in which it is sold from shops, kiosks or barrows. They make one lick or suck: the more 'sophisticated' children or childish adults bite off the narrow end of the cone and treat it as a nipple through which they suck down the ice cream.

In view of this symbolic closeness we wrote a note on the significant features of the mother–child relationship for the agency and the manufacturer to help them understand the dynamic they were dealing with. I will discuss below how some of these features actually appear in the consumers' relationship with ice cream. The note was as follows:

SOME BASIC PSYCHOLOGICAL AND SOCIAL FACTORS
A note on the mother–child relationship
One of the most important features of the mother–child relationship is the provision of food, with the child in a completely dependent position. Another way of looking at this situation is the provision by the mother of all-pervading love and security. For the child the two things are not distinguishable as they are for the adult. Food is love and security. His thinking is concrete: in his mind love is loving acts and good things, particularly the good breast. He is not as yet capable of making the abstraction from that to love.

The emotional and intellectual life of the child at this time has a number of important characteristics which distinguishes it from those of the older child and adult. Contrary to general belief, the child's emotions are characterized by their great violence, by the way that they in turn blot out everything else so that the child's world becomes all-happy or all-sad, and by the rapidity with which he swings from one emotion to another. Thus the hungry child whose crying is not immediately answered may become entirely absorbed by terrible anger against the longed-for, but absent, breast. But he may become instantaneously and completely absorbed by pleasure the moment it reappears. However, he is not merely angry. In phantasy he destroys the object of his anger and since he cannot distinguish between phantasy and reality, he believes he has destroyed it in reality. In its absence, he suffers from guilt about its destruction, anxiety that he has altogether lost it, fear of retaliation from the attacked object, and so on. He needs the reappearance of the breast to allay these feelings and part of his pleasure then lies in the feeling that he has now omnipotently re-created it, undone his destruction, made friends with it again. The omnipotence of the baby in phantasy is only equalled by his powerlessness in reality. Deprivation of the breast, then, leads to aggressive omnipotent phantasies which are followed by guilt, depression and anxiety. The breast and the good food it gives have complete and immediate power to assuage these feelings.

At other times the baby feels unable to control his greed and in phantasy will bite up the breast or even steal it from the mother. Again he believes he has really done this and needs the assurance of the reappearance of the good, sound breast to assuage the depression and anxiety related to his omnipotent destructiveness.

Another characteristic of this situation is the lack of effort which the baby in reality makes to get food. His wishes are enough. He wishes for food, the wish perhaps stimulated by the actual presence of the breast or expressed by a cry, and the breast is his as if by magic. This becomes for him the situation, his wishes have magic power, and he never thinks of doing anything himself to get what he wants, or that his own efforts can have any relation to it.

These characteristics are very different from the way the adult approaches reality, but traces of them remain in even the most mature, well-adjusted adult and can be revived by certain situations and certain objects.

A NOTE ON PLEASURE FOODS

Ice cream belongs to a group of products which may be described as pleasure foods. Other products in this group are chocolates and sweets, alcoholic and soft drinks, and many kinds of preserves, sweetmeats and desserts. Closely associated, though not actually eaten or drunk, are tobacco and chewing

71

gum. These products are related to certain psychological and social factors and characteristic of them is their ability to gratify oral desires and, like the breast with the infant, change depression and anxiety into pleasure.

The concept of pleasure foods represents a fusion of Lewinian field theory and psychoanalysis, a fusion that became deeply embedded in the Tavistock tradition (Lewin, 1935). Trist introduced Lewin's theories to members of the Tavistock whilst they were still in the army; this had a profound effect on their thinking. Thus the concept of pleasure foods brought together the environmental influences, the 'field' and the internal situation through which the consumer responded to field forces.

This kind of oral gratification serves, then, as a method of alleviating current anxieties and depression which are in part the derivatives of the infantile anxiety and depression connected with the actual loss of the breast. Compensation for this loss is sought in the consumption of substitute objects, the pleasure foods. Thus the need for them becomes particularly great when contemporary difficulties awaken again the residues of the earlier situations which to a greater or lesser extent exist in everyone.

Many pleasure foods have good food value,[2] but this is of secondary significance in relation to their function and the actual eating pleasure is primary – that is, the emotional 'food values'. A good deal of the insistence on their food value is guilt about pleasure and the apparent lack of usefulness.

An outstanding characteristic of consumer behaviour with respect to pleasure foods is the combination of a number of them in one situation so as to achieve the greatest pleasure, to make life all pleasure, like the infant's. For example, at the cinema people smoke and eat sweets and ice cream, one after the other. At the pub people smoke, chew and nibble, as well as drink. There the pleasure foods add greater pleasure to a situation expected to be pleasurable in itself. Alone during the day the housewife nibbles from the larder, adds a sweet and a cigarette, from time to time: they help her to overcome the aloneness, the boredom and frustration of routine housekeeping. This behaviour is the adult representative of primitive infantile greed, and the need to reassure oneself by having all the good things for oneself.

In contrast to pleasure food is what may be called plain or 'real' food which is eaten for the more utilitarian purposes of building one's body, of enabling one to work, and is less intensely connected with primitive pleasure situations at the breast, though some connection remains. In our Protestant society, like other Protestant societies, the split between food that gives pleasure and food that has food value is deep and somewhat rigid. Pleasure foods belong very largely to the kind of eating and drinking which goes on between 'proper' meals and intrudes only slightly into such meals, which are designed to give food value. The expectation of food from pleasure eating or pleasure from 'real' food is minimal. The split is less evident in upper than in lower income groups.

ICE CREAM AS A PLEASURE FOOD

In some ways ice cream may be regarded as the pleasure food *par excellence* – above all in the extent to which it can reinstate the infantile pleasures to the loss of which the adult has never become quite reconciled. It has great power to act as a substitute for the breast, to wipe out anxieties and depression.

One may begin by noting the massive quality of the consumer's physical sensation. Optimally experienced, this is so complete as to blot out all other concerns so that, as for the child at the breast, there can be no bad things left and reality consists only of the good substance and the pleasure it gives. Ice cream has a capacity to provide this all-absorbing experience extremely vividly. Related to this is the suddenness of the onslaught of the state of delectation which ice cream again shares with the breast and the immediate quelling of the woes of an angry, hot infant the moment he is put to the breast. Proof is here given of the power of the good breast to overcome all ills and harms, a demonstration of its infinite power to provide good experience and total and all-pervading security.

The coldness of the ice cream produces both the initial delectable shock and the massiveness of the persisting sensation;

it thus reinforces other factors relating ice cream to the breast, such as its apparent milkiness. Neither of these magic effects is produced without the co-operation of the cold receptors in the tongue and the mouth. If, on the other hand, the ice cream is too cold, the taste sensations succumb to overwhelming cold sensation, pleasure becomes neuralgic pain, good turns to bad. All is disappointment, just as when the cold is insufficient. To allow full realization of the specially delectable ice-cream experience, the temperature of the product has to be gauged with exacting finesse.

This means that the ice cream must be eaten almost immediately after it is out of its container, which acts as the good breast that keeps the milk in good condition. It is most satisfying when the act of taking it out is witnessed and there is immediate handing over and consumption; this seems to bring back most easily the experience of the restoration of the lost or stolen breast.

The next important effect of the coldness is that it inhibits the use of the teeth. The breast is preserved against attack and destruction by greedy, devouring biting. Also, since the product melts in the mouth, no mastication is necessary. The cold shock should be great enough to inhibit the teeth but not so great that the outburst of pleasure sensation is in any way marred as the melting in the mouth occurs. Clear experience of this sequence is responsible for the delicious surprise which emotionally is proof that the good substance has passed in intact and unharmed, reaffirming its wholeness inside the mouth.

Lastly, the coldness produces contractions in the stomach walls. The effect of this is to produce sensation of the ice cream going in intact and almost alive in the stomach. There could be no more perfect technique for proving that eating up the good thing and so taking it completely inside oneself does it no harm. At every stage the magical emotional meaning is directly proven to the consumer by the physical sensations he experiences.

Closely connected with the power of ice cream to reinstate the breast is the attitude of helpless dependency which the consumer shows towards it. People feel that the desire for ice cream should be enough to conjure it up magically like the breast: no effort on their part should be necessary; that is not part of the bargain and spoils the fun. It is impossible to stress too strongly the need for the distribution system to fit itself as fully as possible to this attitude, taking full responsibility for making the product available. Everything must be set for the magical appearance of ice cream as best suits particular circumstances.

Another consequence is the consumer's infantile concrete attitude to ice cream; it is largely either in sight and in mind or out of sight and out of mind. The appearance of ice cream or even of advertisements for ice cream is very likely to arouse the need for it, which then becomes imbued with a primitive, intolerable urgency. Also moods of depression and anxiety or deprivation and frustration are quite likely, in favourable circumstances, to lead to sudden notions for ice cream. On the other hand, if ice cream is not available to satisfy the impulsive desire this will touch off violent infantile hostility against the ice cream manufacturers, especially if they create the desire for ice cream in circumstances where they are then unable to satisfy completely the resulting consumer demands. Ice cream too easily becomes 'I scream'.

Quality and purity
Anything which so closely represents the continued existence of the breast has to be very, very good. Any ice cream which fails to match up with consumers' expectations with respect to taste, supposed quality of ingredients and coldness is met with the most violent hostility. However, these attitudes are strongly countered by the dependency of the consumer. Easy availability, the magic appearance of the breast on desire, is apparently more important than the need for a taste which implies quality. In fact, an essential part of the goodness of good ice cream is that one should get it when one wants it. Otherwise it ceases to be really good, for it has let one down and something of lower quality which shows its goodness by being available will be preferred. The consumers' dependency also affects attitudes to action to prevent the sale of low-quality ice cream: the consumer himself will take no responsibility but demands that someone else,

particularly the producers of high-quality ice cream, should do it for him.

Ice cream as a pleasure food would predictably have found it particularly difficult to move into the family meal system, orientated as it was on a different food/pleasure balance with emphasis on being well fed or fully fed, especially in the less well-to-do households where getting enough food could be quite a problem. Attitudes were also still affected by wartime shortages and continued rationing, which really did make it difficult to sustain a nutritious and sufficient diet. The emphasis was on being well – that is, nutritiously, even if boringly – fed, rather than enjoying oneself.

While this was true, there was another apparently contradictory dynamic at work: wartime shortages and rationing had particularly deprived people of the pleasure foods, sweets and chocolate and ice cream itself. There was a pile-up of deprivation and longing for satisfaction which indeed broke through in the late forties and early fifties when supplies were approximately back to normal. There was a deep split between these two objectives and the ways of achieving them which would have been difficult to bridge in terms of having the pleasure food, ice cream, as part of a nutrition-orientated meal, even if in fact it was reasonably nutritious. The housewife, the family gatekeeper, would have tended to keep ice cream apart from, rather than helping it to become a part of, the family meal.

Having ice cream with meals at home was sometimes experienced as rather an assault on the role of the housewife as provider of food: she had to do nothing to prepare it; gave nothing of herself. This had similarities with the actual fate of a cake mix where the housewife had to add only water to the powder: it failed to catch on. A later version of the same product to which milk and/or eggs had to be added was a success. It was more maternal. Ice cream was a competitor to the custard the housewife made herself. The housewife's need to please her family by giving them what they wanted, or what she thought they would want – ice cream – was thus in conflict with her wish to sustain her feeding role. There was another factor in the custard/ice cream conflict. Ice cream was felt to be much more expensive than custard and so might be beyond the budget. This impression was exaggerated by the fact that custard *apparently* cost nothing – custard was made from 'free' ingredients already in stock whose cost was not taken into account.

By contrast, ice cream cost visibly 1*s*. 6*d*. or two shillings. Ice cream was often seen as a total addition to meal cost – as it probably was, in fact – rather than a substitute, costwise, for something else. The cost of ice cream, then, might really have broken the family budget. There were many complaints about the amount of ice cream one had to buy. A 1*s*. 6*d*. block was too big – and remember there was no way leftovers could be preserved. Custard, by contrast, seemed infinitely elastic. The alternative to the block – a number of small portions, one for each family member – was also rejected: it did not allow 'mother' to serve the 'pudding', nor did it allow for 'seconds'.

There were also a number of practical difficulties about having ice cream with home meals that linked closely with some of the patterns described above and in 'Psychosocial aspects of eating'. Most important was the fact that only 3 per cent of homes had refrigerators and there were virtually no home freezers. There were difficulties, in other words, in getting ice cream into the home and available for meals in the first place. So there was a kind of teasing quality about the advertisement's encouraging the consumption of ice cream as a food in meals when there was no practical way of getting it. (Note, from the description above, the importance of ice cream, like the breast, being easily and quickly available when wanted.) The result was considerable negative reaction to the advertisements and to the products from consumers who discussed the advertisements with us.

There was the 'It's beside the point' reaction: 'All this has nothing to do with us.' Behind this there was a lot of suspicion and hostility held at bay. 'Why are they tempting and teasing us?' The hostility showed too in complaints. 'Why don't [they] give us back the tricycle men?'[3] 'They must have gone over to the refrigerator class.' People felt they could not possibly be the target of such advertisements. They had been dismissed, annihilated. Mother did not care! This provoked an excluded group reaction and made consumers very hostile to the manufacturer and the advertising agency. They knew they did not have the necessary conditions to keep ice cream for meals in the home, and envied the often imaginary people who did. The manufacturer first deserted them and then tortured them with what they had lost – 'weaning' with a vengeance. The whole idea of ice cream in the home became unreal because they saw no reality in it for themselves. What was denied to them they denied to everybody else, including the fortunate possessors of refrigerators and high incomes. They withdrew from the whole idea of ice cream in the home meal system, the best escape from the pain and frustration of wanting it and not being able to get it.

An additional insult was that their 'own' newspapers carried these advertisements: 'All this ice cream in the *Daily Mail*, or in *Hulton's Weekly*. It's no use to me.' Worse, of course, the newspapers stimulated the wish for ice cream and did nothing to meet it. The danger again was that ice cream in the home would be written off, the wish for it being too frustrating and painful to be sustained. Probably the last straw in all this was advertising the delight of having ice cream with the Christmas dinner, a meal with high pleasure expectation. But with the shops shut and no refrigerator, there was no way that people could get the ice cream. The reaction was furious.

The quality of these reactions showed their roots not only in the current situation but as derivatives from the powerful positive and negative reactions of the infant in his relationship with the original pleasure food, the breast, and its possessor, the mother. There was real danger to the manufacturer in the present and also in the future in making people aware that ice cream was around when they were not to have any and could not get to it. Respondents felt that the manufacturer was indulging in wish-fulfilment at their expense – his wishes for higher sales taking no real account of what he was doing to them. They kept insisting that he should make the product more accessible: 'Get the tricycle men back'; 'Make the blocks cheaper.' The advertisements seemed to be working up a conflict between the manufacturer and the consumer, between the manufacturer's wish to sell more ice cream and the consumer's wish to have more ice cream when the manufacturer did not provide him with the wherewithal actually to get it.

The consumer did not really need a stimulus to his appetite – in the aftermath of wartime shortages and in current rationing he had more than enough appetite. He needed practical help in satisfying it and he felt it was up to the manufacturer to supply this. Without that he would have none of it, the advertising or the ice cream. The danger in all this for the manufacturer was that not only would he fail to achieve his original objective of getting ice cream into the home family system, but that such a negative reaction might defeat his objectives for all time, or at least for a very long time to come.

Having come to that conclusion, we set our minds to considering what could be done instead. There seemed to be two main approaches: first, to try to devise methods of overcoming barriers to getting ice cream into the home meal system; or, secondly, to investigate whether it would be possible to enter new winter markets or enlarge existing ones to take attention off the home, at least for the present. The latter felt and later proved to be the more effective approach for the time being.

Crucial to increasing home consumption was the problem of having the ice cream arrive at the home in prime condition and remain so until the family was ready to eat it. The correct degree of coldness is of the essence in this. Soggy, soft ice cream is just no good at all – worse, it is 'yukky': 'It could put you off for ever.' Ice chips show that the ice cream has melted and refrozen. This is no good – it proves that the provider has been careless: not only of the product but, worse, of one's needs. Too cold and hard ice cream is no good either, so there is no point in freezing it too hard to stop it going soggy. At home, where disappointing experiences of food are especially to be avoided, ice cream had to be just right. People expressed such feelings quite strongly: 'Keep me away from that soggy stuff.' 'It looks worse than margarine when it has come apart: put me off for months.' At the other end: 'You'd need an ice pick.' Even carrying the ice cream from the shop to the table takes away its first freshness.

As well as being in prime condition, ice cream has to be available just where and when you want it without apparent effort . . . like the breast for the baby. As if by magic, the good mother anticipates the baby's need by that fraction of a second so that he never actually has to realize he needs her. There was considerable resistance to having to wait once one felt one wanted an ice cream, and to the effort of going to fetch it. One respondent lying on Brighton beach had not had an ice cream for several years: she suddenly felt an overwhelming desire for one. The nearest sales point was some yards away up some steps, so she went right on daydreaming but did not go to get any. Perhaps she only wanted a dream anyway, since she had not eaten ice cream for real in years. Anything that signals ice cream, like the tricycle bell, arouses desire, but it should also offer satisfaction, like the man with the tricycle.

Bringing together these and other points about demand and supply, we considered how ice cream could be supplied to the home in perfect condition so that it could be available at the point where it was wanted and with minimal effort. I do not think, looking back, that we ourselves ever found any of the possibilities very hopeful or even relevant. They were likely to be expensive and quite troublesome, as well as limited mainly to the well-to-do and to special occasions. Basically this effort would have had to be centred around containers which would have been owned by the family or supplied with the order on loan or hire from the sales point. In fact, work did not go ahead on developing such possibilities and efforts were concentrated on outlets other than the home where winter sales might be increased. Referring back to assumption 3 (p. 69 above), it seemed clear that bringing about such a change in food habits in such circumstances would be beyond the resources of the advertisers. Some other objectives would have to be found that were within their resources.[4]

Other possible outlets would essentially be indoor outlets which were heated and so negated the seasonal changes in temperature out of doors: public places where people had meals or engaged in pleasurable activities where ice cream would enhance the pleasure. Many of these seemed to be particularly suitable for the sale of ice cream in psychosocial terms. It seemed more practicable to encourage the favourable trends in such places than to fight against the formidable barriers to entry into the home. The seasonable trends in those places were not always so great as in the home, so that evening them still further might not be too difficult.

We set ourselves, therefore, to explore a number of situations which already had an appreciable winter consumption of ice cream. Within each category of possible outlets we found some that had a high winter consumption and others with a low consumption or none. This was hopeful in indicating that there was potential for development, and also pointed to the need to investigate the reasons for the differences between establishments. Our investigations included cinemas, indoor functions and activities, institutions that provided meals for staff and/or clients like factories, schools and hospitals and restaurants serving midday meals to factory, office and shop workers.

Ice cream was already consumed in quite large quantities in the cinema, which appeared to be a particularly suitable outlet. The darkness and relative anonymity provided some protection for people, especially men, who might not want to be seen eating ice cream, considering it childish or self-indulgent. Solitary gluttony was also hidden. Ice cream added to the other pleasures: the film, smoking, eating sweets, holding hands. It seemed to figure quite importantly in the weekly ritual of a man taking his wife or girlfriend to the cinema, especially in the working and lower middle classes: helping to consolidate the good relationship, often giving the man an excuse to be a bit 'cissy' because he was only joining his lady in her pleasure.

Interestingly, however, some of the same negative feelings appeared here too. The ice cream was too expensive, more than in the shops – so much the worse that the man would be buying for two. But really, ice cream should be free, like the good breast. Respondents felt strongly that the ice cream sold in the cinema was inferior to that sold in the shops, as indeed it sometimes was. They felt that a captive audience was being exploited by cinema managers and suppliers – an unforgivable sin in this context. There were also complaints about the inadequacy of supplies: none on some evenings, running out on busy evenings like Fridays and Saturdays: not something that should happen to ice cream. How strongly these complaints illustrated the comments above about goodness, the need for perfection, the anger at being teased and tantalized if the possibility of having an ice cream was offered but the ice cream was not available – and immediately!

The cinema definitely offered ample scope for the development of winter sales, especially by reputable manufacturers whose name gave a guarantee of goodness. Cinema-going is at its peak in winter. Sales could be stimulated by appropriate screen advertising, bearing in mind the immediacy of reaction and demand for ice cream. We stressed the importance of supplies never running out. There seemed little doubt that the attitude of the cinema manager to providing ice cream was crucial: his own interest in it, how he saw it fitting in with his overall provision for his clients, how much trouble he was prepared to take, its profitability. Such a gatekeeper figure was to emerge as being of great importance in all the indoor situations. This raised marketing issues beyond advertising – the need for salesmen who could work effectively with the gatekeepers.

Every community has indoor activities mainly concentrated in the winter: regular meetings like youth clubs, indoor sports or social clubs, women's groups, the occasional formal and special function. Some kind of food and drink was likely to be served in all of those. Here again there appeared to be very good psycho-social conditions for the sale and consumption of ice cream: places where people meet for pleasure and where ice cream could add to the pleasure and help people to indulge themselves. Individuals would often be buying for one only and the cost would not seem too high; the need to be fully adult might be somewhat relaxed; ice cream would sometimes add to and finish off a meal in pure pleasure because real food had been so well provided in earlier highly nutritious courses. Further, many of these situations are the winter equivalent of summer situations where ice cream would be provided almost to the point of being a conventional necessity. Thus a cultural carry-over would not be too difficult.

Some of these situations, particularly the clubs with regular meetings, might have problems like those in the home: no refrigeration or possibility of delivery so that getting supplies of perfect ice cream would have been very difficult. However, there seemed more possibility for the provision of ice cream in such institutions for the occasional formal event: the annual dance, Christmas parties, weddings. It has been the custom, in fact, for ice cream to be delivered for such events in special containers: for example, the ice-cream container embedded in an outer container filled with ice; small portable refrigerators or freezers that could be plugged in; or refrigerators or freezers already there could be used. The cost of this in the institutional setting would be less inhibitive than for home consumption, especially in the special-treat atmosphere.

Ice cream served in such situations tends to be more than simple vanilla. It is often made into a 'dish' in combination with other food like fruit, meringue, cream. The ice cream may indeed be 'own-made' – the chef, like mother at home, preferring to make it himself for his diners. More variety also appears in the ice cream itself: more, and more exotic, flavours – ice-puddings. The pleasure element is emphasized and the food value played down (although realistically it is high) when the course follows a rich and satisfying main meal: 'I don't really need anything more.'

The situation is very similar in expensive restaurants serving evening meals: ice cream adds great pleasure and the possibility of an exotic note after a rich and satisfying dinner. The exotic note seemed important to counteract the feeling of childishness in eating ice cream at a sophisticated function. In both situations, ice cream is established traditionally as a light sweet in the course system of the formal meal. These explorations led us in turn to question the second assumption of the advertisers: that ice cream could easily enter the family meal system in its current form, mainly plain vanilla. The more exotic kinds made for the formal dinner might be more appropriate.

It seemed again to be a matter of stimulating demand, both by appropriate advertising and by deploying salesmen who were skilled at working with gatekeepers, club officials or possibly their caterers. The additional service offered – containers provided as well as the ice cream – could also be advertised and promoted.

There were many and varied ways in which ice cream appeared in meals provided by institutions. Looking first at hospitals, we found the position of the gatekeeper particularly striking: the person who planned the meals and decided what resources should be devoted to ice cream, anything from none at all to a considerable proportion of the still-rationed sugar and fats which were given to an ice-cream manufacturer in exchange for ice cream. That caterer believed it was an important addition to the diet, nutritionally speaking. But it was also an emotional food – it was 'motherly'. For patients it was an aid to dealing with anxiety and stress, a sign that the hospital cared, a nourishing, nurturing, easy-to-digest pleasure. For nurses, too, it was more than a food – it was a reassuring, nurturing pleasure in the stress of their occupation.

In other words, ice cream could have an important place in institutions where stress and anxiety are high for both staff and clients, and the need for nurturing objects is particularly high. This market appeared worth cultivating. On the other hand, staff who served ice cream got pleasure from that: it made them feel loving, kindly and nurturing. They also, at the time, tended to regard ice cream as nutritionally excellent for helping to build patients up and foster recovery; this view would perhaps be questioned nowadays.[5] The amount of ice cream served in different hospitals varied considerably; it seemed to be closely connected with the attitude of the individual gatekeeper: the dietitian, chef, matron or whoever.

Many people who determined the menu in schools also favoured ice cream in meals. In their case, this seemed to be connected with a wish to be, and to be seen to be, good to the children: not to be seen as the purveyor of conventionally awful, dull school meals, a kind of grim and unappetizing lesson. But there was conflict. An analysis had shown that ice cream did not contain the nutrients needed to balance and complement other nutrients in the meal. Milk content was too low! (Never mind cream.) This provoked anger and grievance both about the failure of the ice cream itself and about having to give up serving it. Would it be worthwhile to make a more nutritious ice cream for schools which might also have been more acceptable to hospitals or even ordinary homes? The difficulty would probably have been expense.

Finally, midday restaurants and industrial canteens: various points about the psychosocial setting for ice cream suggest that ice-cream consumption might be high in such places and could easily be stimulated. Eating in such places is characterized by the use of pleasure-food extras to compensate for having to eat away from home, and to keep as high as possible the home-substitute quality of the meal. The canteen seemed to function as a quasi-maternal institution in contrast to the more brisk, paternal, authoritarian environment of the factory or office. Regression was tolerated as an accompaniment to a home-substitute environment.

This appeared to be connected with the fact that there did not seem to be the same marked differences between the ages and sexes of consumers, or in their occupational status, as are found in other consuming situations. Their absence argues in favour of a strong common influence being exerted in these situations. An interesting exception to this was a group of women technical assistants in a laboratory with strong masculine identifications, as though such scientific pursuits were essentially masculine. Their consumption was low and they seemed unaware that they differed from their male colleagues, whose consumption was within the factory norm.

Canteens tend to be quite cheap and money is left over for the price of an ice cream. The cheapness of the meal may, however, lead to some dullness, lack of imagination and variety in the menu, so that the consumer does not feel quite satisfied or well enough fed and needs some addition such as a 'maternal' pudding. In the canteen, the individual is almost certainly buying for only one person so that serious cost issues do not arise. The fear and embarrassment about it being childish to eat ice cream do not appear to have much influence here: a man will not be seen by his wife and children indulging in a childish or effeminate pleasure, and it is good to regress when life is stressful.

The actual consumption of ice cream varied considerably in different canteens and restaurants; in the very cheap canteens it seemed beyond the price range of customers and was little in demand. Getting real food was too serious a business. In the more expensive canteens consumption went up and it was high also in expensive restaurants. The attitude of the gatekeeper was, of course, again very influential in affecting sales in general and the amount of seasonal fluctuation in particular. Consumers also varied considerably in their attitudes to ice cream. Some could reasonably be described as addicts: they had ice cream every single day; there were occasional consumers whose consumption varied quite a bit; and there were people who never used it – 'wouldn't touch the stuff'. The nature of the use also varied. Ice cream often had a 'custard' function eaten with the dessert, whatever it was: fruit, apple pie, steamed pudding. Sometimes it was eaten alone as a dessert; sometimes it was picked up at the snack counter and eaten 'on the walk'.

On the whole, the population of canteens and even midday restaurants was fairly stable; this meant that the culture around ice-cream consumption tended to be built up and maintained. Newcomers fitted into it. So once the regular amount of consumption was built up, it too tended to remain fairly stable. When people left there was a chance that they would take the ice-cream culture with them and might influence other places.

All in all, it seemed to us that there was considerable potential for building up good winter trade in canteens and midday restaurants, both by a direct approach to the consumer and by sales efforts directed at gatekeepers. A combined approach seemed desirable in view of the strong negative feelings that arise when awakened desire is not met.

At the end of our explorations we had little doubt that winter sales of ice cream could be stimulated by due attention to outlets other than the home. The home itself was possibly one of the worst outlets at that time in view of the practical difficulties of getting ice cream there in good enough condition. In fact, the client followed our advice and built up winter sales outside the home. We also felt that if sales were successfully established in these other outlets, this might ultimately have some influence on the home if and when the practical difficulties could be overcome – for example, by gradual growth in the domestic use of refrigerators.

Subsequent developments were interesting. As the effect of wartime shortages and rationing has declined, rather compulsive use of the pleasure foods has also eased off and the demand has plateaued, but still at quite a high level. The psychosocial picture has not changed much, although changes in external circumstances have influenced the way it is deployed. Consumption has remained at a good level in all the non-domestic situations, but in addition consumption has greatly increased in the home now that there is almost universal ownership of refrigerators and high ownership of home freezers. Storage is little problem.

Ice cream has now moved into the position of being almost a conventional necessity in some homes. It is always in the freezer ready for use when wanted as a pleasure food, as part of a family meal, or whatever. Further, as discussed above, the former sophistication of the upper-class restaurants has filtered down through the social classes. Sometimes the housewife adds the sophistication herself, sometimes she buys it from the wide range of exotic ice creams now provided by the manufacturer. Present behaviour justifies our rejection of assumption 3 and our feeling that to enter the home ice cream needed to provide a wider range of flavours and combinations of ice cream and other ingredients. Interestingly, however, in spite of this, the 'custard' function has stood up well in the home.

Life would be almost inconceivable nowadays without ice cream, even for people who hardly ever or never use it. It has almost become a part of our heritage, like unconscious memories and phantasies of the prehistoric past of our own lives – the good object must always be there, even if it is not noticed or used.

POSTSCRIPT (1988)

When this paper was originally written, pleasure foods, with the possible exception of alcohol, could be regarded as a relatively innocent way to relieve anxiety and distress, with good nutrition as a bonus. Unfortunately, this is no longer the case; so many of the ingredients of the pleasure foods are now suspect: sugar, animal fats, chocolate; tobacco can actually be a killer, and alcohol can be dangerous except in small amounts. As regards ice cream, the more 'genuine' it is the worse. A move is afoot, indeed, to popularize ice cream that is more genuine, part of a move to take food in general nearer to the 'natural' – ice cream that would contain more real cream (Stack, 1988). The projected products sound delicious, but at what cost . . .?

So the good – or thought-to-be-good – turns bad, the benign mother-substitute turns out to be dangerous, the specially good turns into the specially bad. As yet, society has not really faced up to this problem. People still tend to deny the potentially bad effects of those so-much-needed pleasure foods. In the case of ice cream this has kept sales up, particularly in Great Britain. There is pressure too to sustain the denials and maintain consumption. The *Guardian* quotes the manufacturer of a rich, genuinely creamy ice cream as saying: 'Ice cream is full of protein, vitamin A and calcium. It isn't balanced, but if you are going to eat pudding you may as well eat ice cream if you want to stay healthy' – the 'good food' argument in an up-to-date form (Stack, 1988).

On the other hand, life is felt to be becoming more and more difficult and dangerous . . . the need for support, sustenance and comfort is increasing. But what is one to do when the supporting, sustaining, comforting mother-substitute is herself dangerous? So far, society has come up with no safe, healthy substitute for the pleasure foods. The attempts to use drugs or more alcohol instead only make matters worse. This is a sad dilemma for society.

NOTES

1. It is historically interesting that this particular manufacturer had begun to produce ice cream to balance another food product with high winter sales, and the pendulum had swung too far.

2. For further discussion of food value see Postscript, pp. 87–8.

3. Travelling ice cream salesmen who went round the streets.

4. There was one cheap and easy way of keeping ice cream in a good state for at least long enough to get it home and keep it while the rest of the meal was eaten – by wrapping it in many layers of newspaper – but it did not feel quite right: ice cream is not fish and chips.

5. See Postscript, pp. 87–8.

II The purchase and consumption of chocolate*

This study was carried out in 1959, some ten years after the ice-cream study (see above, pp. 68–89). During that time a number of other major studies on the subject of pleasure foods had been done, and our experience and understanding of their psychological position had been considerably extended. In particular, we had completed several studies on various chocolate products.

The client for the study reported here was the manufacturer of a well-known chocolate product, a product which had long been held in high regard – almost a 'household word' – but, strangely, never had very high sales: a product rather unique in its design, different and in a rather higher class than most of its close competitors. This product had disappeared during and immediately after the Second World War, had then been in short supply and unofficially 'rationed', and was now coming back fully on to the market. Its reappearance had met with only limited success and the client was naturally anxious to discover why that should be and to find ways of extending his market.

We considered it relevant to do a study bringing our experience of pleasure-food consumption in general, and chocolate in particular, up to date. So we began with a wide general survey of the chocolate market, consumer attitudes and behaviour. We then considered how the specific product fitted into the market, and how its marketing could be related to consumer patterns.

Our report to the client began with a discussion of the concept of pleasure foods which will not be included here since it has been rather fully described in the ice-cream paper. In this paper, we discuss more extensively the negative feelings surrounding the consumption of pleas-

---

*Revised version of a paper originally entitled 'Some social and psychological aspects of the purchase and consumption of chocolate'.

ure foods and the defences, personal and socialized, that the consumer uses in order to be able to pursue his pleasures without suffering too severely from the negative feelings.

CONSIDERABLE DOUBT, disappointment, guilt and anxiety are stimulated by giving, receiving and eating food, especially pleasure foods. The infant may experience his activities and phantasies about feeding as aggressive and destructive, especially if he starts feeding with angry feelings or feelings of being unloved. Sucking may be experienced as overexcited and greedy, exhausting the mother and depriving other people; the infant often experiences biting and chewing as destructive, especially if they develop precociously – that is, before teeth come and solid food plays an important part in feeding; the infant's longing for a very good feeding experience may lead to an idealization of feeding which dooms him to disappointment.

The infant may feel acute envy of the mother as the source of the vitally important food supplies which for him mean both love and life, emotional as well as physiological satisfaction. He often feels very possessive about his mother. He feels guilty about his attacks on others, and fears that they may really destroy or spoil the source of his own food and the food itself. Eating the 'spoilt' food may be experienced as dangerous: this is the source of many eating difficulties in later childhood and even adulthood and contributes to the strong feelings of dislike which individuals often attach to specific foods. The infant expects punishment and counterattacks. In his phantasies, the food itself will hurt him and produce bad effects. The inevitable digestive upsets of infancy may be experienced in this way. His possessiveness leads to fears of being possessed in return, and losing his own freedom.

In discussing sweets and chocolate, adults and older children made consistent and repeated references to modified, more mature forms of these same anxieties. Disappointment was frequent and bitter, and provoked great anger against the giver or manufacturer. Idealization of sweets as a source of satisfaction was common, the idealized sweet usually being connected with something eaten in fairly early childhood and remembered. Sometimes they say the sweet has now 'disappeared'. People often claimed that a sweet had disappeared when it was in fact still readily available. At other times, people admit that the sweet is still sold but claim it is not what it used to be. Sweets which appeared regularly as childhood idealized favourites included whipped cream walnuts, certain Cadbury products, especially milky ones like the milk flake, and Sharp's Kreemy Toffees. One respondent who was very idealistic about them remarked that they were not what they used to be and that 'Mr Sharp must have died and taken the secret to the grave with him'.

The feeling that sweets are not what they used to be was typical of consumers and covered a complicated set of feelings. It is doubtful if the sweets ever gave the satisfaction they are remembered to have given, being themselves already an unsatisfactory substitute for a remembered even earlier idealized feeding satisfaction, which in turn was never so good as the memory or phantasy. Older children and adults who are reasonably mature would not in reality find food so much at the centre of their pattern of satisfaction as the infant does. The exciting, satisfying experience they seek would arise in activities and relationships other than feeding, the most obvious being satisfactory mature sexual relationships. The greatest idealization of sweets in older children and adults tends to appear in people who are somewhat immature or whose lives are temporarily or permanently disappointing.

Other manifestations of the early problems were common. Greed and attempts to control it were obvious. Wide-eyed 'Oohs' were a typical response to our offering chocolate, or 'Oh, gorgeous!' and a kind of lunge at them. But it was often difficult to induce people to eat very much or take a broken bar away. People were afraid of being enticed and too excited by the chocolate, and often felt they were on the edge of a dangerously overexciting experience if they let themselves go. Fears of being possessed or compelled by sweets, especially chocolate, were very common: 'It gets you'; 'You can't stop eating till it's finished'; 'It fascinates you'; 'You start by buying one bar a week and find you are buying one every day, so you have to take yourself in hand.' There were many fears about what would happen if one overindulged: teeth would go bad; one would get fat; one would get spots.

In phantasy, these consequences were closely connected with retaliation and punishment for greed and were feared not only because they spoiled one's appearance and so lowered one's self-respect, but also because they were conspicuous and exposed one to censure from other people. General opinion connects fatness with overeating in a simple and direct way, and medical evidence which shows that no such simple relation exists is disregarded. Spots and bad teeth are both commonly taken as evidence of overindulgence in sweet, sugary foods. Such real connections as exist were greatly exaggerated. The expectation of disapproval was reflected in such common phrases as 'Nobody loves a fat boy', and shown in the merciless teasing to which a fat child is subjected by his peers, often in itself a sign of envy and jealousy that he has had so much more than they have.

As with ice cream, anxiety about the condition of the food was apparent in discussing sweets and chocolate. Much time was spent discussing what sweets were made of, whether the ingredients are 'genuine' and 'natural' – for example butter or margarine, real fruit or artificial flavouring, real liqueurs or just alcohol flavour. People were very suspicious and readily believed they were being cheated by substitutes. The condition of the sweets or chocolate was of vital importance: it must not be stale. People talked of avoiding small shops because the turnover was too low, asking before they bought when the stock had come in, and buying something else if the sweets were too old. Bloom on chocolate was a major cause of disappointment and anger: few people admitted to eating chocolate with bloom, although in fact it makes little difference to taste. A significant number of respondents said that they had absolutely refused to buy the same manufacturer's chocolate again, even when a formal complaint had produced immediate replacement of the spoiled chocolate.

A similar manifestation of anxiety arose in the handling of chocolate: people worried about chocolate melting and being messy so that they would get hands, faces and clothes stained. Mothers worried about children getting messy and often gave them other sweets in preference to chocolate for this reason. People worried about how chocolate breaks and disliked crumbs which could not easily be caught in the wrapper.

Fears of being exploited were common. People tended to be somewhat suspicious about price, size, shape and presentation, in relation to value for money. Price and size were intuitively balanced and one product compared with another. Criticisms were made of manufacturers who spent too much on wrappers and detracted from the value which went into the product itself. Respondents criticized wrappers which made products look bigger than they were and led to a feeling of being disappointed and cheated when opened. People were not generally aware of the weight of the product, but this situation seemed to us to be changing in the direction of growing awareness, and the expectation that packaged products would either cost a round sum like 6d. or 1s. for a declared weight or that they would be a defined fraction – 2 oz, 4 oz, 8oz, 12 oz or multiples of a pound – at the appropriate price. Fears of exploitation were most clearly expressed against sweets described as 'rubbish' which unscrupulous shopkeepers would sell to unsuspecting children, but were undoubtedly at the ready in relation to all confectionery products.

Too great an interest in pleasure foods made people feel childish; this embarrassed them, and made them expect criticism from others. Older boys and men often felt it as a reflection on their masculinity since it implied an excessive dependence on food, which unconsciously evoked the mother. A persisting close tie between mother and daughter is more acceptable in our society than a similar tie between mother and son, and women are permitted the symbolic expression of such a tie through pleasure foods more than men are. Greed and possessiveness were felt to have possible adverse effects not only on the person who supplied the food, but also on other people whom they deprived, and gave rise to feelings of guilt and expectations of censure and punishment.

Excitement was closely connected with sexual excitement and aroused the same kind of personal and social restraints, though to a lesser degree. We found that an excited relationship with a food product which is strongly masculine in connection may be a socially acceptable way of expressing displaced sexual excitement. For example, adolescent girls who were struggling to cope with strong sexual feelings, which by custom could not be expressed directly, ate many sweets and often those with strong masculine connotations – for example phallic in shape, hard as masculinity is hard, with male-sounding names, and so on. The same is true of adolescent boys, who are anxious about direct expressions of their normal sexual wishes towards other boys or men. They seek to develop their masculinity by eating such 'masculine' products and so becoming like them. Familiar phrases imply that one becomes like what one eats: 'You will turn into a strawberry, fish, biscuit, etc., if you eat any more'; 'You'll begin to look like a cow if you drink so much milk'; or 'People begin to look like people or animals they live with.'

Disloyalty to a product aroused feelings similar to disloyalty to a friend or sexual unfaithfulness. People felt ashamed and expected some criticism if they showed interest in or knowledge of too many varieties of the same pleasure food – for example chocolate bars, where the range was very large. The phantasies came very close to prostitution and sexual promiscuity. They were the more alarming because such desires are general, although the majority of people disown them and hold them in check in the interests of other relationships and satisfactions. Again it may be noted, however, that more 'disloyalty' or 'promiscuity' is permitted in relation to pleasure foods than sexually. The typical pattern of consumer choice was to have a group of fairly regular products – 'friends', one might say – possibly not all liked to quite the same extent, but all consumed fairly regularly. Products entered and left this group and occasional sorties were made to buy other products.

Following this theme, one can see the anxiety about fatness and spots as implying specifically, in so far as eating is sexualized, anxiety about illicit pregnancies, the result of secret extra-marital affairs: these phantasies apply to both sexes, though they are more prevalent in women, for the unconscious has little understanding of the real biological difference between the sexes. Dental decay and spots were also experienced as a direct assault on one's sexual attractiveness as a punishment for one's indulgence, and people felt correspondingly embarrassed and upset. Dental decay aroused anxiety that the penalty for overindulgence is diminution of ability to indulge in the future – for example, through the common experience that it was quite difficult to eat toffees if one had dentures.

The consumer, then, was faced with the need to find methods of holding at bay his anxiety about consuming pleasure foods – chocolate in this case – so that he could continue to consume and enjoy them, even satisfy a craving for them. Consumers developed a number of characteristic devices which resolved the anxieties or contained them at a tolerable level. They gave both rational and irrational explanations about the pleasures and benefits derived from eating sweets, and possible ill effects. So heavily were the rational elements permeated by the irrational, however, that we came to talk about a 'consumer mythology' which developed around the whole topic of pleasure foods.

A favourite rationalization for eating pleasure foods is that they are 'good food', 'nourishing' and 'good for you'. This applies to chocolate *par excellence* – both because there is a real element of good food about it, especially the milk, and because chocolate stands very high as a giver of pleasure. Milk was also important to 'domesticate' chocolate which, in its purer state, was felt to be an exotic product with a strong erotic aspect. More important than the real 'good food' element in chocolate was the need to deny that it was eaten because it gave such intense pleasure. One might almost say that the greater the element of pleasure-seeking in consuming the food, the more likely it was to be justified on grounds of being good for one or necessary. Need was stressed rather than greed or desire.

This device is reinforced by projecting one's own feelings in reverse into the product. The person was not greedy or sensuous: the product was tempting or fascinating. This was particularly true of chocolate. It compelled one to eat it, one ate it because it was there – almost it demanded to be eaten. Many people felt quite unable to stop eating chocolate until there was none left. Such tempting behaviour had to be resisted and controlled, of course – for example, by buying small quantities at a time so that one was not too far tempted, or by rituals such as how much one might eat at a time or when one might have it: for instance, so many pieces after a meal.

Alternatively, people attributed the consumption or greedy wishes to other people. Categories of consumers varied in the extent to which consumption was permitted. Greed and indulgence were relatively easily permitted to children. Their consumption might be controlled, but their greedy and sensuous wishes were much more tolerated. Women were more easily permitted such indulgences than men. A familiar pattern was that people tended to deny or minimize their own interest and consumption while stressing how much other people consumed. Adults talked of children as the main eaters. Men talked of women and children as the main eaters. Thus people evaded guilt and anxiety about their own consumption, and often succeeded in evading actual knowledge of how much they did consume. They also evaded the need to worry about being childish or, in the case of men, effeminate. Consumption was achieved in this situation by identification or association with the permitted category of consumer: 'I only buy them for the children, and we [husband and wife] eat them because they are there.' An important element in the buying of sweets by adults for children or by men for women was the expected shared consumption without the taint of childishness or effeminacy.

Anxiety about being childish was evaded, particularly by women, by the technique of 'occasional lapses'. They admitted that occasionally they would have an urge to eat some very childish kind of sweet, or to eat sweets in a childish way. However, this was not regarded fully as a part of themselves, not their ordinary behaviour, but something separate and limited in time and amount, and easily discarded or controllable. It seemed likely that children, women and men could indeed be arranged in that decreasing order of consumption, but the differences were by no means as great as people would have liked to believe.

97

A similar pattern existed in relation to socioeconomic classes. Generally, it was 'non-U', in contemporary parlance, to show too much interest in pleasure foods, especially the simpler and more childish varieties. Consumption tended to be attributed to lower classes. People in the upper classes criticized the lower classes who 'waste their money' on excessive quantities of pleasure foods instead of buying sensible foods. The author can remember this accusation being made against the unemployed in the 'Great Depression'. There was some reality in it, too. Chocolate consumption in Wales was unexpectedly high in view of the level of incomes. It seemed that the need for pleasure, consolation, compensation for misery, overcame ordinary common sense about food provision. People in the middle and upper classes tended to feel 'de-classed' if they ate a lot of pleasure foods or were observed to do so. Again, we felt that there was probably some validity in a decreasing order of consumption going from the lower classes, except the very poor, to the upper classes, but it was not nearly so extreme as one might have expected to hear people talk.

Social anxiety about overindulgence in pleasure foods was often handled by secret and solitary eating. The extent to which people bought sweets for solitary consumption seemed to us considerable. This would not so easily deal with guilt, which was a personal matter, but it did deal with disapproval and censure. Even people as intimate as husbands and wives often knew little of each other's habits in consuming pleasure foods. For example, a wife had no idea that her husband frequently ate two sixpenny chocolate blocks instead of lunch when travelling. He was rather embarrassed and ashamed to disclose it to her under our questioning. Eating alone in this context means really being alone, except for one's internal society – eating sweets by oneself but in the presence of strangers, for example in a train, was universally acknowledged to be embarrassing and shame-making.

The fears about childishness, effeminacy and de-classing were also counteracted by seeking products which intrinsically negate such fears and/or had been given an image which negated them. People consumed sophisticated, elegant, adult products, or 'masculine' products, and insisted that children, or the lower classes, would not like one's own choice or would prefer something simpler. This pattern was surprisingly marked with regard to chocolate. Many adults insisted that children are not too keen on chocolate. They said it was too rich, or sickly; that children preferred coloured, attractive sweets; that children would not spend their own pocket money on chocolate because they could not get enough for their money. These same adults were quite likely to enthuse about how they had liked chocolate when they were children, but did not seem to see the inconsistency.

Adults kept certain sweets for eating when the children were not there, often in situations which were lightly disguised preludes to marital relations. This not only reflected some possessiveness and greed aimed at getting a bigger share of a scarce or expensive sweet but also, by implying that the sweet was not suitable for children, made it an 'adult' thing to eat. Sweets were often described as not suitable for or not liked by children which are in fact perfectly suitable and liked, chocolate itself being the best example.

Likewise most respondents, but particularly middle- and upper-class adults, struggled hard to establish the 'U' standing of their preferred sweets. In middle- and upper-class groups, the discussion often became quite a fierce competition about who could demonstrate the most 'U' consuming pattern. Many people sought smart, sophisticated, elegant or exotic products through which they could establish their own sophistication and knowledgeability. Some de-classing results from too open interest or too public consumption of 'ordinary' products such as most Cadbury's lines, although certain products like Bournville and Almond Dessert gained prestige through being plain (that is, dark) chocolate, which was more adult, sophisticated and masculine than milk. On the other hand, Cadbury's milk chocolate was the everyday chocolate *par excellence* for the working classes, who do not need to be 'U'. But the upper and middle classes consumed more 'ordinary' chocolate than they were prepared to admit, to themselves or to other people. They tended to deny the extent of their own consumption and to buy such chocolate for solitary consumption or for consumption along with intimates whom they did not mind knowing their weaknesses.

People also sought help in dealing with anxieties from the product itself and from its image, advertising and so on. We have referred to some aspects of this already in discussing the anxieties, but will mention them again here for the sake of completeness. They sought sweets which are not 'messy' – for example chocolate which does not melt easily in handling, or flake or crumb. In addition, they avoided eating chocolate in situations where it was particularly prone to these difficulties: in hot weather, on summer outings, in hot cinemas or theatres. Or they chose their chocolate accordingly. One reason for the choice of boxes rather than bars or blocks for theatre or cinema was that bars and blocks are difficult to handle cleanly in such circumstances, and may become so soft that they are difficult to break.

People preferred sweets that could be eaten easily and inconspicuously and without what they felt as 'making faces'. They avoided too big sweets or blocks which break into too big pieces, although they sometimes ate them when alone. Mars bars are such a product, and our evidence was that many people who would never have eaten them in public ate them in private, when they tackled the bar whole and bit and chewed large pieces.

People sought protection from fear of making a greedy, destructive onslaught on the product. The wrappers should come off easily and the product break easily if it needed to be broken, so that one was not made to feel one must ravage it to get at it. Wrappers which were difficult to undo and products which were difficult to break tended to make people feel frustrated and irritable, and increased their fears of being aggressive. On the other hand – and somewhat inconsistently – wrappers should be a thorough protection to the product to ensure its goodness and relieve anxieties on that account, and for preference should be completely sealed. They should not appear to cost too much in themselves, otherwise they were felt to detract from the value put into the product and the consumer's ready anxiety about being cheated was stimulated. Wrappers or other containers should not be too big for their contents or make the contents seem bigger than they were, otherwise angry disappointment and feelings of being cheated would ensue. There were many bitter comments about boxes of chocolates whose lower layer proved to be half filled with paper. Too much paper was difficult also because it is liable to be noisy. This made one feel conspicuous and caused acute embarrassment in situations like theatres and cinemas where quiet is important. For sweets consumed by adults – at least publicly – an adult, elegant, sophisticated presentation was desired.

Advertising and the general presentation of the product should avoid excessive excitement, especially in potentially 'sexual' situations, and should give reassurance against greed and its consequences: fatness, exhaustion, and so on. It seemed inadvisable to show vast quantities of the product; to show a 'badly' – that is, aggressively – bitten or broken product; to show wide-open, excited eyes or mouth; to show gestures or movements which lend themselves too clearly to a sexual interpretation. Emphasis on the product being good or 'good for you' relieved anxiety, as did information about its ingredients, but this must not be too 'obvious' or it will arouse suspicion instead of allaying anxiety. We were interested to find that consumers were mockingly disbelieving of recent sweet advertisements which claimed the product did not make you fat or did not take away your appetite if eaten between meals.

People needed reassurance against fears that they would be acceptable only because of the sweets they gave, 'cupboard love', instead of for themselves. This fear must not be stimulated by claiming too much for sweets in creating or facilitating a relationship. There was violent hostility to some Black Magic advertisements which gave the impression that Black Magic, and Black Magic alone, was responsible for a successful 'courting' evening and gave no credit to the young couple for furthering the relationship themselves. The human relationship needs to be kept in the forefront of the situation and the chocolate accorded the role of facilitator or aide: 'Chocolates can help to make a good evening, or add just that extra touch, but they can't make it themselves.' This point might be generalized, to state that it is important not to collude too much with the consumer's own tendency to idealize sweets. Restraint is necessary in describing how good sweets are, not only to avoid overexcitement but also to avoid bitter, angry and hostile rejection of the product if it does not come up to expectations.

We felt that our description of this situation was valid at the time. However, our client was clearly concerned also – or even more – with future trends, so we were interested to consider how the patterns we were studying were likely to develop, particularly how the deployment of the basic patterns might change in relation to changing circumstances. At the time of the study, national consumption of pleasure foods, chocolate in particular, was very high, higher than in any other country except the USA.

However, we did not regard this situation as giving any grounds for complacency to the industry as a whole, and certainly not to any individual manufacturer. We predicted that the market would become a much 'harder' one, for reasons which stem from both supply and demand. The market's very strength was evoking a great upsurge in supplies; both old and new manufacturers were flooding it with more and more products. Competition was becoming increasingly fierce: not all manufacturers might survive, and certainly not all products would.

This situation was likely to be compounded by a fall in demand which seemed probable for a number of reasons. We anticipated that the upsurge in demand in the late forties and fifties would work itself out and that as frustration and deprivation faded, demand might well fall. Shortage of food had been a real experience for many people in this country. Only children under about ten escaped direct experience of wartime and postwar rationing. Many people in economically depressed areas had suffered from having too little food or food of inadequate nutritional value for much longer.

The following sequence of changes in food habits seemed likely to follow such lengthy deprivation when food became more available. The first reaction would be increased consumption of foods traditionally regarded as 'treats' – that is, the pleasure foods: possibly a vast increase, as on the first and second occasions when sweets were de-rationed after the war. This might take some time to work itself out, especially if money is reasonably plentiful, but satiation point would ultimately be reached. This is certainly true of individuals eating pleasure foods. Few people can have escaped the experience of eating themselves to a rather sickly standstill on a favourite sweet, and having a marked reluctance to eat it again for some time.

Regular high consumption of pleasure foods, as contrasted with the occasional 'binge', is likely to lead to an unbalanced diet. Experimental evidence suggests that sensitive physiological processes may then tend to direct the individual to other sorts of food. Tastes and preferences change; more high-protein foods, fruit and vegetables are chosen. Some evidence of trends in this direction already existed in various official publications (HMSO, 1956). Trends in health education are likely to reinforce higher consumption of such foods at the expense of the traditional pleasure foods. More pleasure from such food in meals is likely to reduce the need for compensation from pleasure foods.

Some degree of deprivation arises inevitably in the early mother–child relationship and tends to leave some permanent psychological consequences to be worked out in eating patterns among other things. However, it is to be hoped that recent trends in paediatrics will lead to less emotional deprivation for the infant, since they teach more permissive feeding patterns with greater adaptation to the infant's own timing. This is followed by an early childhood period when actual pleasure foods are more readily available to the child than they have ever been before. Economic conditions support better and more pleasurable feeding throughout childhood. One could have predicted, therefore, that less compensation would be sought in later life for early deprivation through consumption of pleasure foods; that there would be less need for rather naïve oral pleasure through sweet, milky foods; and that there would be more expectation of satisfaction from other sorts of pleasure, in sublimated forms of activity and from more sophisticated eating and drinking experiences.

Signs of this change were already apparent. To some extent they were class-linked. Middle- and upper-class people tended to be relatively more interested in such things as wines or smart or exotic foods, generally savoury, eaten at mealtimes. Their taste in actual pleasure foods tended to the more 'tangy' and stimulating – for example, bitter chocolate. The general pattern of relationship between the social classes is for the lower classes to follow the upper classes after a time lag, and we felt that the upper-class leadership was likely to be followed in behaviour about sweets. Lower-class food patterns generally follow upper-class; this would lead to food-consumption patterns which make extras in this form of pleasure foods less physiologically and psychologically necessary.

Another element in the situation was that there had been a fairly abrupt rise in the real and money incomes of the lower economic classes. In many cases, their overall spending patterns had not yet been adjusted to this increased money. Their perspective about how their increased incomes might be built into a new pattern of living had not yet developed. This left a considerable amount of money free for 'pleasure', a great deal of which went on pleasure foods. This situation would not last indefinitely, however, and already selling sweets had become 'harder' on new housing estates where people were heavily committed to hire-purchase payments.

To summarize the market trend: we anticipated that it would become increasingly hard to sell in the chocolate market and that there would be greatly intensified competition between the main manufacturers. In such a situation it seemed likely that the weaker manufacturers would in time be squeezed out of the market, which would come to be shared between a smaller number of economically more powerful firms. This had already happened in a number of other markets. Advertising and marketing would be a critical weapon in the struggle, and it was likely that the producers who survived would be those who were able and willing to allocate considerable finance to 'buying' themselves a place in this market, and showed sensitivity to 'consumer mythology'.

It seemed probable that the balance between different products would change and the consumption of the more sophisticated, elegant and possibly expensive products would increase. Indeed, this trend was already visible. All respondents knew about a number of the more expensive brands of chocolate and sometimes bought them. Although working-class respondents regarded Cadbury's as 'their chocolate', they did experiment with others for special occasions or in certain moods, and undoubtedly found an extra pleasure and prestige in them. Middle- and upper-class consumers carried that pattern further and to some extent used the special, more expensive products for ordinary consumption, although they still relied mainly on Cadbury-type products.

This trend might well demand changes in the products themselves as well as in extraneous features like packaging and advertising; more sophisticated fillings, with more tang, seemed likely to be sought: coffee; nuts; liqueurs; peppermint; ginger. Many people expressed dislike of too sweet and gooey fillings, like orange and other fruit flavours, and old-fashioned violet and rose flavours. Preferences about the chocolate itself were changing towards more plain chocolate. We had found unmistakable signs of a trend in this direction over a period of years, although it was a slow trend and was most marked in the London area. Retailers often commented on noting that trend in their sales. 'Milk', with its more infantile associations, seemed to be declining somewhat in importance as a selling point, and giving place to preferences for something with more 'bite'.

The strength and prevalence of the plain-chocolate preference was much greater than one would expect from actual sales figures. People who preferred plain chocolate were probably somewhat smaller consumers than those who preferred milk, being in general less sweet-toothed. Plain chocolate actually was quite hard to get. All retailers kept some, but only specialist high-class retailers kept a large variety. A consumer who wanted a particular kind of plain-chocolate product might have difficulty finding it. Two choices were then open: he bought nothing and might or might not pursue his search elsewhere, or he took an alternative; if this was another chocolate, he might have to buy milk. The second alternative is the more likely. The desire stimulated by wanting chocolate and being in a sweet shop probably requires some sort of satisfaction without further effort and waiting.

Sales of milk chocolate were artificially raised in relation to real consumer preference. People had gradually begun to seek out the shops where they could get what they wanted, and sales of plain chocolate were concentrated on such shops: one of them reported that in the last few years his milk:plain sales ratio had changed from 3:1 to 1:3. It seemed likely that most retailers preferred and pushed milk-chocolate sales. They preferred to stock milk not only because turnover is generally better but because it is generally more consistent with the notions of their own roles. For an unspecified request, milk is almost always supplied. There seemed to us to be a kind of circular effect here – milk sells better because it sells better. Nevertheless, plain was making slow inroads into the market. In fact, we felt this trend to be so strong that our client should take note of it and develop his products accordingly.

Later developments in the market proved that we had anticipated correctly and there was a considerable swing from milk to plain chocolate. In a sense this was a swing back to the pre-war situation when there was a dominance of plain chocolate. The production and sale of milk chocolate as the dominant product was partly due to the wartime fall in the amount and quality of raw material. It was not good enough to make a really good plain chocolate.

When people heard we were working on chocolate, they very frequently and spontaneously commented: 'Oh, why don't people make more plain chocolate?' The context of these remarks and the way they were said conveyed more than merely a reference to the fact that plain chocolate was rather hard to get. The respondents almost seemed to be seeking permission to eat plain chocolate; such permission would be given by the manufacturers supplying it plentifully. The wish to eat plain chocolate is strong, but so also are the restraints against it. It may seem too exotic and exciting. It might be rather risqué to choose it.

In a group discussion some older respondents complained bitterly that they could not get plain chocolate, but at the same time made clear their envy and jealousy of the pleasures younger members of the group could have and they could not. In this context, it seemed clear that plain chocolate was unconsciously linked with the young adult sexuality which the older people in the group could no longer enjoy. Plain chocolate, then, becomes easily invested with sexual phantasies and problems. Milk is safer and less exciting, more 'domesticated'. The use of 'plain' seemed sometimes a deliberate, if unconscious, self-deception – that is, people were eating something 'plain', not exciting. They seemed to want a total product constellation which made the consumption of the longed-for plain chocolate more permissible. Work needed to be done to facilitate and develop a general trend to more sophisticated, mature pleasure foods, and a producer who contributed in a major way to that development would gain a great deal of consumer goodwill.

Our general recommendations for the development and stabilizing of a position in the chocolate market were, therefore, that the development of sophisticated, elegant products be continued and that consideration be given to the kinds of chocolate to be used with greater emphasis on plain, backed by adequate and appropriate advertising. These considerations were particularly relevant for our client, who was already in the more expensive sector of the market.

Both our study and previous studies on pleasure foods suggested that the relationship between consumers and retailers, and between retailers and their suppliers, are complicated and can easily become difficult. This was especially true of consumers and specialist confectionery retailers, who were the biggest single type of outlet for confectionery.

Customers and retailers would like to establish a good relationship with each other. The customer tended to approach the shop with eagerness and high hopes about what he would buy. He wanted interest, help and advice. The retailer wanted to satisfy his customers and to feel that they relied on him. Some shopkeepers and customers did establish and sustain such a relationship. However, the situation was fraught with potential dangers. Customers readily felt they were being childish, especially when buying simple sweets in small quantities for themselves. Typically, the adult customer would 'let the shopkeeper think' that (s)he was buying the sweets for a child. The customer expects censure or contempt for his childishness and some retailers did express this attitude, which the customer resented.

The inequality between customer and retailer in the possession of sweets also caused difficulty. Typically, a shop is crammed with goods of an almost unbelievable variety, a large proportion of which are on show. This tends to evoke intense feelings in the customer, close to his infantile feeding experiences. These could be difficult for him to handle and predispose him to expect the hostility from the retailer which he often met. He experienced greed and longing to obtain the full potential gratification from the shop, but he could choose only a small part, must be disappointed, and grudged and envied the retailer the possession of the rest. He thus tended to approach the retailer fearfully and defensively, expecting censure for his greed and retaliation for his envy.

The retailer, on his side, had mixed feelings about selling sweets, and experienced considerable conflict. He wanted to sell sweets because he hoped to enjoy the giving it implied and wanted to please his customers, as well as for ordinary economic motives. He took pride in the vast quantities of pleasure he could provide, a situation which bears obvious resemblance to being a good mother. But the desire for possession conflicted with the desire to give, and retailers might sell their goods grudgingly, envying the customer who bought them. One retailer said: 'I can't sell a quarter of chocolates without having one myself.' (The sweet retailer's wish to have the sweets for himself is described vividly by George Eliot in the short story 'Brother Jacob'.) The retailer tended also to be afraid of the customer's greed and to protect himself by giving grudgingly. He feared the exhaustion of his stocks, and the possibility of replenishment only partly modified these feelings. Retailers feel grateful to suppliers who keep in close touch and guarantee quick replenishment of stocks, and whose role can be that of a constantly supportive supplier rather than a comparatively rare visitor who seems mainly interested to sell on his own behalf. Retailers felt that Cadbury's representatives most easily filled that role because of the market position of their products.

The difficulties were intensified by the customer's virtual

certainty that the retailer would not be able to satisfy him, and the retailer's intuitive awareness of this. It was remarkable how often respondents commented that 'sweet shops never have what you want' and quoted examples of sweets they had not been able to find. This stems partly from reality and partly from phantasy. No sweet shop can possibly carry the full range of products, and a customer who wants anything other than one of the relatively few stock lines may easily fail to find it in a particular shop. But the customer often did not ask for what he really wanted, because what he wanted – the idealized sweet, as described above – did not exist, except in phantasy. The unformulated ideal was not related to a concrete product although the customer hoped that, as if by magic, the shopkeeper would produce it.

The retailer, on the other hand, intuitively recognized that he could not give his customer exactly what he wanted, either in quantity or quality, despite his wealth of supplies. He could not give all; he had not got the ideal sweet. He anticipated dissatisfaction and criticism and tended to be aggressive: for example, 'take it or leave it' as a defence against his customer and a means of dealing with his own guilt and inadequacy. Retailers were very ready to tell us how difficult their customers were – fastidious, capricious and dilatory – while they described themselves as patient and helpful, as indeed a few of them were. Retailers tended to thrust something at their customers in order to get rid of them, or alternatively pay no attention to them, while customers tended to point at something in sight or reach, or said the first name which came to their mind in order to escape: 'If the shopkeeper asks what you want and you don't know, you ask for one you have seen advertised.'

These attitudes and habits emphasized the importance both of having products well displayed in shops and of establishing direct links between the product and the customer by advertising and other methods, so that the product's name would come easily to the rescue. The retailer tried to deal with his own problems about failing to meet demand by blaming the manufacturer who did not ensure that he got exactly the right product or supplies at the right time. Maintaining his goodwill by ensuring supplies is, therefore, very important.

The confectionery purchaser is particularly prone to enter a shop not knowing what he really wants. His craving is for something sweet, often more psychological than physical. He is met with the bewildering variety of sweets in the shop and may well become even more uncertain. Children are particularly prone to this and may dither indefinitely about how to spend a few pence. When the customer turned to the retailer for help or suggestions in making what was felt to be an almost intolerable choice, he was often met with unwillingness and hostility. Retailers admitted to a certain unwillingness to give advice. They pointed out that tastes were very individual and this made it difficult to be sure of a recommendation. They were anxious about recommending something the customer would not like – and rightly, when one remembers the angry disappointment people feel when given the 'wrong' sweets.

There was a discrepancy in the perception of the importance of the transaction which made for difficulty between customer and retailer. The retailer saw his business as a multiplicity of small transactions on each of which he made only a small profit. He felt those transactions should be accomplished quickly and without much fuss or effort on his part. The psychological seriousness of the transaction for the customer was often out of all relation to the sum spent. He felt – and often acted – as though he was buying something of the greatest importance, as indeed psychologically he might be: love, or the means of expressing and attracting love. He was liable to take a lot of time and care over his decision. There might be a clash of objectives: the retailer would get cross with a customer who acted as though she was buying at least a washing-machine when she would spend only a couple of shillings; the customer would get irritated because the retailer was not more co-operative in her major decision.

Some of the feelings about retailers expressed by respondents were as follows: 'They expect you to know what you want straight off . . . if you don't, they're not interested.' 'You can't see the place for sweets. You can't see all that's there . . .' 'You can't go into a shop and buy a measly quarter of a pound, but you don't want to buy a lot . . . the assistants are unhelpful.' 'They are frightening, that is the main thing.' Housewives complained that retailers let their children buy rubbish – indeed, provided rubbish for them to buy. Children complained that shopkeepers were not interested in them, and only wanted their custom. Anything the manufacturer could do to help in the establishment of good relations between customer and retailer would be welcome to both sides: for example, to facilitate clear identification of the product for the customer so that it came more readily to eye, hand or mind when he was trying to think of something to buy, or, better still, helped him set out with the actual intention of buying it. Likewise, it would help if the retailer could feel sure of recommending a product, not only because he liked it himself but because he was clear about what kind of product it was, how it was perceived by consumers, what psychological and social roles it played, when it was eaten, for what reasons, for whom it was generally considered suitable, and so on.

Other typical features of the customer–retailer relationship followed from the difficulties described. The dissatisfactions and anxiety about the relationship were transferred to the product: the customer distrusted the care the retailer took of the product and was anxious about cleanliness, hygiene, freshness. He readily suspected that the retailer's disregard for him would be matched by a disregard for the goodness of the product. He feared that his own anger with the retailer would spoil his enjoyment. These feelings were also transferred to some extent to the manufacturer and manufacturing processes. Such anxieties go far beyond the few real difficulties or bad experiences of unsatisfactory goods. Much could be done directly by the manufacturer to allay the consumer's anxieties: for example, by using advertising and other methods to build a product image which implies goodness, cleanliness and freshness, and by assuming responsibility publicly, through packaging and otherwise, for the safe arrival of the product. The direct relationship established by the manufacturer with the consumer would be important to bypass the consumer–retailer relationship. Cadbury's had, of course, achieved a very enviable position in the market here. Their general image was closely linked with the goodness and naturalness of farming, milk and so on, their general reputation as employers conveyed care for people, and their high sales were understood to imply quick turnover and guaranteed freshness.

It is clear from what has been said above that both manufacturer and consumer were very dependent on the retailer in the matter of final purchase. This came to some extent from advice, but perhaps more from the hasty choice forced by the retailer who was anxious to get rid of a slow customer, or by the effect of the retailer's display in determining the choice of a customer anxious to escape. It was rare for a customer to leave a shop without buying something. Thus, he and the manufacturer were limited by what the retailer stocked. The effect of this might go beyond the immediate purchase. Disappointment and consequent anger if a particular sweet was not available might inhibit a future purchase – as, indeed, might the forced choice of something else which might permanently replace the original choice.

The implications of this situation were, in a way, obvious: for example, to strengthen the direct links between the consumer and the manufacturer. It also seemed obvious to try to get the retailer to provide the best possible display position. However, we felt that this needed to be handled with care. Few important manufacturers were unaware of the importance of display and positioning. The retailers were consequently beginning to feel somewhat beset by the competitive onslaughts of the representatives of different firms, all trying to get the best display. They were beginning to feel at a loss to know how to deal with the number of products and with the supplies of display material and dispensers. We felt that the less pressure which needed to be exerted in this way, the better. It would be preferable, if possible, to have the consumer exert the pressure by asking for the product than the representative putting on pressure to display it. But it might have been hard for most products to achieve the enviable position of Penguin chocolate biscuits in a school tuckshop we visited. They sold in such vastly greater quantities than anything else that they were not displayed at all.

If this position can be established, it can convey other benefits through the kind of relations made possible between the representative and the retailer. We found that relations between retailers and representatives varied considerably according to whether the representative was felt to be pressing the retailer to buy supplies of a product the demand for which is uncertain, small, spasmodic, or coming only from casual or very special customers, or whether the representative was felt to be offering to help the retailer by giving him the supplies which he needed to satisfy his customers, to meet a demand which was certain, reliable and regular – in other words, whether the representative was felt to be orientated more to his own need to sell or to the retailer's need to be supplied.

The latter alternative created a more satisfactory situation for both retailer and representative and led to better sales, for it was based on mutual co-operation rather than conflict and so maintained the retailer's goodwill and wish to sell the product. Both parties felt easier and more satisfied if the retailer spontaneously gave a large order than if he gave a small order which might yet be slightly larger than he really wanted. Our client was in some difficulty here in that he was meeting a small, spasmodic, specialized demand.

There was another reason why it might be important for the manufacturer to establish as far as possible a personal relationship between himself – that is, the product – and the consumer. Selling was becoming increasingly mechanized and depersonalized. Chain stores and self-service stores, together with packaging and dispensers, were taking much of the personal-service element out of shopping. Such selling methods had advantages – in speed and cheapness, and, for lower-class shoppers, the absence of class distinction in favour of the 'good': that is, better-to-do customer. However, many customers keenly felt the loss of the satisfying relationship with the retailer. One woman made the interesting complaint that the self-service store was too 'clinical' and complaints about their being too impersonal were common.

For the middle- and upper-class customer there may be an actual loss of something (s)he had or could have: for example, being a 'good' customer to a family grocer; to the lower-class customer it may be more the loss of an illusion, something (s)he longed for. The customer liked to feel that somebody cared whether (s)he got what (s)he wanted and would come back for

113

more. It is an important reassurance about being liked and valued. Conventionally, the family grocer cared: the self-service store does not. A manufacturer who could take up this friendly service position himself would greatly strengthen goodwill: for example, if his products became the recognized, familiar friend in the self-service store, recognition of which would help a customer who was feeling rather confused and helpless, with no assistant to advise.

Consumers tended to divide chocolate into two categories: chocolate bars or blocks and boxes of chocolates. Their uses were quite distinct and differentiated. It would almost have been true to say that consumers divided chocolate into 6d. bars and boxes. Other products – of which there are many, some of which sell quite well – seemed to live in a kind of uneasy no-man's-land between these two main sections of the market, fitting satisfactorily into neither and lacking the well-defined roles and functions of 6d. bars and boxes.

The 6d. bar gained its strong position to a considerable extent from being an individual-sized unit of about 2 oz. One person could consume it all at once without feeling unduly greedy, full and sickened or dissatisfied and frustrated. It was neat, convenient and inconspicuous, fitted easily into a pocket or a handbag and could be broken and eaten without much obvious fuss. Sixpence was an acceptable price unit, a reasonably small sum which created little conflict about whether one should or should not spend the money, unless the individual found himself spending the 6d. too often. People often said that price was no object in buying sweets, a remark which we treated with some scepticism. We felt that people have an intuitive, rather unconscious relationship with price which means that they operate within certain defined limits without making conscious decisions. In these terms 6d. for unit-size bars was good value and convenient.

There were many uses for 6d. bars. They fitted well into the need for solitary and secret eating and large quantities were bought for this purpose. People who lived alone might buy one on their way home to eat later during a possibly lonely evening. They were much used in 'transitional situations', on a train journey or car-driving: quite a number of men 'confessed' to eating a 6d. bar on their way home from work, to ease the transition, deal with impatience about getting home and take the edge off appetite lest they should greedily 'attack' the home-cooked food of which they have been deprived all day. Bars were used to alleviate the boredom or frustration of waiting. As one woman said: 'You get tired when you have to wait a long time for a train and so you buy a 6d. bar of chocolate.' A 'long' wait on the line she used could not have been more than ten minutes.

The bars filled 'gaps' between meals and were used to tide one over if a meal had to be delayed for any reason. In those roles they were closely rivalled by chocolate biscuit count lines and Cadbury's Snack. They substituted for meals which had to be missed altogether. They were taken along to eat as a 'sweet' – that is, a pudding – after carried snack meals, for example, on hikes or picnics. Their convenience for packing was very import-ant. Like ice cream, they were often eaten after a meal bought out, especially in rather unsatisfactory circumstances such as in a poor works canteen or an indifferent restaurant. They took the place of the sweet or were an extra. There was therefore, in the consumption of 6d. bars, a high element of seeking solace, compensation for deprivation, help in dealing with loneliness, boredom and frustration. In these roles, they were essentially something which an individual provided for himself. Buying for others was not common, except for children, nor was shared consumption. Sharing a 6d. bar if it was all one had was a depressing and irritating experience for many people.

For some occasions on which bar or block chocolate was used, one 6d. bar would not be enough: for example, a substitute for lunch, or on a long walk, in which case many people preferred to buy two or more 6d. bars. They felt that one 6d. bar was enough of one variety; after that they got tired and wanted a change. Several bars rather than one bigger one avoided the difficulty of carrying around opened and reclosed packs which might be messy or 'leak'. People liked to feel that as they ate their stock, what was left became smaller, neater and less conspicuous. The 6d. bars were usually easier to break into portions than the larger blocks, especially the solid chocolate blocks like Bournville, most of which could not be broken simply and inconspicuously into mouth-sized pieces.

The 6*d*. bar was essentially, then, an individual-centred product, not much used to mediate social relations but rather to deal with their absence or the absence of other food which represented them. They were a solitary rather than a shared experience. They were largely 'utilitarian' in function and were bought, for the most part, with specific limited purposes in mind and for immediate consumption or at least total consumption in a foreseen and limited situation.

Boxes of chocolates were in direct contrast. They were used almost entirely within active social relations. They were given for presents, they were taken on outings of various kinds, especially to theatres and cinemas, they were bought or given for entertaining. For the latter, middle- and upper-class consumers often bought handmade chocolates or other special sorts loose, sometimes in assortments of their own choice. Boxes were not usually intended for total consumption on one occasion; even on outings, some chocolates might be saved and taken home. Boxes of chocolates are intended to be passed round and shared. They were expected to be more expensive than blocks. Again people tended to claim that price was no object, but this, too, operated within unconsciously defined limits. Furthermore, a hierarchy of prices, types, uses and recipients usually exists. There were a lot of 'workaday' boxed chocolates, like Cadbury's, Rowntree's and Caley's, which would be bought for ordinary shared family consumption: the special weekend sweets, for example. For middle- and upper-class families something a little more 'U' is sought: for example, Terry's.

This division of the market put our client in some difficulty, since his principal product did not fit easily into either category. The product was rather smart, but expensive, so that a small bar of the size of the 'standard' 6*d*. bar would have cost appreciably more than 6*d*., or to sell a 6*d*. bar would have meant it would be too small. Within the 6*d*. bar context, his product would have been regarded as poor value for money. His larger blocks were occasionally used in the way boxes of chocolates were used: on outings, at the cinema, for a family treat at home. But these uses did not amount to significant sales. Basically, this was not an 'ordinary', 'everyday' product but something which was bought on special occasions, for a special treat, when the ordinary price/value concepts were relaxed. Our findings indicated that it would not be easy to move from that position – price and the rather 'special' image would prove a barrier. We recommended that sales efforts would be more effective if directed to strengthening the roles of the larger block and creating a differentiated sub-market, close to boxes. A possible way of doing this would be to pick up those situations already known to be considered suitable by consumers, and to strengthen the consumer's sense of the product's relevance.

There were other weaknesses in our client's position. The product was well known and well regarded, except by a small minority of consumers who claimed to hate it. It was rather exciting and evoked happy memories, especially among the over-twenty-fives who had known it before it disappeared during the war. However, these positive feelings did not really promote sales. The product tended to remain a happy memory. It was a kind of 'household word', which again is not necessarily a healthy position. Household-word products may be seen as very good and reliable but also as rather old-fashioned, not quite keeping up with the times, rather like elderly and affectionately regarded parents. They may literally be 'left on the shelf'.

Some of the enthusiasts had not eaten the product for some time and did not always like it if they ate it again. It came dangerously close to the idealized sweet that no longer existed, or if it did, one would not risk disappointment by trying it since it was certain not to be as good as it used to be. The affectionate childhood memories also tended to raise the anxieties about being childish, which were intensified by the sweet and milky nature of the chocolate.

Some people liked the richness, smoothness and milkiness but many others found it too rich, too milky, too gooey. Although it was a continental product, its actual qualities did not make it seem very sophisticated or exotic, qualities needed to defend against childishness. It was relatively expensive. People said that the shape and packaging were such as to defeat attempts to carry and eat it inconspicuously. It did not always break easily and cleanly. It was difficult to wrap up again if some of a block was left.

In view of this situation, we advised reconsideration of the client's policy of keeping the small block as the central product of the group on which the main selling efforts were to be concentrated. The company had more power of manoeuvre in the design of other products and was better equipped in other areas to meet the increasing sophistication of the expensive, high-class sector of the market, in which its prices inevitably place its products. We considered also that with the marketing conditions prevailing at that time, any such developments would need to be backed by sufficient and appropriate advertising.

It will be clear that we considered that our client had a difficult task ahead if he seriously wanted to establish his main product in a strong market position and, supported by that, to establish a number of other lesser products. Advertising would have to be the main instrument, although the importance of the representative–retailer relationship should not be completely overlooked. It will be clear from the ice-cream study that we had considerable reservations about how much advertising can accomplish.

We concluded our report with comments on possible advertising approaches. These summarized and extended earlier references in the report. There would be much to be said for some short, vivid phrase which could become closely connected with the product, a slogan or other idea that could overcome the consumer's inertia by its sheer psychological relevance and easily come to his mind at appropriate moments or act dynamically even if unconsciously on choice at the point of sale. Cadbury's 'Bridge that gap' slogan is one of the best examples in recent years. It is more difficult to achieve this kind of slogan for a product which is versatile in its uses.

When considering pleasure foods, people tend to be in a mood determined by the psychological constellations described above: they feel rather than think, they want to be indulged, irresponsible, dependent and coddled. In this mood, they are likely to be most influenced by copy and presentation the impact of which comes from apparent simplicity and immediacy, although in fact, of course, it describes complex psychological situations. Few potential users of pleasure foods are in a mood conducive to working and they will probably not take the trouble to read a lot of complicated copy. A little more effort may be made by people who are thinking of providing pleasure foods for others, especially if copy offers some support and help in the problem of providing.

Because of the situation in retailing, we felt that advertising needed to be orientated to building up the direct relationship between manufacturer and customer. The tone of this relationship could well be developed around the theme of the product and the manufacturer as trustworthy, reliable, affectionate, friendly, concerned with people's well-being. This must be backed in the retail networks by the development of selling techniques orientated to a supportive rather than pressure-selling role for the representative with the retailer; this should become progressively easier if consumers' spontaneous requests for the product increase.

In general, the tone of the approach would need to suggest pleasure or potential pleasure, the quality of the mood being affectionate, companionable, almost comforting in an interesting way. To introduce open excitement into advertising would sway the mood too much towards the unconscious sexual components of the feelings about chocolate and arouse too much anxiety. This tone may be conveyed not only in copy and general terms, but perhaps even more importantly by the visual presentation of the mood and relationships of the people in the advertisements. In a previous investigation of advertising copy, we found that pictures of pop-eyes and wide-open mouths provoked great anxiety about greed and, unconsciously, about sexual excitement. Consumers found it difficult to identify with the people in the advertisement and tended to reject the product.

Within the general framework, however, it would be possible to vary the balance of excitement and affectionate interest according to the people and the circumstances presented. The desirable balance in each case would be determined by conventions and customs and the objectives of eating chocolate. For example, children are permitted a good deal more excitement and boisterousness than adults, and this may appropriately be picked up in copy. In contrast, the excitement needs to be muted in situations showing mixed groups of young people, since sexual problems are important and difficult at that age. Eating chocolate together may well be an aide to young people in developing friendships with the opposite sex, but this should not be expressed too clearly. A semi-overt reference to the underlying aims might raise anxiety and tend towards rejection of the product. In presenting solitary situations, also, advertising should subordinate excitement to themes suggesting affection and companionship.

Advertisements which show some resolution of conflict or anxiety and avoid stirring up further problems are most likely to stimulate goodwill. For example, in 'longing' situations, hope of satisfaction may be stressed in words and action: 'I wish I had . . .' is less hopeful than a phrase like 'Now for . . .' or 'Now I'll have . . .'. The first phrase leaves some doubt, while the others assume the existence of the product and its probable possession. Purposeful, active movements towards something are important, implying hope, even if the person is tired, lonely or bored. The hope should not, however, suggest false assurance or greedy anticipation. In 'finishing the job' and 'break' situations, the sense of a job well done, a reward or an anticipated and deserved pleasure are preferable to boredom or frustration. The former imply that the person has the capacity to enjoy things and to accept the challenge of work as well as more dependent pleasures.

Permission to indulge oneself and others is useful, if it is not overdone. It should be implicit rather than explicit, suggested situationally, perhaps, rather than expressed verbally, or shown by means of a person who looks as if he can enjoy himself without anxiety. Idealization of the product may be dangerous: it reinforces the consumer's phantasy and may provoke hostility against the product if it fails by being 'only' very good, not perfect. It is advisable not to suggest greed, too active biting, or overindulgence. This requires, among other things, caution about the subtle messages conveyed, mainly unconsciously, by the visual aspects of advertisements: for example large quantities of chocolate, chocolate broken in an untidy way, or a person holding chocolate in a way which suggests it will melt in his hand.

Approaches to consumers' anxieties must not be too direct and open. It is better to avoid making the anxieties fully conscious if possible and approach them obliquely and through their resolution: for example, healthy, slim people obviously liking the product are more reassuring than statements that it will not make you fat and spotty. Reassurances about anxiety or greed may be given by showing people who, without being prim or priggish, 'know when to stop', as one respondent put it. Reassurance against messiness and damage can be given by fresh, clean-looking visuals and a related company image. Care should be taken not to convey to the consumer that the manufacturer shares his anxiety or is himself anxious about it. This would reinforce the consumer's doubts and tend to make him suspicious of the product. The manufacturer might convey his own anxiety to the consumer by too open references to the consumer's anxieties, by too much direct reassurance against them, by false or exaggerated claims for the product: for example, that it is an upper-middle-class product if only the working class use it, and by overinsistence on the product's qualities.

Our advice was to build on known user situations and not to try to develop new ones: this stemmed from our feeling that if the advertisement deviated too much from accepted uses it might be seen as unrealistic and raise doubts in the consumer as to whether the manufacturer really knew his own product. This would tend to have adverse effects on sales. For developing new products, we felt that first approaches might be made through using known 'experimental' situations: for example, when people are away from home or out of their usual routine. Such situations give opportunity for buying without 'commitment': for example, if one does not expect to revisit the same shop. Thereafter, more 'ordinary' situations can be developed. Young people are more likely to experiment than older people.

Caution would be necessary in approaching certain categories of consumer. It is risky to show men eating alone, except possibly working-class men, who would not, in any case, be relevant to the product. The presentation of women alone is difficult, though not impossible; they would need to be shown in a way which reassures against childishness. Men and women together is a relevant situation but must suggest neither childishness nor sexuality. Children would need to be handled with care, since adults dislike associating chocolate with children. Social classes would also need to be handled with care. We do not feel it would be advisable to use the upper class, since neither they nor other people associate them with much interest in pleasure food. The sophisticated middle class, being a little bit 'special', is probably the class objective since it allows the lower middle and upper working class to join in also.

POSTSCRIPT (1988)

We were defining a very difficult task for our client, a task which might prove virtually impossible. The basic design of his product and its cost made it extremely difficult for him to gain a significant position in the market, especially against powerful competition from very well-regarded 'native' manufacturers whose products were better value for money and against other continental manufacturers who were more truly foreign and exotic. The product has in fact continued up to the present time to hold a small position in a rather specialized part of the market. It is now made in dark as well as milk chocolate. Production has been taken over by a different manufacturer.

6 Safety on the roads

Two papers

The author, with colleagues at the Tavistock Institute, did a series of studies in the late 1950s and early 1960s on driving and road safety. Some of this work was carried out for motor manufacturers and was particularly concerned with design of cars and accessories. The later work was financed by the British Safety Council (London), the Transport and Road Research Laboratory (Crowthorne, Berkshire) and the Institute. This work concerned safety-belt usage, drinking and driving, and the high casualty rate among young motorcyclists. I would like to express my gratitude to the British Safety Council and the Transport and Road Research Laboratory for their help and support in this work, and to many anonymous drivers who eagerly took part in it. The drivers were mostly male, as will become obvious in the papers.

The two papers that follow deal separately with findings that concern car drivers – 'The driver's dilemma' – and motorcyclists – 'Growing up on two wheels'.

I The driver's dilemma*

'THE DRIVER'S DILEMMA' describes the psychological conflict that faces drivers. On the one hand, driving offers a unique combination of pleasure and satisfaction. On the other hand, these can be realized only by entering a situation fraught with dangers, real dangers that in their turn arouse unconscious phantasy danger situations that give rise to anxiety greater than the real danger warrants. To realize the positive opportunities in driving, the driver has to find ways of keeping his conscious sense of danger and anxiety at a tolerable level.

PLEASURE AND SATISFACTION IN DRIVING

Drivers characteristically feel very committed to driving and set a high store on its rewards. They were probably the most enthusiastic and forthcoming of any respondents we encountered in this kind of research work. There was never any difficulty in getting them to talk. They never bored each other or us. It was usually difficult to bring individual or group interviews to an end. We frequently found them later still eagerly discussing among themselves: for example, out on the street after the interview ended. There was always more to say. Driving is

*The three original papers were: 'A note on driving and road accidents (including a critical evaluation of the Ministry of Transport's Christmas 1964 poster campaign)', London: British Safety Council, 1965; 'Drinking and driving. A note on drivers' reactions to the proposed Bill making it an offence to drive with a blood-alcohol concentration above a prescribed limit', London: British Safety Council, 1966; 'Some social and psychological aspects of road safety', London: Tavistock Institute of Human Relations, 1967.

central in a driver's activities. Many of the drivers seemed to regard themselves almost as addicts.

Some of the pleasures and satisfactions seem to be connected with earlier experiences and fantasies, some long forgotten: the frustrating inability of the baby to move and go where he wants to; his joy and pride when he can crawl and then walk and thus gain more control over his environment and make more use of its opportunities. Later, there is a long history of struggle to gain skills, joy and pride about mastering them, but some disappointments about failure, limits to what is achieved, longing to have done better. Unachieved goals may drive one to further efforts. Mastery is never complete.

Driving seems a rather natural field in which to deploy some of these dynamics and the things drivers say show the derivatives from these roots. Being in control of a car gives an exciting and reassuring feeling of added mobility and power. The extremities of the driver's limbs are applied to controls that harness the car's power and mobility on his behalf. (So different from a push-chair, when someone else is in control and the child is immobilized.) The car gives great results for minimal physical effort. Rapid acceleration and speed with power in reserve accentuate this feeling and in turn arouse dormant feelings of exultation and omnipotence. The driver feels he can cope with anything – an important antidote to any lingering doubts he may have about his competence or potency.

Such feelings are particularly noticeable when the driver has effectively established his skills and can deploy them successfully. When this becomes automatic and manoeuvres can be carried out without conscious thought and planning, the driver really begins to feel as though the vehicle is himself. The controls and power of the car are mastered and become his servants in a way no human being ever will. Confidence in the ability to control the car as a powerful extension of himself adds to his sense of status; he becomes a bigger and better man. Drivers were often opposed to devices that make driving less of a challenge and reduce the driver's control, notably automatic transmission. They reduce the driver's feelings of competence and masculinity, hence such remarks as 'Automatic transmission is all right for women – they can't manage the gears anyway.' The very fact that women can also drive, and drive well, is felt by some men drivers as an insult, an invasion of territory that should be exclusively for the exaltation of their masculinity. Women drivers should be 'rabbits': slow, confused, overcareful. Their better accident record is somehow converted into a disability.

As driving skills and habits of car usage develop, drivers greatly enjoy their increased freedom and extended range of opportunities. Car mileage tends to increase over the first few years as they learn to exploit these features. Driving extends the driver's geographical and experimental horizons as walking does the child's. Drivers can go to places and do things that the non-driver cannot or will not because it is too much trouble. They feel free and independent as no one else does, even habitual car-passengers. They are free of the increasing inadequacy of public transport – inadequacy, however, exaggerated by unfavourable comparison with one's own car. Drivers feel their mastery in this respect too: 'You can just get in the car and go.' They can indulge their impulses as non-drivers cannot.

There is, however, another and apparently contradictory side to the driver's enjoyment of driving. To return for a moment to our imaginary baby – his progress is not continuous; there are ups and downs, failures as well as successes, disappointments and anxieties. At such times he may feel like giving up the struggle and want to retreat, to go backwards for a time, to seek comfort and reassurance. He wants his mother to hold and coddle him.

Shades of this also appear in the car-driver. He feels the car does or should offer him protection and the chance to be dependent. While its engine and power give him a sense of potency, by contrast the body of the car becomes a separate object into which he can go – retreat, one almost feels – and in which he can be safely enclosed. Drivers have compared the car with a house, a little universe, a home which they take around with them and in which they shut themselves away, like the baby in his pram or his mother's arms.

A car does more than protect one from the difficulties non-drivers have to face, like going out in bad weather or the inadequacies of public transport. It also protects and comforts a driver against the ordinary anxieties of life: things that go wrong at work, family problems, political situations – even anxieties about driving itself: 'Once you have shut yourself up in the car, you can just forget about it.' Or: 'I worry about accidents when I am not in the car, but once I get in the car, it's all right.' Being contained, sheltered, protected in the car is wonderful, a kind of armchair or pram comfort. These experiences are best realized when the driver is alone in the car, and drivers sometimes bitterly resent intrusions such as passengers or worrying behaviour by other road users.

DANGER AND ANXIETY

The almost gloating enthusiasm about the rewards of driving is, however, infiltrated by direct and indirect expressions of anxiety, often quite severe. Drivers are preoccupied with the threat of danger. Some of the anxiety is conscious, but a great deal is not and tends to appear only in disguise, as it were, emerging in the form of defensive statements such as denials of danger or the attribution of bad driving to other drivers, not oneself. The conscious anxiety tends, because of the defences, to be less than the real difficulties and dangers warrant; the unconscious anxiety greater. As was discussed briefly above, the driving situation acquires anxiety displaced into it from other sources with which it is linked symbolically: that is, from unconscious phantasy systems which give rise to intense and primitive anxiety.

The description of the pleasures of driving above will have suggested that the car is a mixed object in symbolic terms. The engine with its power is a masculine symbol linked essentially with the father and his potency: the body and inside of the car are maternal. The whole car therefore represents a joint parental figure and so is likely to arouse residual anxieties about oedipal problems. The child who wishes to acquire father's potency to have better control or possession of mother is likely to become anxious lest that borrowed or stolen potency get out of hand because he cannot manage it – or, worse, lest the father take revenge by attacking the driver. A surprising number of drivers would never open their car bonnets if they could possibly help it or almost dreaded touching their engines, as though they really would attack. There was almost a forbidden masturbatory quality about concerning oneself with the engine. It was also surprising to find how much car choice seemed to rest on the body and especially a big boot, although little might be carried in it except perhaps once or twice a year on holiday.

Drivers frequently described a car as a lethal weapon, linked again with the stolen, forbidden power that might get out of hand. The responsibility to control the power and not let it get out of hand was heavy. Projected into the car were fears about the driver's own murderousness and his anxiety about controlling it once he had such a powerful weapon. Behind that again are intense primitive feelings and phantasies: children freely hate and want to kill, even if only temporarily. Who has not heard a child say to his nearest and dearest: 'I'll kill you', or 'Drop dead'? Feelings of power, exaltation and omnipotence are terrifying as well as exhilarating. One may be carried away: drivers sometimes are, and consciously or unconsciously know this. They are aware that they may not be able to hold their murderous feelings/lethal weapon at bay either because of impulses inherent in themselves or because of external events that may stimulate their anger, particularly the behaviour of other road users.

Many uncertainties confront the driver. Very important among these is having to sustain continuous relationships with other road users. Many of them are strangers and their behaviour tends to be regarded as unpredictable. The presumption is that they may well do something awkward or even dangerous which may threaten oneself or require a rapid reaction to prevent an accident. The behaviour of road users is to some extent governed by explicit prescription and regulations. These help a little, but not enough. Road users do not always follow them – indeed, most drivers know that they do not always follow them themselves. In addition, there is scope for a wide variety of unpredictable behaviour, even if people do obey the rules. A driver is entitled to pull up suddenly for completely private reasons, not obvious to a following driver whose responsibility it nevertheless is not to run into him. Such behaviour causes the minor contretemps dreaded by drivers and requires alertness, which is difficult to sustain consistently. If the driver cannot cope, disaster threatens. These intrusions into the pleasurable image of driving frighten and anger the driver, which in a sort of circular way makes matters worse.

There are also non-human uncertainties: one's own car unexpectedly develops a fault; someone else's car bursts a tyre and swerves across a motorway. There may be invisible or almost invisible hazards in the road itself: a pothole turns out to be deeper than it seemed; a bend turns out to be much sharper than the road sign or the terrain indicated. Drivers feel that the highest level of skill is inadequate protection in such circumstances, and many doubt their own skill anyway, if only secretly.

The mechanical soundness of cars is another source of uncertainty and anxiety; drivers may feel totally and rather helplessly dependent on mechanical soundness for safety. We discussed above how difficult many drivers find it to 'interfere' with their engines, an inhibition that may well extend to other working parts of the car, its mysterious insides. They tend to do little inspection or maintenance themselves and often do not feel qualified to inspect or judge whether a garage is doing its job efficiently. Yet they are dependent on the garage. The driver may not know the person who does the actual work and cannot judge his efficiency and integrity. Drivers tend to feel very much at the mercy of such factors, and this is frightening.

Drivers' views of their garages reflect their unconscious phantasies and anxieties. They talk of the contretemps resulting from bad maintenance and repairs, usually by big – that is, powerful – garages almost as though they are uncaring or positively hostile – the vengeful father. By contrast, they talk with affectionate longing of 'the little chap round the corner', a caring but not powerful father figure who knows and is felt to love them and their cars personally. There are people who buy not so much cars as garages: having found a garage that is efficient, reliable and caring of car and owner, they always buy cars for which that garage holds the franchise. Some of this reliance on other people's maintenance, despite the anxiety about it, reflects the feeling that the car should protect and care for the driver rather than demand care from him. It is as though father should care for mother so that she in turn is kept in good form to look after the child.

In spite of – or in contrast to – feelings of omnipotence and power, many drivers feel very unsure of their ability to drive well and safely in all circumstances. They feel at the mercy of their own moods or psychological states that may adversely affect driving. They are aware that anger may make them drive less safely. They are tempted to or do actually take it out of one road user for something another has done to them. The protective power of the car does not always remove all the stress, tension and fatigue they take into it with them. They know that this may affect car control and make them drive badly. Drivers find it difficult to deal with this situation but unable to abstain from driving. It is a rare driver who stays at home.

An important stimulus to anxiety and anger is what the drivers regarded as features that make driving unnecessarily difficult and hazardous. Drivers often talk as though they are helpless to do anything about them other than complain. They project their own responsibility for performing the more than usually difficult task into others, most often 'authorities', who are then held totally responsible for doing something about it – not an attitude which is likely to improve driving. If the authorities do not do what drivers think they should, drivers feel inadequately pro-tected and supported and antisocial moods develop.

There was considerable agreement that 'three-lane highways are a death-trap' and that the authorities should do something about them. Poor road signs, warning signals and street lighting, missing street names and house numbers make drivers feel lost and confused, inadequate, anxious and angry. Such feelings are particularly acute when the driver is in strange territory, so much so that some drivers seem to find it almost impossible to venture outside their own localities. The driver's demand to be looked after is very forceful: the demand to have things made easy for him so that he can enjoy driving without anxiety, the demand for a benign (parental) authority who does all this. Authorities which do not are regarded rather as neglectful parents who do not protect the children from avoidable danger. There was comparatively little sign of response to challenge or of more adult attitudes like accepting the responsibility to cope.

ATTEMPTS AT RESOLVING THE DILEMMA

The ways that drivers try to resolve their dilemma are many and varied. I will comment on only a few of the most common, defensive techniques intended to keep anxiety at bay so that the driver can drive and enjoy it. Some of these have already been mentioned in the foregoing discussion and I will try to bring them together now. In so far as those techniques are defensive they do effectively reduce the conscious level of anxiety, but at the same time prevent the anxiety from being confronted and worked through. They also inhibit the development of realistic ways of dealing with the real difficulties and dangers of driving. Drivers are left with a vague uneasiness about which they cannot do much rather than an awareness of tasks and problems that could be realistically tackled.

The defences are not only individual – psychic defences – but are also social and involve the use of others: for example as recipients of projections or collusive interaction among and between drivers and others to build up defensive views held in common and so reinforced. The building and joint operation of such social defences is a major motive for the almost compulsive talking about driving.

Denial is a powerful technique: denial of the dangers one is exposed to and to which one exposes others, and especially of the possibility that one could be involved in, let alone cause, an accident. 'It couldn't happen to me' attitudes are prevalent. Some drivers admitted that they deliberately put the thought of danger out of their minds since they would not enjoy driving or might even have to stop if they thought about it. 'I forget about the worry when I get in the car, although I must say it sometimes hits me afterwards.'

Feelings of omnipotence are themselves partly a defence against anxiety about not being able to cope. This, together with the projection of one's own shortcomings, contributes to the feelings of unrealistic confidence in being a good driver oneself and in one's own safety. Many drivers bolster this feeling by keeping up a *sotto voce* commentary on the faults of other drivers they encounter, and passengers are expected to be willing participants in this exercise. These measures are effective in keeping conscious anxiety at bay and giving confidence, but at the cost of secondary anxiety about overconfidence and the vague uneasiness described above.

Drivers in discussion almost always reinforce such views of themselves and each other: we here are all good drivers, almost by definition. A man's account of his driving and his accident record would have to make it absolutely incontrovertible that he was a dangerous driver before a group of drivers would question the hypothesis that we here are all good drivers. To sustain this fiction, drivers may also make a distinction between good driving and safe driving. It is not absolutely necessary to be a safe driver to be considered a good driver. The good driver is one who is described as driving with power and panache: he drives fast, he dashes in and out, he seizes opportunities. That he may have a poor accident record, makes himself a nuisance to other drivers and indeed may escape trouble himself only because of their skill and quick reactions counts for little – the macho image gone mad.

The idea that one is a good driver may be sustained by abstaining from making a critical review of one's own driving – it would be a waste of effort anyway, when one is so good! Few drivers seem to do this. In fact, many drivers do not seem to know what criteria might be used. Nor do people often criticize other people's driving openly to them; they only project into and criticize absent drivers. It seems that drivers would hardly dare to criticize other drivers and could not bear to be criticized themselves. This would seem such a narcissistic assault to the core of the driver's being. The less competent a driver, the less he seemed able to criticize his own driving. Conversely, the ability to review one's own driving critically seemed to be a factor in good driving.

Omnipotence seemed to carry drivers beyond the point of feeling that they would never cause an accident, to the point where they believed in and supported each other in the view that they were such good drivers that they had an absolute immunity from accidents. They could always drive out of trouble. A driver's accident record made little impact on these views. Long accident-free history understandably built up confidence, but the feeling could be just as strong in drivers who had had accidents. If one had never had an accident it proved one was immune; if one had had an accident one had 'had one's lot' and so gained immunity, as from an inoculation. Similarly, drivers assume an unrealistic degree of isolation from environmental factors and their effects and lack a real sense of danger and need for care in snow, ice, fog or high winds. Magical thinking and superstition add to the defences: 'If I have a little knock when I'm leaving such as just touching the gatepost, then I'll be all right.' Or: 'I never feel safe until I have seen an accident', as though that means today's accident is over.

Projection is massively used, individually and socially. Drivers talking together engage in collusive projections into other absent drivers and reinforce each other's views. 'They' cause all the trouble. Whole categories of other drivers are scapegoated as though they were all the same, and agreement about who 'they' are is usually quickly and easily reached – Mini drivers, lorry drivers, drunken drivers, weekend drivers, women drivers. Evidence for such views is minimal. Flaws in logic are common: for example generalizing on one case. Someone saw a Mini driver do something terrible yesterday; (therefore) Mini drivers are bad drivers. Arguments become circular: someone was seen driving badly on a Sunday, so he must have been a weekend driver; therefore weekend drivers are bad drivers. Counter-evidence, if produced at all, is likely to be ruled out of court. The discussion may well degenerate to a level below the usual intellectual capacity of the speakers. The objective is not truth but the establishment of convenient depositories for unmanageable anxieties.

In a similar way, external conditions may be scapegoated and *entirely* blamed for accidents when all they do in fact is make driving more difficult and call for more care and skill – or in extreme cases they may mean one should not drive at all, a sacrifice drivers find it hard to make. The familiar hates have already been mentioned: ice, snow, fog, shortcomings of the authorities. These again are convenient depositories for the driver's anxiety about coping and his overburdening responsibility for driving well and safely.

SOME EFFECTS OF THE INADEQUATE RESOLUTION OF THE DRIVER'S DILEMMA

Such massive defence mechanisms used by many motorists individually and collectively are likely to impair the capacity to see what is going on around one, to assess its significance realistically and to react to it effectively. Drivers gave many examples of this, some of which have already been cited. Stories were often told in a slightly manic, humorous way, especially if nothing awful happened as a result. Three drivers had been following a fourth in a very thick fog. He turned into an enclosure where he always parked for the night; the other three 'blindly' followed him. That raised a laugh. Less amusing was an insurance agent's account of how he got an unusual number of claims relating to accidents on the same spot. He went to investigate and found it was a T-junction. Cars entering the main road from the leg of the T could not actually see into the main road from where they stopped, but they acted as though they could. Since they saw no approaching traffic they behaved as though it was not there and caused collisions.

It follows too that anything that raises drivers' anxiety is likely to mobilize even more massive and primitive defences. It is quite normal to regress under stress. However, this also means that when difficult circumstances require more awareness and more effective responses, drivers may well become less able to cope, their judgement and effectiveness impaired by the situation and their reaction. So-called 'motorway madness' in fog is one such effect and may really be a kind of temporary madness in usually quite sane people as they are seized by acute anxiety and mobilize primitive – that is, mad – defences. The rear lights of the car in front in a motorway fog seem so comforting as against being alone in a directionless wilderness that many drivers cling to them, although they know intellectually that if they are close enough to see them at the speed at which they are travelling, they are dangerously close. Being alone or being the leader in a motorway convoy with nothing in front is a horrifying and terrible experience: one's eyes are out on stalks trying to pierce the blackness ahead to find something there at the same time as one dreads finding something there, so suddenly one hits it. One really feels the threat of madness, a fog inside as well as out.

Confrontation with accidents seems to have a similar effect. The immediate shock may breach the defences and confront drivers with the seriousness of their position – there but for the grace of God . . . They may drive with great – even excessive – caution for a time, but the effect is temporary, variably estimated by drivers as three to ten miles, but probably less in fact. As the driver re-experiences the feel of his car and remobilizes his defences, confidence or overconfidence returns. Accidents, after all, happen only to other people.

Drivers tend to suppress the topic of accidents in discussion and certainly do not often spontaneously raise it. There seems almost to be a taboo on such talk. There are exceptions. A recent accident may put some pressure on a driver to discuss it as a means of helping himself to deal with the experience and work it through, especially if he can prove, at least to his own satisfaction, that it was entirely someone else's fault. Intense guilt and shame add to anxiety. Regardless of whose fault the accident really was, the driver feels he should have coped better and saved the situation. He may be left with a feeling of helpless terror: 'There was nothing I could do.' That may be true, but his omnipotence is breached, his competence and masculinity are challenged. It is hard to stay in touch with that and not raise defences against it.

Even quite firm efforts to get drivers to talk about real or imaginary accidents produce little reaction other than flight into another topic. If set a more general task of discussing the problems and difficulties of driving, drivers give little attention to accidents. They are more likely to elaborate on minor frustrations and difficulties – 'little niggles', as one man called them – of the kind already described. These are much easier to address, especially since they facilitate projection. These minor contretemps are, in a way, the stuff of driving. Drivers do have to deal with them a great deal and can realistically expect to have to do so, since they are happening all the time. So it is understandable that they talk about them a great deal. By contrast, one may really never have been in an accident; many of the drivers certainly claimed to have accident-free records. Hopefully, or magically, one never will be. So why should one worry? In other words, the attention given to 'little niggles' is also to some extent a defence against the greater worry about accidents.

The obverse of avoiding thinking or talking about accidents is that drivers seemed to pay very little attention to safety. They even said that most drivers are not safety-conscious. They cannot emotionally afford to be, because that would imply being danger-conscious. Many drivers felt that they would not enjoy driving if they had to think about safety all the time. This seemed to lead to some real disregard of safety factors.

Safety features were little mentioned in relation to car choice. Indeed, drivers did not seem to know much about safety features in cars they were considering buying. A very reputable, expensive car was being advertised with emphasis on safety features. Drivers would have loved to have that car if they could have afforded it, but the safety features were totally disregarded as a reason for the choice. Drivers seemed to feel that a car should automatically be safe and give full protection, rather like a mother whose goodness should not be doubted. To suggest that some cars might be safer than others or that one might give some attention to safety features seemed a rather bizarre idea, or even an insult. Car manufacturers have long been of the opinion that 'you can't sell cars on safety'. The same goes for car accessories. Safety belts were low on most people's lists, if they appeared at all.[1] Popular accessories were those that eased the driver's task – like wing mirrors or better screen washers – or added to comfort and pleasure – like good heating or radios. Drivers professed to be interested in good driving, which may or may not include safe driving. It often does not. Safety seems to be such a touchy subject that it often has to be ruled out of consideration.

SOME IMPLICATIONS OF THE RESEARCH FINDINGS

I would now like to consider the implications of this research for attempts to improve driving and reduce accidents. The general conclusion that seems to emerge is that propaganda based on provoking or increasing anxiety may very well arouse resistance. Drivers are quite anxious enough already. The effect of such propaganda might well be to strengthen many drivers' defences, risking further impairment of their reality sense and their performance. By contrast, drivers welcome an approach that shows some understanding of their predicament, offers some relief of anxiety and mobilizes support in facing the difficulties and dangers. They also welcome offers of more enjoyment. In so far as such approaches reduce anxiety and increase rewards, they lower defences and benefit reality sense and performance. This conclusion was supported by the specific findings in the safety-belt and drinking-and-driving studies.

Hostile reaction to the use of safety belts was widespread. Intensive propaganda about their effectiveness in reducing the number and severity of casualties in accidents largely fell on deaf ears. The majority of drivers did not know details and tended to react apathetically – 'I suppose it must be a good thing if they say so.' Many people did not remember what they had read or heard. There were sometimes active attempts to disprove the data, usually by highly suspect arguments such as generalizing on one case again: 'He would have been killed if he had been wearing a safety belt; he only saved himself by diving into the passenger seat.' There was exaggerated confidence in the speed of one's own reactions and one's ability to save oneself. There was a great deal of anxiety about being trapped in a car – possibly a burning car – by the belt after an accident. Much was made of the difficulties and dangers arising from the belts themselves, like lying across the throat and choking you in the event of sharp braking; people tripping over belts and hurting themselves; belts kicking about the car floor and dirtying your clothes.

Small kernels of truth in these complaints were greatly exaggerated. The reactions were sometimes really quite paranoid, the belt itself becoming rather a phobic object. Far from being safe and protective, it became a source of mysterious and horrible danger, a trap, a threat, a source of contamination. The hoped-for protective mother turned into a horrible witch. In other words, it looked as though the name 'safety belt' was being interpreted as 'danger belt', itself imbued with all the dangers it could help to prevent and confronting the driver with what might happen to him. This raised anxieties and militated against usage. *Safety* belt was an unfortunate choice of name; the more neutral term 'seat belt', which gradually replaced it, was a better platform from which to launch the move to compulsory usage. It is interesting to compare this with motorcyclists' use of crash helmets at the same time, which was almost universal and without compulsion. Crash helmet, or skid lid, conveyed the macho image beloved of the young male motorcyclist.

The widespread image of the habitual safety-belt user was much in contrast to that. He would be a kind of old woman, overcautious, fussy, priggish – not, of course, a good driver. Drivers could not identify with him. There was also a contrasting image with which they could also not identify, a kind of negative version of the 'good' driver. This was a man who would wear a safety belt to enable him to drive dangerously in the macho way: he would ensure his own safety through the belt, would be so well-to-do that he did not have to mind if he wrecked his car, and by implication did not care either if he wrecked other people and their cars. Drivers felt that safety belts were an insult to the masculine image of the driver, and the certainty that he was a good and responsible driver who did not need safety belts because he would never be in accidents.

There were notable exceptions to this picture, however, though not in large numbers. These tended to be middle- or upper-middle-class drivers who prided themselves on being well informed and realistic. They read 'good' newspapers, listened carefully to radio and television and thought carefully about what they learned. They followed the 'propaganda' and installed safety belts. But even some of them admitted to having taken a long time actually to get the belts once they had decided to do so, and to taking even longer to develop usage once they had them. These people derived some moral support against the general hostility from the feeling that they had 'friends', people like them: that is, other drivers they saw wearing belts. One woman said she felt she belonged to a kind of club.

Some important findings emerged from discussion with those drivers. They experienced what we came to describe as 'bonus' factors from the use of safety belts, factors related to pleasure and comfort. They liked being held firmly by the belts, felt the car was more containing and protective. Some felt the belts helped them to sustain a good driving position. This was most extremely expressed by a very tall man who drove a Mini. He said he would not have been able to avoid crouching, a bad and tiring driving position, but his belt kept him upright and relaxed. In general, it was felt that belts contributed to the reduction of driver and passenger fatigue in that they made unnecessary or less necessary a lot of the minor adaptations to the movement of the car: to braking, swerving, taking sharp bends. Drivers particularly liked the fact that their passengers did not 'bob about' so much, such bobbing tending to make the driver feel he was not driving well or looking after his passenger properly. Safety came up in a different way. Drivers felt that belts helped them to drive better and might actually, therefore, contribute to accident avoidance even better than to casualty reduction. It seemed that an approach to *seat*-, not *safety*-belt usage along these lines might have been more effective in increasing usage than the safety-and-accident-based approach.[2]

The drinking-and-driving campaign studied was the 1964 Christmas campaign which basically consisted of a horror road-accident poster and the slogan 'Don't ask a man to drink and drive'. This campaign was internally inconsistent and evoked confused and contradictory reactions from drivers. The effects of the horror poster were reminiscent of seeing a real accident. There was some immediate shock which was sealed off and defended against. Although the poster was truly horrific, drivers sometimes complained that it was not horrific enough: there should be 'lots of blood and gore'. That would have had no more, or perhaps even less impact in our opinion. Enough of horror is enough.

The slogan had a very different effect: it was in many ways a relief. It did not isolate the driver with his almost unbearable responsibility but mobilized social support for him. It recognized the reality that drivers do not usually drink alone but in a social situation where how much they drink is not only a personal matter but also a function of how much pressure others put on them to drink and how much support there is for abstention. The slogan seemed somehow to rescue the driver from an uncomfortable position as a social isolate who was also a potential or actual delinquent or criminal to be dealt with morally and punitively, an approach that only too often creeps into drinking-and-driving campaigns. An ordinary, reasonably responsible driver is not likely to accept that view of himself: he may well disclaim any connection with the driver to whom the advertisement is addressed, and project the problem into the 'real drunken driver'. This disclaimer may, however, lead him to drink more than is sensible or even legal, so he might indeed become a delinquent through his own denials. Since he was treated by the slogan as though he was an ordinary member of society who cared about what he did, he was more likely to behave as one. This seems really to have happened. Drivers we saw at the time reported that they felt there had been some impact on events like office Christmas parties, which were more 'sober'.[3]

This paper describes the driver's dilemma, which is to optimize the rewards of driving in spite of the real and fantasy dangers in the driving situation. Psychic and social defences are developed to keep at bay the anxiety aroused by the dangers, defences which may make it more difficult for the driver to perform his role and task as effectively as he might. The paper suggests that the most effective way to improve driving performance is to facilitate a better resolution of the dilemma by attempting to modify the anxiety and defences and increase the rewards. This would allow the driver to approach driving more realistically and apply his judgement and skills more safely and effectively.

NOTES

1. This study was done before seat belts became compulsory fittings.

2. These findings came out of a situation where most of the belts in use were of the static variety. Inertia belts do not give the bonus to the same degree, since they firm up only under impact. The belts now in use are almost entirely inertia. The change may well have been a concession to the paranoid reactions described above. I myself feel somewhat regretful about this change, which deprives drivers and passengers of some advantages. There is also some evidence that static belts are marginally safer.

3. This slogan part of the campaign seems to have made it one of the most effective drinking-and-driving campaigns. Sadly, more recent campaigns seem to have reverted to treating the driver as a social isolate and a potential delinquent. We are not surprised that they have not been very effective.

II The motorcycle: growing up on two wheels*

I WOULD LIKE in this paper to concentrate attention on the way that psychoanalytical experience and insights can illuminate one's understanding of people and their behaviour in situations other than the consulting room, and deepen one's understanding of what goes on in society at large.

To illustrate the point I will select some of the findings from a research study of young male motorcyclists, ranging in age roughly from sixteen to twenty-two. The study was commissioned by an organization that was concerned about the alarming accident and casualty rates among these young motorcyclists, and sought guidance about what action might be taken.

We assumed that it would be of central importance to try to gain access to the kind of data more easily accessible in one's consulting room: that is, to the unconscious phantasy systems that lie behind the conscious thoughts and feelings and behaviour. A fuller understanding of such unconscious phantasy systems would illuminate the transactions between the motorcyclist and society, in particular with his motorcycle, the roads, other road users and the relevant authorities and, we hoped, would elucidate why these transactions so often end in disaster.

For this purpose our main research instrument was the long discursive interview with individuals and groups. It would not be true to say that the interviews were not guided, but they were certainly not guided by preconceived questions or topics intro-

*This paper was one of a series of public lectures organized by the British Psycho-Analytical Society in 1969 on the subject of 'Sexuality and aggression in maturation: new facets'. Dr. S.H. Klein chaired the series of lectures and edited the book in which the papers were collected for publication (Klein, 1969).

duced by the interviewers. Instead, after a general introduction to the topic the interviewer made a continuous series of near-clinical judgements about where the immediate focus of interest or anxiety was for the respondent, and having done that tried to guide the respondent through as close an exploration of it as possible. This meant, of course, that there could be, and were, considerable differences in the topics dealt with by different respondents.

Which brings me to the question of the analysis of the data. Such an interviewing method will not provide statistical data, nor was it our intention that it should. Rather, we were concerned to understand the forces operating in the situation, the springs of action.

I will go on in a moment to give some examples of how we analysed the data, but first I would like to make a theoretical point concerning one way the individual uses his environment as an aid to the resolution of intrapsychic problems. The individual seeks out relevant situations in the external world which he can identify, usually unconsciously, with psychic situations within himself. The two situations must resemble each other to some degree before this can happen. Once it does happen, elements of the external situation come to symbolize elements of the internal situation. The individual then experiences an external situation partly as it objectively exists, and partly in terms of the internal fantasy systems he has psychically put into it. Successful mastery of an external real and symbolic situation aids the resolution of the internal situation and gives reassurance to the individual that he can cope.

To come now to motorcyclists. Those with whom we are concerned are involved in the typical social and psychological problems of adolescence and early manhood. They have chosen their motorcycling as one relevant external situation into which they can project their private versions of these problems, and through which they seek help in solving them and in dealing with the associated anxiety and distress. This is what these young men have in common. But they are also a cross-section of society and vary very much among themselves – for example personality, intelligence, social class, their place in society and their ability to use the resources of society. These variations, as I hope to show, result in great differences in the way they use motorcycling.

I will go on now to comment on some of the social and psychological tasks of the adolescent and how these are deployed in the motorcycling situation.

1. RELATIONS WITH PARENTS AND AUTHORITY

The adolescent, moving towards manhood, has to revise his relations with his real parents and with other people and institutions in society that symbolize them and their authority. He must detach himself to some extent from actual parental authority, and make relationships with more distant and often impersonal authority such as the legal system, the moral code and conventions of society, the police and magistrates. He must also re-evaluate the nature of his own conscience and how it will function. These processes involve, *ipso facto*, the reworking of oedipal problems.

What happens, then, when such problems are taken on the road? Many different things, of course, but let us look first at an extreme version: at the kind of boy who reaches adolescence with inadequately resolved oedipal problems, including an envious and hostile relationship to father figures and to authority, and very limited capacity to contain and work over such problems within himself. He is a doer rather than a thinker. He usually owns a fairly powerful machine with which he acts out his problems in a massive way on the roads, often with disastrous consequences.

He tends to regard car-drivers as his natural enemies, as successful and sexually potent males whom he cannot hope to emulate. He tends also to regard scooter-drivers as younger versions of car-drivers heading towards successful manhood. (In this view he is quite right, as I hope to show later.) So they are also his natural enemies. All his latent oedipal hostility is therefore re-evoked towards these other drivers.

There is no need for these other drivers to do anything provocative for the attack to be launched. As one such motorcyclist said: 'A few of us were out and we saw some scooters and somebody said, "Come on boys, let's cut them up." ' They often tease car-drivers much as small boys do their fathers, in this way trying to deal with feelings of inferiority and to triumph over the more successful older man. They may act out their oedipal fantasies in such a way as to contribute to accidents in which the car-driver is technically responsible. For example, such motor-cyclists seem adept at riding in a car-driver's 'blind spot', invisible in his mirrors. When the car-driver signals a manoeuvre they are at his side and he may hit them. It is legally his fault. These motorcyclists also seem to collect stories of the large damages paid them by car-drivers after such incidents. The whole atmosphere is of fixing, exploiting and triumphing over the hated father figure, the car-driver.

These motorcyclists also have an immature relationship with authority. They cannot identify positively with authority, nor envisage ever exercising such authority themselves. They appear also as relatively 'conscienceless' and therefore without good internal authority. They are, in other words, people whose conscience is primitively harsh and punitive to the point where it cannot be borne internally; hence it is denied and emotionally evacuated into external authorities which are perceived as the more harsh and punitive in consequence. As a result these motorcyclists feel impelled to defy authority and to break the rules it makes. Police and magistrates are also natural enemies.

The motorcyclists defy the rules of the road and experience little conscious guilt or anxiety about doing so. 'Getting nicked' for a driving offence, far from being a disgrace, becomes a kind of decoration for gallantry. They complain bitterly about what they regard as the unfair attitudes of magistrates, insisting that motorcyclists suffer unfairly heavy fines, or even that magistrates impose very heavy fines in order to get motorcyclists off the road, because they cannot afford to pay the fine and run a motorcycle at the same time. They described this in terms that suggested it was almost like castration by a revengeful father. One can see how easily this may create a vicious circle of law-breaking, punishment experienced as unfair, and further defiant law-breaking.

But there is another less overt attitude. Such defiance is hard work, and these motorcyclists seemed to long for a supportive, protective and indulgent authority, more like a kindly mother than a stern, punitive father. They were like children in spite of their age, and tended to claim the privileges of a naughty child who would not be treated so harshly as an adult for the same offence. They hint, for example, that fines should be orientated to the driver's capacity to pay, not to the offence. Hence car-drivers should pay more because they are better off. It is almost as though they want to be treated like children being aggressive with toys, not like adults aggressively handling potentially murderous weapons.

In total, then, one can see a situation which is geared to bad driving and a high accident rate.

But by no means are all motorcyclists like this. Contrast another kind of motorcyclist, a young man who has relatively successfully dealt with his oedipal problems, whose envy of successful older men is emulative rather than destructive, who relates positively, though not necessarily uncritically, to authority and has probably had positions of authority already himself. He has a reasonably well-developed capacity to work over his problems intrapsychically rather than through impulsive and ill-considered action. He very often owns a scooter, which he may experience rather more like a mini Mini car than like a motorcycle. He suffers relatively little from the compulsion to act out crudely on the roads. One would not claim that he is totally immune to the temptations of acting out his oedipal problems, but when he does his reactions are different to those of the first type. He is likely to feel shame, guilt and anxiety about giving way to those impulses, not triumphant and omnipotent. He is likely to learn from such experiences and improve his performance in future. He does not take punishment lightly, let alone proudly. He may not always blindly obey the rules, but at least he usually attempts to assess them realistically and is judicious about how he breaks them. He may not religiously observe speed limits any more than car-drivers do, but he is unlikely to exceed them grossly, or just for the sake of doing so.

He regards authority as on the whole benevolent and sees the police and magistrates as part of a legal system that is orientated to maintaining reasonable order, discipline and safety on the roads. Such motorcyclists accept responsibility on the whole as adults, and are much less prone to claim indulgence as naughty children. They are able to relate fairly realistically to other road users and their needs, and to show concern for them. They are orientated, therefore, to driving well, and are not accident-prone. Such evidence as we had suggested, indeed, that their accident rate was closer to that of car-drivers of the same age than to that of the first type of motorcyclist.

2. PROBLEMS ABOUT SEXUAL POTENCY

Male adolescents are typically beset by anxieties about their sexual potency, the state of their sexual organs and their sexual functioning. They are also beset by anxieties about an actual or potential sexual partner, about whether they will satisfy her and be satisfied, about the possible dangers of the mysterious vagina. Added to problems of their lack of experience, or limited experience in sexual relationships, are very primitive irrational anxieties stemming from infantile sources in the personality.

Motorcycles and the road again lend themselves well to symbolic representation of these problems. To return now to the first type of motorcyclist, and first a general comment about his capacity for symbolism. This is ill-developed and crude. In effect this means that his relationship with an external object tends to be overweighed with qualities attributed to it from the psychic object it represents. The obverse of that is that his capacity to relate realistically to the objective qualities of the real object is limited. For such a motorcyclist the motorcycle becomes crudely symbolic of the genitals, and he acts out and tries to deal with potency problems very directly on his vehicle. He says, for example, that it is a part of yourself, you can feel it between your legs or, even more obviously, it is marvellous to feel that power between your legs. He contrasts the motorcycle proper with the scooter and says contemptuously, but enviously: 'It's like a chair, you sit on it.' In other words, it is a separate object.

The possession of a powerful cycle and hope or plans for a yet more powerful one give him reassurance that he is sexually potent – not, however, by real maturation but by attaching to himself, in a rather magical way, a crude potency symbol. The ability to control this powerful object reassures against anxiety that he may be carried away and damaged by his own sexual impulses. In this context the 'ton' – 100 miles per hour – is often talked of in a way reminiscent of orgasm: dared, achieved, and survived. Such motorcyclists are often highly knowledgeable about their vehicles' capacities, and have a high degree of skill in driving. This provides further reassurance symbolically about sexual competence, but is unfortunately no guarantee that they will deploy their knowledge and skill safely on the roads. They are, indeed, often carried away by their impulses, since those would-be magical ways of coping with them are not really effective.

The relative emotional immaturity of such motorcyclists makes it difficult for them to orientate their sexuality to making relationships with others; hence remarks like: 'It's a part of yourself', and the contemptuous envy of the scooter-driver who makes a relationship with his scooter as a separate object. Their relationship with their motorcycles is, therefore, very masturbatory. For example, they sometimes become preoccupied with maintenance, spending much more time in taking cycles to pieces, cleaning and servicing them than seems necessary, sometimes more time than they spend driving. They give the impression of being always at their cycles, and preoccupied with the state they are in. A lot of erotic pleasure is derived from this activity. This was highlighted by one boy who spoke with evident pleasure about how nice it was that he could work on his motorcycle in his bedroom. No car-driver could do that. Work on the cycle is sometimes aimed at actually increasing its power beyond the manufacturer's specifications: for example, by boring out feed pipes to increase capacity. Maturation for these boys is seen in terms of owning a yet larger and more powerful motorcycle. It is much more difficult for them to envisage maturation in terms of successfully developed heterosexual relationships and marriage.

Damage to the cycle is felt as a terrible narcissistic wound. They seem to care for the cycle almost more than they do for themselves – they *are* caring for what again emotionally is experienced as a vital part of themselves. As one boy said after an accident: 'When I saw my bike was damaged I sat down on the pavement and cried.' It hardly seemed to matter that he himself was uninjured.

When they ride their cycles these boys are forced into a relationship with real objects, for example the roads, into which they project much of their anxiety about females. Road problems symbolize sexual problems; to deal with these they often become experts in road conditions: the effects of wet, grease and ice or bumps, irregularities and holes. They are often unduly anxious about such things, as they project into them fears about bodily products in the sexual zones and of the female body. Many references were made to the dangers of night driving, particularly of falling into holes in the road, and envy was expressed of car-drivers whose four wheels carried them safely over such hazards.

However, their expert knowledge of road conditions and their somewhat paranoid preoccupation with the dangers of the roads are no guarantee that they do in fact respond realistically to them and drive appropriately. On the contrary, the crudely symbolic nature of their preoccupation and the high degree of anxiety associated with it tend to mobilize a primitive omnipotence about their capacity to cope and denials that 'it could happen to me', which intensify accident-proneness.

Fear of entering into a committed relationship with a female also appeared in a curious relationship with the motorcycle. We were struck by how few of the motorcyclists came to interviews on their motorcycles. They were very unlike car-drivers in this respect. Their explanation for their behaviour seemed to show fear of fusion and confusion: they would get lost in unfamiliar territory, particularly in one-way streets. Also they showed fear of attack; for example, very often they said that if they brought their cycles into town they would be stripped down. Both of these anxieties reflected real situations but were greatly exaggerated and seemed to reflect anxieties, on both a sexual and a personal level, that if they entered into a committed relationship they would be lost and would lose essential elements of themselves. Their motorcycles were described as being used mainly for going out – that is, out of town, away from it all, escaping into the safety of open spaces with largely homosexual companionship.

Contrast again the other type of motorcyclist. His use of symbols is much more sophisticated, which means that his relationship with his vehicle and the roads is less dominated by crude sexual symbolism. He has a more realistic appreciation of the capacities and limitations of his vehicle, and of the opportunities and problems of the roads. His vehicle is regarded primarily as a means of transport which, however, he enjoys using. He is able to deal with his sexual development and anxieties more directly by testing them out with real females. Indeed, his vehicle is often used as an aid to such activities, carrying him easily to and from places where he meets suitable girls. The fact that motorcycles are regarded as inappropriate means of transport for nicely dressed girls on dates is likely to precipitate an early decision to become a car owner, a decision to which he is probably tending in any case. Not for him the phoney attempt to reassure himself that he is making sexual progress by getting a bigger cycle as a potency symbol. Realistic success in committed sexual relationships is much more possible and important for him.

This kind of motorcyclist deploys a good deal of care and concern towards his machine. One could almost say that he respects and cares for it as a thing which is unconsciously associated with people who have cared for him well and to whom he responds with gratitude and concern. He also does his own maintenance because, as he says, it is easy and cheaper, but he is fairly realistically orientated to keeping his vehicle in good working order, and is not concerned to increase its power beyond its original capacity. In return he expects good service in practical and realistic terms, good performance and freedom from breakdowns.

All this adds up again to the fact that the motorcyclist of this type is likely to be a good driver, realistically in touch with what he is doing on the roads and well orientated to other road users.

3. AGGRESSION AND DEATH

It need hardly be said that adolescents are aggressive, nor that the adolescent is very frightened of his aggression. The whole upheaval of adolescence frees powerful aggressive as well as sexual drives. Anger is easily provoked in the adolescent as a reaction to the confusion and dilemma of his position and to the people who he feels hinder his development or fail to solve his problems, and have given him a terrible world to live in. So powerful can these feelings be that one often has the impression that adolescents need to live dangerously, to challenge death and survive, involving both themselves and others in the process. The increase in physical strength, in intellectual knowledge, and in opportunities which can be used to express aggression may terrify him. A three-year-old, experiencing temporary murderous feelings acted out physically towards his mother, is protected by some awareness that he is unlikely really to be able to murder her. A sixteen-year-old boy does not have this protection. Acting out aggressive impulses by crashing toy cars on an electric circuit is one thing. Having the opportunity to act out the same fantasies with real vehicles on the road is another. Revised modes of handling aggressive impulses and trying to subject them effectively to the direction of libidinal forces are now necessary.

Motorcycling is again an obvious area for the development of such problems. Our first type of motorcyclist is in severe difficulties here. His internal resources to contain his aggression are meagre. His capacity to mobilize positive feelings is also meagre. He is forced to act out aggressive impulses directly, and often physically. Sophisticated symbolic expressions of aggression, like intellectual debate or disciplined organized sport, are intellectually and emotionally beyond him. Further, his position in society deprives him of opportunities. He so often lives in the interstices rather than the networks and institutions in society, and cannot find, or cannot join, organizations that would give him opportunity for socialized discharge of aggression. He cannot play rugby for his old school or join a tennis club. He cannot look forward to fighting intellectual battles as a lawyer or expressing his sadism constructively as a surgeon.

One almost feels he is condemned through lack of other

151

outlets to antisocial activities such as acting out aggressive impulses on the road in ways that endanger himself and others. The roads are unfortunately suitable outlets. I have already referred to the aggressive interplay between the motorcyclist and car- and scooter-drivers. In addition they act out their aggression on the road in very aggressive rivalry with each other, endangering both themselves and other road users in the process. Some of them indeed dislike group runs, or even refuse to go on them because they realize the dangers of mutually aggravated aggression. The need to challenge death is powerful, and is associated with massive denials that it could happen to the self. The motorcyclists seemed engaged in a constant attempt, not always successful, to prove that death was for others. If they talked about death on the roads it was almost always other people's death. Thus they succeeded in projecting their fear of death connected with their own reckless aggression into other people and denied that they themselves were in real danger. The noise and smell that emanate from the cycle, usually from the rear, are also a very crude symbolic representation of the way the baby experiences his aggression through his phantasies about the purpose and effect of his anal activities.

The 'ton' in this context implies going to the brink of death and surviving, with some kind of guarantee that therefore one will continue to survive. Accidents partake of similar meanings in lesser degree. They are often regarded as a kind of initiation rite, 'you are not really a motorcyclist until you have had one', they say. There is also relief after having an accident. Very often the reality is less bad than the fantasy about what *could* happen. At least one has not died. Such an accident may also be regarded as a kind of inoculation that guarantees immunity against other similar experiences. The effect of accidents is minimal in sobering these motorcyclists down and making them more careful in future. Their capacity to learn from such experience is limited.

The other kind of motorcyclist, as one might expect, is again better off. He is in less danger of being overwhelmed by aggression. He has more capacity to sublimate it, and to harness it to positive ends. Also he usually has more opportunities open to him to express it in constructive ways and is better able to use them. He can play competitive games, he can take up relatively dangerous sports like skiing, climbing or sailing which serve similar purposes but much less violently. He is less easily provoked into angry responses by the bad behaviour of other road users, and less prone to think he is being badly treated by other road users or authorities when he really isn't, and to react aggressively. If he takes pride in beating other road users away from lights or by weaving in and out of traffic jams he is more likely to do it safely and without being overwhelmed by aggressive competition. If he does behave aggressively and dangerously he is likely to feel guilty and frightened and resolve not to do it again.

Such motorcyclists are less likely to push dangerous acting out to the limits. No 'ton' for them, even if their vehicles were capable of doing it, which they usually are not. Their relation with top speed is more realistically orientated to the power of their machines and to road conditions. They do not need to prove their manhood in such ways. They can achieve real success in other ways: by intellectual and professional achievements, by holding positions of responsibility. Their basic self-respect is greater, they feel more faith in their own survival and have less need to challenge death to reassure themselves about it.

They take no pride in accidents or death. Accidents do not initiate them into any group which they value. Indeed, unlike the other kind of motorcyclists, they do not feel they belong to a motorcycling fraternity. It would seem silly to them to belong to an official or unofficial club, concerned with so mundane and useful an activity as motorcycling. It would be like a housewife belonging to a refrigerator club. Defying death on the roads holds no glory for them, as one boy said after he had seen an accident with casualties: 'It [that is, death in an accident] seems such an insignificant way to go.'

INDICATIONS FOR ACTION

It is not my intention in this paper to go in detail into what can be done about these problems. However, I will comment briefly on what seem to be the implications of the data I have discussed. In a sense one may say that the whole problem resolves itself into one of maturation. The more mature the boy or young man, the less likely he is to act out his developmental problems with a motorcycle on the roads. Of this general point there are two aspects in practice. The first I have already discussed: that the quality of driving is closely associated with the motorcyclist's degree of maturity. The second I have mentioned incidentally in passing: that the actual choice of vehicle is often also linked with the degree of maturity. This affects not only the choice between different two-wheeled vehicles but also the choice between the motorcycle and a car. If one could get more motorcyclists into cars sooner the casualty rate would go down at least, even if the accident rate remained the same, because cars are safer vehicles and their drivers and passengers less vulnerable. Unfortunately, the less mature the motorcyclist the greater appear to be his difficulties in moving to a car.

Other research work with car-drivers has shown clearly that the car represents a combined parental symbol: the body maternal and protective, the engine paternal, potent, and possibly dangerous. To be a car-driver one has to have the capacity to make an effective relationship with this joint parental figure. Unresolved oedipal problems and difficulties with father figures and about potency may make it difficult to do this.

The motorcyclists most dangerous to themselves and others are unfortunately, therefore, those who are least likely to be able to make the transition to the safer car.

How, then, to help the young motorcyclist to mature more quickly and effectively? I will consider action only within the framework of his own chosen area of symbolization: that is, motorcycling. Evidence from other work on accident reduction suggests that action directed towards the accident-prone only is not likely to be very effective. Indeed, in the case of the accident-prone motorcyclist such singling out would be likely only to increase his paranoid reactions and defiance of authority. In any case, other motorcyclists are not so safe that they would not also improve. So action needs to be orientated to changing the whole institution of motorcycling, not only to the motor-cyclists themselves but to their environment, including the roads, authorities, and other road users. The responsibility for taking initiative lies primarily with the relevant authorities. For example, they might develop attitudes more supportive and protective and less punitive, giving, for example, more care to vehicle and road development with two-wheeled vehicles in mind. They could consider processes whereby effective models could be provided for identification: men who ride with skill, dash and daring but with safety and concern for others. Alternative types of distinction and decoration might be offered, such as high performance in trials. This could then be linked with the provision of more sporting facilities for motorcyclists which might encourage them not to use the roads for sport motorcycling.

Very important here is the question of the age of first licence. At present[1] it is sixteen for the motorcyclist and seventeen for car-drivers, which inevitably conveys a message that it is easier and safer to ride a motorcycle, although people know rationally that it is not. It seems very likely that there would be a change in the car/motorcycle balance if there were a different relationship between the age of first licence. Action would be neither easy nor quick, but it does seem important in view of the accident and casualty rates.

Within this context I want to conclude now by commenting briefly on our responsibilities as adults to these young men and as car-drivers to motorcyclists. I raise this question lest we, as adults and car-drivers, become smug, regard ourselves as only the innocent victims of the acting out of disturbed adolescent motorcyclists, and reject our own responsibilities. It is important for us to consider our own blind spots, both literal and metaphorical.

Literally it is easy for car-drivers to forget that motorcycles are less easy to see on the roads than four-wheeled vehicles, since they are so much narrower. Car-drivers do have a tendency to identify with their own kind as road users, and forget, or do not allow for, the presence of cycles. Motorcyclists can be blocked from direct or mirror vision by parts of the car or small objects on the road that would not completely prevent one seeing a car or larger vehicle. The presence of motorcycles on the road, combined with the speed at which they legitimately travel, makes extra careful looking round blind spots desirable.

But perhaps more important are metaphorical blind spots – that is, our incomplete awareness of the factors in ourselves that may lead us to initiate difficulties for motorcyclists, or enter into mutually acting-out activities if a motorcyclist initiates some difficulty.

We car-drivers also suffer from envy. Envy of motorcyclists may lead us consciously or unconsciously into attacking them: 'I won't let him pass, however much he hangs on my tail.' So I hug the crown of the road in the face of oncoming traffic when I could perfectly well move over to the left. By so doing I am likely to stimulate the only too easily provoked paranoia and aggression of the motorcyclist and encourage him to take undue risks to get past.

Such envy arises from a number of sources. For example, many car-drivers have owned motorcycles in the past and still have a hankering after them, especially in fine weather, on open roads, or in close traffic. The car-driver envies the motorcyclist's speed and manoeuvrability, his power and skill, his youth and dash. He envies the challenge and danger of motorcycles, the very things that attract the young. The car-driver envies the motorcyclist his freedom and independence on the roads, which is interpreted, at least unconsciously, as freedom from the cares and responsibilities of adult life.

Car-drivers also project into motorcyclists psychic problems they have not completely resolved in themselves, although they may have coped reasonably well in terms of what they have been able to do in life. For example, not all married men have adequately resolved their own oedipal problems, or problems of heterosexual commitment. Such car-drivers may well project these problems into the motorcyclist, who is a suitable external object. The car-driver may then act in such a way as to provoke an oedipal battle with the motorcyclist, trying to beat him away from the lights, or hooting noisily at him for no good reason. Such behaviour would again be likely to touch off reactive aggression in the motorcyclist.

As car-drivers, most of us do not like to entertain the idea that we ourselves may be bad, aggressive or dangerous. We seek opportunities to find those faults in other drivers. Motorcyclists are in every way a natural for this role. The danger is that we then treat the motorcyclist unduly harshly and unfairly, censoring him not for what he is or has done but for the way we have seen him in terms of our own projections. The authorities are not immune from this problem either, since indeed many of them are car-drivers and may identify with car-drivers and adopt those unfairly harsh attitudes to motorcyclists.

Added to these emotional difficulties is real ignorance, sometimes motivated, about the special properties of two-wheeled vehicles and the needs of their drivers. For example, some car-drivers act as though unaware that for safety motorcyclists may need more consideration than cars. A following car can usually reckon that if a car in front brakes sharply it will proceed further before stopping. If a motorcyclist brakes sharply he may fall off on the spot, becoming an easy and only too vulnerable target for following traffic. If a car makes another car swerve suddenly its four wheels usually make the manoeuvre quite safe, but a motorcyclist may come off.

One is left with the feeling that the battle of the generations is fought out on the roads as elsewhere, and that perhaps we, as the older generation, are not as understanding as we might be. Motorcyclists are exceedingly vulnerable, both emotionally and physically; it will not help them to make emotional progress or reduce their danger on the roads if their problems are met by subtle encouragement to act out, if they are provoked into paranoid reactions by other road users behaving badly or primitively, or if they are really unfairly treated by authorities. Sympathy, understanding, or even indulgence from us as their elders are more likely to be effective.

NOTE
1. 1969, as it still is in 1989.

7   Recruitment into the London Fire Brigade*

IN 1965 the London Fire Brigade was in difficulty about recruiting men and women to keep the Brigade effectively manned. 1965 was, of course, a time of reasonably high employment, so there was a good deal of competition from other employers. The Greater London Council therefore sought help in devising more effective methods of attracting recruits to the Brigade, basically by designing a recruiting campaign. From the point of view of the Tavistock Institute there was a novel element in the situation, one we rarely experienced. Because the work was for a local authority it had to be put out to competitive tender. After submitting our proposals to the Council we were duly summoned to be examined by a committee and found ourselves in a waiting room with a number of colleagues, known and unknown, mainly from advertising agencies, who were our competitors.

We never knew why we were the successful competitors, though we used to joke to ourselves that it was because we were the only agency that put up an all-woman team[1] and they liked the idea of having more women around. At that time there were few women in the Brigade, and they were mainly engaged centrally and in communications and not on stations as women are now. Be that as it may, we were made to feel most welcome and had much kind and willing co-operation from the officers, men and women of the Brigade and from a number of the men's wives. I would like to express my gratitude to them for their help

*Original title: 'A study to investigate recruitment into the London Fire Brigade'.

and my profound respect for the way members of the Brigade carried out their difficult and often dangerous work.

I suspect that the Greater London Council may have regretted their choice, since we certainly did not tackle the problem in the way they had probably expected. We did not, in fact, accept *ab initio* even that the Fire Brigade had a recruitment problem, let alone that the way to deal with it was to devise a more effective recruiting campaign. It was not Tavistock practice to accept the client's own diagnosis of his problem, or necessarily to implement the prescription he wrote for himself. We sought to explore the situation for ourselves and come to our own conclusions about what was wrong and what would seem an appropriate way of tackling it. We hoped to be able to carry our client with us and help him to develop a new understanding of his situation, then to move towards effective action. In this we probably differed from the other tendering agencies who might have pleased the Greater London Council more by doing what was asked.

To further this exploration, we spent a great deal of time with officers, men and women at all levels in the Brigade and in many different locations: Command Headquarters, the Fire Brigade Training School, fire stations in different locations which had different demands on them and different problems. In all we saw some two hundred members of the Brigade – not a large proportion, but the consistency of their responses led us to believe that we had obtained a fairly accurate picture of what was going on. We also spent a great deal of time on fire stations and saw the situation for ourselves. We saw a very different set of problems from those originally presented to us – almost the reverse, in a sense. If the Brigade could keep the men it had and make more effective use of them, the recruitment problem would have become insignificant.

In what follows I try to describe significant features of the situation in the Brigade, as seen largely through the eyes of its members. The Brigade's image of itself was a complicated mixture of positive and negative views. At that time, trends both within the Brigade and in its social context were tending to swing the balance more to the negative. The Brigade's image was deteriorating both within the Brigade itself and among the general public, the public view often stemming from the Brigade's contact with them. The possible effects of this, both on labour turnover within the Brigade and on potential recruits, were obvious.

Loyalty and devotion to the Brigade were widespread and strong. Many complaints were made, but they were made without real bitterness and with an undertone of hope that voicing them might lead to some improvement, a hope perhaps stimulated by our presence.

The men felt they were performing an essential public service that carried heavy responsibility for the protection of human life, and secondarily for property. They accepted and enjoyed the responsibility and the status it brought. They valued and enjoyed the training, experience and skill that enabled them to carry that responsibility with success. They feared, but also welcomed, the danger in their work; dangers met and overcome reassured them about their own safety and capacity to overcome such dangers. They did not exactly enjoy the grimmer aspects of their work, sometimes very grim indeed – ghastly road accidents, bringing the terribly burned, dead or dying from burning buildings. But they drew strength and satisfaction from being able to carry out these grim and disturbing tasks. 'All part of the job', they said, with a kind of proud nonchalance. The stoicism and pride with which the men faced these situations should not, however, blind one to the enormous cost to them in pain and horror that often stayed with them for long periods. It is interesting that more notice is now being taken of this problem in terms of support for firemen and other rescue services to manage the awful horrors they experience.

Firemen tended to triumph over other people who have not proved their capacity to deal with such situations. They had a rewarding sense of fellowship with others in the Brigade with whom they shared them. The author's stock went up markedly with the men in one fire station when in the course of discussing rescue training by lowering or being lowered by comrades from the top of the station's practice tower, they discovered that she really knew what they were talking about since she had done it during Air Raid Precautions training during the Second World War. In their own eyes firemen are an elite, a view which I tend to share, having got to know them. This feeling was intensified by a widespread view that the London Fire Brigade was the cream of brigades.

The Brigade provided its members with comradeship and companionship of a very special kind, based on continuous and intimate contact with the same people, sometimes over long periods, and in shared difficulties and dangers. Mutual respect and trust are dominant in this comradeship, as they need to be for safety. The men had tested each other out in situations of difficulty and danger as well as in the long, sometimes monotonous interactions of station life: they knew each other well, respected each other's strengths and tolerated each other's weaknesses. Crucial to this situation is the 'watch', both for those firemen who are still members of watches and for senior officers who began their life in the Brigade and developed their basic loyalty to it as members of watches.[2] The men themselves attached great importance to the stability of the watch group: 'Our lives depend on each other, so we must know how far we can trust each other and when.' We were impressed by the way the Brigade maintained permanence and stability in the membership of watches and share the view that this is crucial – the more so since we are familiar with the difficulties encountered in hospitals where the ward group of nurses, a rough equivalent of the watch, constantly changes in membership (Menzies, 1970a; vol. 1, pp. 43–85).

The men enjoyed the 'variety in the job': 'No two fires are ever the same.' 'You are always learning.' They felt they were always facing challenges, which was very satisfying. They had a sense of freedom in spite of the discipline, which did not feel very irksome, and felt they had escaped from the repetitiveness of industrial work. Although there is a good deal of monotonous routine in station work, they lived in the hope that the routine would be interrupted 'when the bells go down': that is, when they are summoned to a fire or other emergency.

Firemen had a sense of security in the Brigade. They related this to such factors as economic security and certainty of pensions, but it was wider than that and was connected with belonging to an organization that takes a good deal of responsibility for one's well-being. The Brigade was contrasted with what the men regarded as typical industrial or commercial organizations which, they believed, did not take this kind of responsibility.

Finally, and very important, there was fire-fighting itself and all the activities connected with it. Fires are a constant source of interest and excitement at all levels of the Brigade, excitement that the men felt few other jobs provide. This was catching: we soon felt the same. When no fire is actually happening, there are past fires to remember and future fires to hope for. We were constantly astonished at the long memories firemen had for fires and the wealth of detail in accounts of long-past fires. Their language is interesting. They talked about 'good fires' or 'decent fires', when the civilian population would talk about bad or terrible fires. Fire-fighting represented all that the men came into the Brigade for: the moment of fulfilment, the reward for all the training and waiting. This situation is not, however, without its conflict. Firemen know that although fires are exciting and satisfying for them, they mean trouble or disaster for someone else, so while they long for fires they also feel guilty about doing so. As one man dramatically put it: 'I was sitting here feeling a bit bored one afternoon and wishing there would be a fire, and then there was the "X" fire [a fire in which several people died]. I felt terrible. I've never been able to wish for a fire since.'

The actual activities involved in fire-fighting also gave a good deal of satisfaction and added positive features to the image. Handling of heavy, powerful hoses, pumping large amounts of water, scaling ladders, entering smoke-filled buildings, carrying out victims, evoked a sense of power and achievement that built up a man's image of himself.

In summary, there were many features of life in the Brigade which had power to attract men into it and to satisfy and retain those men who had joined it.

However, the men also disliked many aspects of life in the Brigade, some of which were experienced as intrinsic concomitants of Brigade life: often the obverse of the positive aspects. These negative aspects were often powerful and sometimes on balance outweighed the positive aspects and so contributed to the labour turnover that was making recruitment a problem. For example, the same fire-fighting activities that gave rise to pride also tended to give rise to shame and embarrassment. Firemen felt, and believed the public to feel, that some of the things they did and delighted in were childish or rather foolish. One firemen said: 'It *does* sound childish, but we actually love playing with water' or 'The public feel we just squirt water.'

Firemen have a painful suspicion that they are not really wanted or valued: 'Nobody thinks anything of us until they have a fire; then it's different, they can't do enough for us then.' It was as though they felt the public identified them with disaster and rejected them on those grounds. They felt bitter that not more recognition is given to their bravery and the hardships they suffer: 'Other people get the credit.' 'It's always the police or the public who get the praise for being brave.' The men tended to blame Brigade public-relations policy for this. Firemen have to face failure as well as success in their efforts, the worst failure being failure to save human life, especially the life of a fellow-fireman. Depression, anxiety and guilt result even if everything humanly possible was done, the more so if it was not. Responsibility for human life is burdensome as well as rewarding.

Long periods of inactivity or of doing duties not immediately connected with fire-fighting or emergencies diminish the fireman in his own eyes and, he feels, in the eyes of the public: 'They think we just sit around and play cards all day.' The kernel of truth in this makes it all the harder to bear (see p. 164 below). Pride in physical fitness and skills was offset by fears lest the public think they are, as they often said, just 'tough morons' or 'all brawn and no brain'. This idea of what the public might feel reflected, however, the fireman's own fears that this was just what he was, or that this was all he needed to be – a view of himself that he found degrading and resisted by emphasizing how much he needed to know and what a technical job fire-fighting was; as indeed it was.

However, the more significant difficulties lay in certain elements of the structure and functioning of the Brigade – elements not intrinsic to its primary task but derived from the particular way the Brigade was organized to carry out that primary task. These stemmed from the Brigade's history and from its response to current pressures from the surrounding social and economic environment.

Discussions with members of the Brigade strongly suggested that they felt the role and function of a fireman, and consequently his prestige and status, were being further diminished, both in their own eyes and in the eyes of the public. Many members, particularly ordinary firemen, were very sensitive on this point. The main features that appeared to us to contribute to the diminution of the prestige and status of the fireman and of the Brigade are discussed below.

Firemen could be regarded as having a less than man-sized job. This may seem a curious statement in view of the technical knowledge, hard physical effort, courage and endurance demanded of them, but it stems from other aspects of the job, such as the number of hours firemen effectively worked, and the nature of much of their work.

The fireman's duty roster was a repeated six-day cycle. In those six days he was on watch on two days from 9 a.m. until 6 p.m.; he then had twenty-four hours off. Next he worked two nights from 6 p.m. until 9 a.m. and finished the cycle with two full days off (forty-eight hours). This meant he had forty-eight hours on duty in six days, usually increased by eight hours' overtime. That seemed a lot, but he would not actually be working for a great deal of that time unless out on a call. Only two days out of the six were effectively working days, plus the three hours between 6 p.m. and 9 p.m. when he was on night duty. The men were permitted to go to bed on the night shift provided there were no calls. Mealtimes and other breaks accounted for several more hours. Thus the effective working time out of the fifty-six hours might well be thirty hours or less. In terms of the men's experience, only two of each six days were 'really working days'. Many of the men were rather sensitive about going to bed on duty. They explained that they could not really sleep, they just rested; or they expressed some of their own feelings by projection into public opinion: 'They say we get paid for sleeping' or 'They think we just sleep all night.' This situation appeared to make the men feel diminished in their own and other people's eyes.

The inconsistency between the nature of the job and its 'size' in terms of hours seemed serious in relation to the fireman's self-image. We rarely heard a complaint that the actual fifty-six-hour working week was too long, and a number of men said explicitly that they did not feel a fifty-six-hour week too long. When we questioned the men about how they would feel if a recruiting campaign were successful enough to make overtime unnecessary, they usually said they would not like to lose the overtime. The way they discussed this seemed to make it clear that they were not only unwilling or unable to do without the additional earnings; they were also unwilling to give up the extra duty *for its own sake*. The men quite often voiced to us a suspicion that the 'officers' did not want more recruits. Once again it seemed that they were projecting implicit views of their own, this time on to the officers. On the whole, the men did not really want many more recruits. The fifty-six hours' duty in six days suited them quite well.

A problem intimately connected with the duty hours was the comparative dearth of calls per man-week to fires or other emergencies – for example, on one station seventeen calls in a 'quiet' month, less than one per twenty-four hours. This frustrated the men and diminished their value in their own eyes and, as they felt, in the eyes of the public. The situation was the more painful since their whole training and self-perception orientated them to dealing with fires and emergencies as their 'job'. It also strengthened their feelings of not being wanted or needed by the people they existed to serve, who truly do not want to need them.

The impact of these problems varied naturally between stations, being most severe in quiet, outlying stations and hardly existing in some of the busy central stations. In a quiet station a watch may have days, or even weeks, without a single call. At the other extreme some of the inlying stations, like Marylebone, complained they were always out on calls. To add insult to injury, a proportion of calls were false alarms or 'silly' calls like chimney fires or grass fires. Although firemen accepted the necessity of dealing with such calls, they found it hard to have too many without a really 'good' fire occasionally. Officers remarked on how morale went down on a station when there had been no 'good' fire calls for some time. Tempers became scratchy and work was done sketchily. The situation was saved by a 'good' fire. Longer hours on duty would *ipso facto* have relieved this problem. Shortening hours, even to the formally agreed forty-eight-hour cycle, would have exacerbated it and further devalued the fireman's image.

To increase hours would have raised a number of other questions: for example, whether the men could then reasonably spend all their duty hours on stations when boredom, monotony and separation from families and friends would have become more serious problems. Some combination of 'on-station' and 'on-call' duties might be considered as an alternative. Whereas sleeping on duty on stations tended to be a source of humiliation to firemen, sleeping on call at home might well be a source of pride, putting the fireman on a par with high-prestige personnel like his own senior officers, doctors, and so on.

Members of the Brigade seemed to feel that stations were overmanned in relation to the total amount of work, including calls. This might be an inevitable consequence of the present method of organizing the duty system. So long as emergencies were manned entirely by men on duty at stations (with the exception of calls that require officers above the rank of station officer) the number of men on watch had to be determined by estimates of possible risks, the cover judged necessary to meet them, and the number of men required to operate the equipment rather than by the total amount of work there is to do, including station work, hydrant inspection, and so on. A really satisfactory solution did not seem to have been found to this problem. On busy stations it worked out reasonably well; on quiet stations it did not.

The practice of having men 'at work' during their day watches made men feel they were kept at work just for the sake of being kept at work and that unnecessary jobs were found for them. This tended to make them feel disgruntled and degraded; they said: 'We are just glorified charwomen' or 'We spend most of our time just playing at being firemen'; for example, they filled in time by doing drills beyond the point where drills seemed to them to be necessary for maintaining fitness and skills. They minded neither station work nor drills at levels they felt to be necessary for efficiency, but did object to doing them if they felt they were just filling in time. Their views about educational activities were roughly similar. They liked to be kept abreast of developments but felt that too many lectures became pointless, especially if they did not get enough opportunity to put their knowledge into practice.

The system tended, therefore, to lead to underemployment of firemen in relation both to effective deployment of their skills and training and to their full employment during hours of duty. The conflict over this was the greater in that the intrinsic features of the fireman's job required active men; the very type of man who wants and enjoys a life where he can go hard at it. When such underemployment develops and persists, it has a detrimental effect on morale and on self-image. It also contributes to labour turnover. A similar situation develops in hospitals, which have a tendency to assess ward establishments in terms of peak workloads rather than average workloads. In consequence student nurses who staff the wards are often underemployed, because they have not enough to do and/or they fill in time with tasks which are too simple for them. The effect on morale is bad and the nurses feel devalued. This situation made a significant contribution to the wastage rate among student nurses of 30–40 per cent (Menzies, 1970a; vol. 1, pp. 43–85). It seemed desirable for the Brigade to explore how to create a system of duties and tasks which would link the method of manning more effectively with the amount and kind of work to be done and the kind of men who did it.

Firemen and junior officers frequently had part-time jobs outside the Brigade, usually on the two days together when they were off duty. There was a time before this study when this was moonlighting and had to be done secretly, but during the study it was 'legitimate' and permitted, a bowing to the inevitable. This practice seemed to stem partly from the men's need to have a man-sized job, though there were other factors such as the need to augment earnings. The official recognition of the practice by the Brigade seemed to imply, to the men at least, a tacit recognition that the fireman's duties and his work cycle did not really constitute a full-time job. This implicit recognition also tended to make firemen feel degraded.

Specific features of the part-time job situation seemed to contribute further to the degradation of the fireman's image of himself and of the public image, since firemen are in close contact with the public in performing their part-time jobs. Most firemen regard the Brigade as their 'job', a job which involves a good deal of responsibility and stress. Therefore they often sought part-time jobs with less responsibility and stress. It was difficult to find jobs other than casual jobs because of the irregular and few hours the men were available. They were often condemned in their part-time jobs to occupations that required comparatively little skill and responsibility. Rates of pay were often, therefore, low, the more so because there was often a kind of tacit agreement between firemen and their casual employers that the men really earned their living in the Fire Brigade and the level of part-time earnings was not so important. In other words, the message to the public, employers and fellow-workers and to the fireman's social group was likely to be that the fireman is a rather low-grade sort of chap.

For an appreciable proportion of their working time many firemen were engaged in ordinary civilian occupations. This tended to weaken their image of themselves as people committed to a highly significant public service, as service personnel. There seemed to be a great deal of confused thinking among firemen about their status and role in relation to the Brigade and civilian occupations. Their standards of comparison and expectations about pay and conditions were surprisingly infiltrated by industrial thinking. There were many complaints like: 'We should get double pay for working on Sundays'; 'If we were doing this kind of shift work in Ford's, we would be earning £30 a week.' On the face of it, these complaints seemed unreasonable since the men joined the Brigade knowing the facts about hours, watch arrangements and pay, and it was not a job like Ford's. They seem reasonable, however, if one accepts the hypothesis that the men were beginning to perceive themselves more as industrial workers and less as service personnel. It appeared that the part-time job system was helping to erode the image of the Brigade as a public service whose relevant comparable institutions are the armed services and police, and to endanger the valuable service traditions of the Brigade.

The men's views about the part-time job situation had a flavour of delinquency, perhaps epitomized in the almost universal use of the term 'fiddle job', especially among former London County Council firemen. There are historical reasons for this, stemming from the time when part-time supplementary work was forbidden and men who did it were breaking regulations and kept it secret. But the continued use of the term also implied its continued relevance to the men's feelings about their part-time jobs: guilt and disquiet and disloyalty to the Brigade. They felt, too, that the Brigade let them down in making part-time work necessary and possible. Such feelings tended to damage their relation with themselves and with the Brigade. Men often said: 'We should be able to manage on one job, but we can't', with reference both to income earned and to workload. They would have liked to feel they were solely firemen, but in the circumstances it was difficult for them to do so.

Maintaining that system of working within the Brigade, with its accompanying part-time job system, raised serious questions. Along with other factors, it suggested that it might be a good thing to consolidate both overtime and part-time civilian working within the hours served in the Brigade with appropriate modifications in work organization and pay, thus eliminating the degrading need for part-time jobs and giving more opportunity to be firemen. However, the difficulties of bringing about such changes would have been enormous.

Discussions with firemen gave a great deal of attention to pay, and there were numerous complaints. Such complaints are quite usual when workers are asked to comment on their jobs, being easier to formulate than more complicated and often vague feelings of dis-ease. However, it seemed that the complaints had some substance in relation to the problem of image. The most general complaint was that pay was too low. This was a complicated problem with many ramifications, and one needs to separate out a number of aspects. First, there is the consistency of the requirements of a job with the standard of living that pay for the job makes possible. There are two images, one of the person in the job, the other of the person living his private life on the pay he gets for the job. The standard-of-living image is arrived at by a complicated series of comparisons and contrasts with people in other occupations and how they live. To have a feeling of equity and of being properly paid, a person needs to feel that there is reasonable consistency between the two images of himself in the job and in his private life, and that he is fairly paid in relation to comparable workers.

For firemen and junior officers this feeling of consistency and equity no longer existed. Firemen used to be in a relatively well-paid occupation; but this was no longer so. Pay in other occupations had leapfrogged over firemen's pay, leaving firemen with the feeling that their pay is no longer sufficient for them to maintain a standard of living which, in comparison with other people, is consistent with the level of job they are doing. There seemed to be some validity in such complaints. Part-time work could be seen in this context as part of an effort to reach the standard of living compatible with being a member of the Brigade – an effort, however, that had the unfortunate side-effects described above.

From another point of view, however, it is possible to argue that firemen are reasonably well paid for what they do – that is if one considers the number of hours a week they effectively work, as against the number of hours they are on duty. For a thirty-hour week their pay was not bad; for a forty-eight-hour week it was inadequate. The adequacy of the pay is interwoven with the problem of organizing duties so that a really 'man-sized' job results. Firemen's pay, overtime pay and part-time pay together gave something like the standard of living to which firemen reasonably felt entitled. It would have been better for the men and the Brigade if both work and pay could have been consolidated within the Brigade.

It is understandable that the fireman's image of himself was affected by his pay. The existing level of pay degraded the image in comparison with other workers. Further, pay makes an important contribution to public image and to recruitment possibilities. It would be naïve to suggest that people do or do not enter an occupation only because of the pay offered, but we are suggesting that pay conveys an important implicit message to potential recruits about the level of the job and the kind of person for whom the job is suitable. The pay offered was likely to convey too low an impression of the level of the job and of the recruit required. This might have been one element contributing to the fact that the majority of applicants were not considered suitable (pp. 180 ff). Higher pay would convey a different message about job level and might well attract better recruits. However, higher pay would need to be linked with internal reorganization to bring the level and amount of work into alignment with the higher pay, including the consolidation of normal and overtime hours and pay.

The fact that overtime pay was lost by men on leave made matters worse. There were many complaints about this. The men were no worse off than industrial workers, but they felt worse off. Their so-called overtime was, in operational fact, normal duty and they therefore felt emotionally entitled to get holiday pay for it and deprived when they did not. A similar complaint was over the fact that overtime pay was paid three months in arrears. It did seem somewhat anomalous that they worked these hours regularly and were not paid regularly for them; once again there seemed some reason for consolidation even while recognizing that factors like union pressure about hours and overtime might make such consolidation difficult.

Important issues centre around pay differentials. Firemen tended to complain that the differentials between the youngest, most inexperienced firemen and the oldest, most experienced firemen were too small. They felt that it took years to become a fully experienced, competent fireman and that this fact was not recognized sufficiently in pay differentials. This also affected their self-image; pay differentials were required to convey the message that it was a difficult thing to become a good fireman and took a long time. Present pay differentials did not do this.

Research work on payment in other fields shows that in higher-level jobs and among people who are capable of filling them, there is an expectation that increases in pay, related to increases in skill and responsibility and the enhancement of the related standard of living, will go on over a longer period and be greater in total amount than in lower-level jobs and among the people suitable to fill them. Too quick reaching of maxima and too little differentiation implicitly convey the notion of a low-level job.

Problems also arose about pay differentials between ranks. Between the men and the non-commissioned officers differentials seemed too small to reflect much difference in status and authority. Between sub-officers and station officers the same seemed true. The differentials do not convey the impression that there is much to becoming a junior officer in the Brigade – little more than being a fireman. We will return to the important question of the differentiation between ranks later (see p. 176).

Finally, the payment system for firemen and junior officers approximated more closely to an industrial than to a service model. For firemen in general a flat rate of pay pertained, without allowances except for those who ran the mess. Two points about this were mentioned repeatedly:

1. The need to recognize specialist qualifications by some extra pay: for example for drivers, turntable ladder operators, and so on. Failure to recognize these extra qualifications was felt as a devaluation by authority, a failure to value not only the skills but the keenness and loyalty shown in the willingness to acquire these skills and to accept the extra responsibilities involved. This particularly affected drivers, who were felt to have the lives of their fellow-firemen in their hands and carried *personally* the responsibility for taking risks and breaking rules in the interests of maximum speed in getting to incidents – for example, by driving through traffic lights at red.

2. The provision of an accommodation allowance. Firemen recognized that their accommodation allowance had been consolidated into their pay, but they regretted this. They felt badly treated by contrast with the police, who still had an accommodation allowance. It did seem in accordance with service traditions that some separate allowance be made. This subject

is elaborated below, when we discuss the question of accommodation for firemen (see pp. 185 ff.).

In general, the men felt that they lost something when they gave up 'police parity'. Not only did they feel financially worse off than the police, but there seemed also to be some loss of being a public service, a diminution in their own eyes.

The effect of pay and conditions in depressing the image of the Brigade seemed to be affecting not only present members but also the quality of potential recruits. This was particularly serious in that all future senior officers had to come through the ranks. The pay and conditions offered to firemen and junior officers were not likely to attract many men of commissioned-officer calibre. One may question, indeed, whether in the existing social and economic circumstances it was reasonable to expect many men of commissioned-officer quality to join the Brigade as firemen and spend at least five years *en route* for the rank of station officer, the first commissioned rank. Most young men of this calibre stayed at school to take GCE A levels and frequently went on to university or other higher education. It is unlikely that many men with such education would be willing to spend an indefinite period, certainly not five years, in the non-commissioned ranks. As one officer said: 'If a chap comes into the Brigade these days with two A levels, he's probably got something wrong with him.'

In having no direct officer recruitment the Brigade put itself at a considerable disadvantage compared with the armed services, all of which had direct officer recruitment and relatively rapid entry into commissioned ranks. Large industrial and commercial organizations also recruited such men directly into management training schemes with a reasonable guarantee of a management post within a fairly short time. The potential officer or manager had the *status* from the beginning, although he was a trainee. In the Fire Brigade he did not.

The opinion widely held throughout the Brigade was that a man must spend several years as a fireman and non-commissoned officer to acquire the knowledge about fires and fire-fighting that he would need as an officer. One respects this opinion – coming, as it did, from men of long experience – but it may be mistaken. It has proved possible in other fields to change from a situation where skills and knowledge have traditionally been acquired through experience over long periods to one where such skills and knowledge can be formulated and verbalized to a greater extent and taught more quickly, especially to people of high intelligence.

The system for acquiring the necessary qualifications for promotion seemed to cause other difficulties in the junior ranks. Many of the men who sought promotion had had comparatively little experience of formal study and found private study difficult. They also had difficulty in finding the time and conditions for study between Brigade, part-time work and family commitments. There was a curious practice: a man would say he had taken his exams for his next promotion. In any other situation one would assume that he had passed these exams. We learned through experience that in the Brigade this frequently meant he had sat them and failed, almost as though showing willing by trying should be enough. The men often seemed discouraged by this situation and although willing, or even eager, for promotion found it hard to contemplate carrying on with study. The situation might have been eased if there had been some formal courses.

Firemen and junior officers must qualify themselves for promotion first and then offer themselves for selection. It seemed open to question whether this was the correct order. The problem partly resolved itself into deciding whether the men or the Brigade should bear the risk that efforts spent in preparing for promotion might not be rewarded. If qualifications came first, the man must bear the risk that he might not be promoted even if properly qualified. If selection came first, the Brigade must bear the risk that some mistakes would be made. It seemed to us more appropriate that the Brigade should bear the risk, selection coming first and training following. This reversal would have carried the message that the Brigade was serious about finding and training the best possible officers, a message that the existing system did not convey. This situation seemed at least implicitly recognized in other organizations including the armed services, where selection tended to precede training for promotion.

Such a reversal would have thrown more stress on the efficiency of the actual selection process. If the Brigade invested heavily in training potential officers, it could not afford too many failures. Highly sophisticated techniques existed and were widely used in other organizations for selection of men for higher ranks, techniques often developed from those used by the armed services in the Second World War. Such techniques also help in assessing potential capacity at an early stage in a man's career. Specifically in the Brigade, they could have helped to spot potential senior officers among firemen, and not only among sub-officers and station officers. This could have reduced some of the discouragement of the long wait for promotion.

Formal training for promotion after preliminary selection would have facilitated broadening the training for officers to include additional elements, particularly man management in its widest sense. Officers and men made it clear that the capacity of the station officer for man management is crucial to the morale and efficiency of his watch. The capacity for man management is also of the greatest importance in more senior officers. Not all men are 'born leaders'. Even those who are benefit from formal training. For those who are not, effective training is most important. The special conditions of life in the Brigade made it very important that the station officer be trained in as wide a view of his role as possible. We elaborate this point further below (see pp. 176–7).

To sum up: there appeared to be a number of problems in the Brigade about the selection and training of men for commissioned ranks. The message likely to be projected by the Brigade is of an organization which does not concern itself too seriously with the manning of its higher echelons. This could not but degrade its projected image. It also put the Brigade at a competitive disadvantage compared with other organizations, including the armed services, which made more use of the best modern practice.

Although formally a station officer held a commissioned rank, our impression was that the role resembled more closely that of senior non-commissioned ranks in the armed services. We asked the men to assess the job in comparison with what they knew of industry or the fighting services and their replies on the whole confirmed our impression. Station officers tended to be seen as roughly equivalent to a foreman, a sergeant or a warrant officer; that is, top non-management and non-commissioned ranks.

In line with the above discussion we found, perhaps not unexpectedly, that the role and status of junior officers was becoming degraded, particularly the role of station officer as it operated in the stations. In operational fact, with rare exceptions, there was no such person as a station officer – that is, an officer in charge of a station. Operationally, there were three 'watch' officers in each station, each the officer of a watch and of the station only during the watch.

The station officer seemed to live too closely with his men and did work too much like theirs to be able to achieve the social and functional distance from them which differentiates commissioned from non-commissioned ranks. Pay differentials tended to enhance this situation. The station officer could not afford to lead a different kind of life from his men, only a slightly better one of the same kind. He was seen to belong to the men rather than to the officers. The fact that a commissioned officer carried out work which appeared to be at non-commissioned level further damaged the image of the Brigade.

This degradation of the station officer might have been a concealed result of the difficulty of getting enough men of high enough calibre to man the officer ranks. The ranks might then have been in the process of being subtly degraded in an effort to match them with the kind of men available to fill them. If this is true, it would have been ominous.

These points added force to the arguments for reconsideration of officer selection and training. The present system seems to jeopardize the performance of certain tasks and to raise questions about the role and position of fire stations.

The issue is whether there were elements in the basic organization and functioning of the Brigade that would have made it more realistic to have a 'station officer' in the true sense of the word, with appropriate subordinates such as watch officers. This would have given the 'station officer' a command which, in size and opportunity for discretion and responsibility, truly merited commissioned rank. In addition, it would have permitted some elevation of the status and functions of the present sub-officer who would presumably command the watch. As regards the new station officers' functions, discussion with officers and men seemed to suggest that certain functions might be allocated to station officers that were then performed by senior officers, were somewhat inadequately performed on stations or were not performed at all.

The role of the station officer is intimately related to the role and function of the station. One might perhaps slightly caricature the situation by saying that there was then no such thing as a fire station in the sociological sense. There was a building with equipment, inhabited and used by three different sets of people at different times by agreement. There was little functional relationship between the three sets and no one locally who was formally responsible for the liaison between them or the overall co-ordination of their operations, although by tradition the senior station officer of the three did what work of this kind needed to be done. This is not a situation where liaison and coordination are likely to be carried out effectively. The men themselves said that their relationships with neighbouring stations on the same watch were closer than with the other watches on their own stations. While this may be to some extent inevitable, since people on the same watch might have operational contact, something important is lost if the station itself is not also an entity to which people can really feel they belong and which has some part in the life of the local community.

Regarding the station as an entity, one may ask whether stations could be given more responsibility for their internal organization and for carrying out their functions. For example, the men repeatedly complained about two tasks which were carried out by higher authorities but which could perhaps be delegated to stations:

1. The question of standby, replacing a man absent from a

watch. The current arrangement for standby was to transfer a man from one station to another on the same watch. Men were sent to stations they did not know to work with watches they did not know, both of which, they felt, greatly added to stress and strain. The men disliked having to travel between stations on standby duties with all their equipment, the more so since transport was not provided: 'You feel a clot getting on a bus with all that gear.' An alternative plan would have been to make the station internally responsible for its own manning, the standby coming from other watches on the same station, outside reinforcements to be called only when the station could not man the watch from its own men. This would have established more identity for the station as such between one watch and another, giving the men a sense of belonging to something more comprehensible over which they had more control.

2. The question of additional leave days. Men complained bitterly about the existing system, by which these leave days were arranged centrally, and said they could never make any plans with friends and families because they were never sure, more than a day or two in advance, whether they would actually get the day off or not. We felt that these things also could probably be more effectively, personally and simply arranged if there were delegation and responsibility to the local station and its station officer.

The existing system seemed to contribute to a feeling among men on stations that they were out of touch with higher authorities, could not communicate effectively with them in either direction and were not sufficiently understood and cared for by them. The lack of social distance between the station officer and his men seemed to contribute to this. As effectively a 'non-commissioned' officer he was not perceived as belonging to the higher ranks of officers and therefore did not constitute an effective liaison with them.

Although the Brigade offered a number of valuable services to the men – such as personnel and welfare services and sports facilities – they seemed to feel that these were not in fact very readily available to them. Some elements of such functions might be incorporated into the role of a station officer, supported by specialist services and with power to call them in when he judged it necessary. For example, he could probably handle a number of personnel problems locally: some personnel training could be built into station-officer training. Such things would also have contributed to the feeling of the station as an entity and added to the satisfaction of belonging to it.

Our data suggested that there might be advantages to the Brigade in strengthening links with local communities. In this the perception of the station as a functioning entity and the role and status of the station officer would be important. This point had particular relevance to the question of recruitment. What did a man join when he joined the Fire Brigade? It seemed that he might well be seeking to join his 'local' Fire Brigade – the station, or one of the stations, in his own area. Conversations with control-room staff supported the view that the public perceived the Fire Brigade as a local service and felt the station belonged to some local authority, possibly nonexistent. Control-room staff frequently found difficulty in getting correct addresses from callers, who acted as though they were talking to their local fire stations: for example, they would give street names but no postal district or town names, or would give instructions like 'It's the first turning on the right over the bridge' – that is, the best way to get to the fire from the local fire station.

If a man went to the local station to find out about joining the Brigade, the station officer could only put him in touch with headquarters. This might have been too distant and impersonal for some men who want to be firemen and are capable of being good firemen. Nor is there any guarantee that the man would be employed in his local station. Organizationally there could not be a 'local fire service', but socially and emotionally there could be something that felt more like it and might be easier to join. In other words, we were suggesting the possibility that more responsibility might be delegated to stations for their own recruitment. For example, the station officer might be given authority to do a preliminary selection interview, giving a tentative 'yes' to an applicant he considered suitable for employment on his own station if he needed recruits, or perhaps referring him to a nearby station if he did not. The tentative 'yes' could be subject to confirmation, following such medical, educational or other tests as are considered necessary to maintain the overall standards in the Brigade. Training for such preliminary interviews could be a part of officer training.

The problem of recruitment to the Brigade might have looked very different if, instead of talking of the Brigade as being, say, 1,500 men short, one thought of there being one vacancy at Edgware Road, two at Manchester Square, five at Croydon, and so on. This links with the question of possible differentiation of officer and other-rank recruitment. Commissioned officers need to be mobile between stations, divisions, Command Headquarters and so on. Other ranks do not need to be so mobile.

A station officer could apply himself to recruitment problems in another way: by general public-relations activities on his 'ground'. Since there would be someone in charge of each watch, a sub-officer or watch officer, a station officer could be free for other duties and might, among other things, devote himself to building up relations with the local community, establishing himself as a significant local figure by such means as talking to local organizations, visiting schools, and so on.

There appeared to be problems in the conversion rate of applicants into firemen. Officers and men believed it to be low. Men repeatedly claimed to have been the only one accepted from their own batch of applicants, or that only two or three were accepted. Other data confirmed that the acceptance rate was low.

Two main possibilities could have contributed to this:

1. The quality of applicants might be low; the conditions described above certainly suggest this may well have been the case.

2. The selection standard might be unduly high.

It seemed likely that 2. might be true. The men themselves felt this. They were puzzled about why so few applicants were accepted and why other men who came up for selection with them were turned down. They tended to feel that the selection criteria were operated somewhat rigidly and harshly. The men's subjective impressions of the selection system are not, in the ordinary sense, evidence. They could not be regarded as expert selectors, especially since as recruits they did not know the Brigade from inside. On the other hand, it might be unreasonable entirely to disregard their impressions. Other factors seem to support them.

Selection standards in the former London County Council Fire Brigade were apparently higher than for the brigades of other authorities. We came across a number of men who had been rejected by the London County Council Brigade but accepted by another authority. Apparently the London County Council Brigade rejected men who were capable of becoming firemen. It seemed that the London County Council was seeking men of higher calibre than was absolutely necessary. If the Greater London Council had taken over the London County Council's standards, as is possible, it might be that men were turned down who were in fact capable of becoming competent firemen.

It is quite legitimate to keep up standards in this way, but it is important to be aware that one is doing so and to recognize the implications. For example, there is the question as to whether the recruit is appropriately matched to the job he will do. If the recruit is too good, difficulties will arise just as much as if he is not good enough, although they will be different. Men of limited intelligence might be quite content to spend most of their time doing station work, just as the low-grade men of the unarmed pioneer corps were content to do unskilled but very useful work during the Second World War. Active men of good intelligence are not and cannot be expected to be satisfied with work of this kind. Work with nurses showed that a major factor in causing discontent and wastage during training was that many student nurses were too good for the work they had to do while training (Menzies, 1970a; vol. 1, pp. 43–85).

The fact that all officers must be recruited through the ranks may subtly have affected selection standards. Without being aware of it, selectors may make some kind of implicit assessment about whether an applicant is future officer material as well as whether he is capable of being a fireman, and accept or reject on these grounds. Officers in the Brigade did not themselves believe that this was happening, but we ourselves still felt it might be. Similar things have happened in other organizations where a similar situation obtained: that is, all promotion through the ranks. For example, hospitals have a tendency to select not nurses but future high-level nursing administrators, which keeps the standards of selection for nurses unduly high.

The men suspected that the officers or authorities did not want too many recruits. We found this plausible. Subtle pressures might exist within the Brigade which played on the officers actually involved in recruitment and selection to make them keep standards up and recruitment, and manning of the Brigade, low. In saying this, we are not attributing any malicious intent to the officers or authorities concerned. On the contrary, we are implying that there might be at work a sensitive awareness of the possibility that the Brgade was in fact adequately manned when it was significantly under paper strength and that the system then worked rather better than if all the vacancies were filled. The exact ways in which such social pressures operate are often hard to tease out in detail, but we have found in other organizations that subtle social pressures of this kind act very dynamically on people who carry out certain roles.

For example, from one point of view the 30–50 per cent wastage of nurses during training was a serious problem. From another it could be seen as a subtle self-regulating mechanism which kept the number of trained nurses in balance with the posts available. Thus the market was not flooded with too many trained nurses, as it would have been if all had completed their training. Unfortunately, the wastage has persisted now into a situation where it is no longer useful, so that there is an actual shortage of trained nurses (Menzies, 1970a; vol. 1, pp. 43–85).

The duty system and leave periods caused quite a lot of problems. When talking directly about the system of watches, officers and men usually expressed satisfaction. They compared it favourably with a previous system of their own and with the police system. In spite of this, however, the men indicated, directly or indirectly, that a number of features in the system gave rise to difficulties. Many of these stemmed from the fact that men on stations, in effect, had a six-day 'working week' as against the seven-day calendar week, everyone else's working week. They could not think in the same 'cycles' as other people did about work and leisure time, and this seemed to cause confusion. They lived in a slightly different world from other people, with a different calendar, although they had to refer to it ultimately in the same terms as other people. This seemed to make them feel more cut off from the rest of the community than they need be by the intrinsic nature of their work.

This was vividly illustrated by a very intelligent junior officer. We asked if he had attended a big fire on another ground 'last Tuesday'. The officer looked confused and then asked: 'What fire?' It was striking that he did not seem to know, in view of the keen interest the men take in fires. In fact, when we explored this, the problem was not that he did not know about the fire but that he did not know what day 'last Tuesday' was. The question we needed to answer was something like: 'What day in the fireman's hypothetical calendar was last Tuesday in the interviewer's calendar?' He then commented: 'You never know what day of the week it is in this job.'

Difficulties arose from the fact that the system implied a repetition of seven six-day cycles over a period of six calendar weeks, each beginning and ending on a different day of the week before a man got back to where he started at the beginning of the next six-week period. The elements in this repetitive cycle were too many and the detail too complicated for men or their wives to be able to keep them effectively in their minds and know quickly where they were about the men being on or off duty. A wife gave a dramatic display of counting off the watches on her fingers before she knew whether they could or could not accept an invitation for a day about a fortnight ahead. This increased the feeling of being cut off and living in a slightly different world from other people, who can look ahead simply and know where they are.

The men were given to stating rather categorically that they never got a weekend off. On inspection this was not quite correct,[3] but the feeling was honest and influential. Feeling that they never had weekends off increased their feeling of being cut off from the rest of the population and treated without respect and understanding by the Brigade authorities. The feeling of never having a weekend off seemed to us to stem partly from the rather confusing situation about the six-day working week. Men did not know when the weekend was. It was also partly connected with the fact that they have Saturday and Sunday off together only once in the six-week cycle, which is very little when they have to fit in with the arrangements of people other than firemen. The situation is exacerbated by the fact that even this weekend is what they call 'not a proper weekend'; that is, they come off duty at 9 a.m. on Saturday, and go back at 9 a.m. on Monday. They complained that it was late on Saturday morning when they got home and were ready to start whatever they planned to do. If they had had a busy night they did not feel like it anyhow.

Similar complaints were made about annual leave. They said they got only the bare fortnight, not a fortnight plus a third weekend as industrial workers do, and they felt somehow cheated and devalued by this. The men felt that this was not only a hardship for themselves, but also placed an unnecessary burden on wives and families and increased the difficulty of maintaining relationships with other members of the community.

Some of these difficulties could have been mitigated and the firemen and their families helped to feel less disorientated in 'ordinary time' and more able to maintain relationships with the rest of the community by some slight modification in what was basically regarded as an acceptable roster. There were possibilities:

1. That a three-week cycle be considered to replace the current six-week cycle. We suggest three weeks because, like six weeks, it works out easily into an appropriate number of watches to cover a week of forty-eight hours plus eight hours' overtime; that is, seven day watches and seven night watches in three weeks. It

also gives a more comprehensible total length of cycle;

2. That within the three weeks the best weekend arrangement would probably be one long weekend off, one long weekend on, and one short weekend off. A good long weekend would amply compensate for a weekend's heavy duty. Annual leave could perhaps also be timed to coincide with the long weekend.

This second suggestion has added interest, since this was exactly what was done when we worked at the Royal National Orthopaedic Hospital with three nursery nurses, three 'watches'. We worked out a roster as suggested here. The nurses found the long continuous duty over the working weekend quite hard going but accepted it because of the long and short weekends they had off duty (Menzies Lyth, 1982; vol. 1, pp. 153–207).

The provision of accommodation for firemen and their families was a complicated and difficult situation. For many years it was the tradition that firemen lived on their station. Tradition dies hard, even when it is not necessarily appropriate to present circumstances. It was doubtful if firemen and their families would then have wanted to live on stations. However, the men felt strongly that the provision of accommodation for firemen and their families would solve the Brigade's recruitment problem. The provision of accommodation could mean either literally providing quarters or providing a substantial accommodation allowance. The men compared their position very unfavourably with that of the police. They knew that they formerly had such an allowance and that it had been consolidated into pay, but this does not seem to mitigate their feelings of bitterness. They felt cheated, even if pressure for the change came from their own union. The loss of men to other brigades that provide accommodation is repeatedly quoted as evidence that provision of accommodation would bring in more recruits.

When men tried to find accommodation they felt most painfully confronted with their prestige and status, and with their public image. Many men worked on grounds where private accommodation, rented or bought, was expensive. This pointed up their relatively low pay and all its complicated implications in terms of their own and other people's evaluation of them. They had no special claim on such subsidized local-authority housing as was available on their grounds, a factor which also tended to cause bitterness since they felt themselves to be servants of the local community and of its local authority. They felt that the community and the local authority did not value their services or understand their needs.

Many men complained of difficulty over mortgages, connected with low estimation of their reliability or status. Men made remarks like: 'As soon as you say you're a fireman, they don't want any more to do with you.' The reason for this was variously associated with the fact that their income was low (their fire-service pay only being taken into account, without their regular 'fiddle' money) or that people think that firemen are just rough sorts of chaps: 'You're not good enough.' There was no question that they felt insulted and devalued by such rejection and made to realize that their public image was not good.

We did not subscribe to the view that the provision of accommodation or good accommodation allowances would solve the manpower problem – it failed to do so for the police. However, we felt that there might be factors in the situation that merited consideration in relation to the way of life of firemen and their families in consequence of the men's job and their image of themselves in relation to it. Its effect on manpower might not be negligible. Our spontaneous reaction to the recurrent demand for accommodation or accommodation allowances was that it was quite unreasonable. Other workers do not expect it, why should firemen? However, further thought led us to believe that this demand, far from being unreasonable, might be quite appropriate to the circumstances of life in the Brigade.

Membership of the Brigade involves a good deal of exposure to danger and grimness compared with most occupations, and considerable exposure to uncertainty. No one knows, when a man goes on watch, what situations he will meet before he comes off watch again – indeed, whether he will survive. The actual risk is small, but the possibility of disaster is always present. In this situation, wide separation of a man on watch from his wife and family may be a real hardship. The wives do not know what is going on on their husbands' grounds and their husbands have little or no possibility of telling them. Anxiety mounts very easily in such a situation. Wives may panic if husbands are late home from duty; husbands worry about their wives worrying. The situation seemed to be dealt with by a policy of relative non-communication between the men and their wives on this topic. The men did not tell their wives much about the danger and grimness they might face, but the wives were not necessarily reassured by this. They 'know anyway' and they may even imagine it to be worse than it is. The men tended to deny that their wives worry, but are aware all the same that their wives do worry.

By contrast, wives who live on a station know when the bells go down, and the men go out to an incident. They may even know where the men are and what the incident is as news filters back to the station: for example, if one appliance returns and the men can relate what the other appliance is doing. Wives who live within easy reach of the station can always pop round and try to find out. They can draw comfort from other wives in the same situation by sharing anxieties about their men. One is reminded of the way mining communities flock to the pithead when there is a disaster, seeking not only the latest information but the comfort and support of sharing the tragedy with others. Mining communities are very tightly knit. Not only would the wives feel better, but the men would too, if they felt that the wives were not isolated from this support and understanding. The feeling of 'community', the sharing of common problems and dangers between families as well as men, was lacking in the fire service.

'On-ground' accommodation can therefore be said to represent a secure holding situation for men and their families in relation to the danger and anxiety of the work, and would contribute to the feeling of security which many men and their families still seek in the Brigade.

Another anxiety that tended to afflict firemen and their families was the possibility of the weakening of the ties and satisfactions of family life. The men were probably spending fifty-six hours a week on watch. Add to that an appreciable amount of travelling time – as much as one and a half to two hours before and after each shift in extreme cases – and a part-time job, and the man is separated from his family for a very large part of his time. If the wife is working or there are school-age children the position is exacerbated, because leisure hours by no means always coincide.

A further threat to family ties was the closeness of relationships between the men on watch. They are bound by the close ties of a shared important interest, of long hours of duty spent together, of shared dangers. It is in the watch that the important process of working over anxieties aroused by the dangers of the job takes place as the men talk over their experiences, learn from them together and get reassurance and comfort from each other. Wives cannot share these experiences as comrades do. The comparison with mining communities is again close.

When wives are geographically separated from each other as well as from their men, as many fire-service wives are, they can neither share with their men nor build parallel supporting groups of wives and families in which the same kind of process can go on, a process which could facilitate the establishment of a community of families within which each individual family would be strengthened. There appears to be some need to facilitate the extension of the closeness of the watch relationship between the men to their families.

This point may also be linked with the difficulties that firemen and their families experienced because of the duty hours. Some relief from the burden of the peculiar duty hours can be attained when wives and families are close to each other and to the station, allowing them the possibility of making mutual arrangements to deal with this situation along with other fire-service families, and cutting down travelling time for husbands.

Some form of provision of accommodation or accommodation allowances seems more consistent with the idea of rebuilding the fire service as akin to the armed services than the present system of a flat rate of pay. Further, if the idea is followed up of a combination of 'on-station' duty and 'on-call' duty, the provision of some kind of accommodation on the ground and near the station is essential. Putting together the evidence at our disposal, it would seem that the most acceptable situation would be to provide accommodation on the ground fairly near the station, but not actually on it.

POSTSCRIPT (1988)

This study represents in some ways a typical example of the way colleagues and I at the Tavistock Institute worked at that time. The case-history described shows that we developed a very different picture of the problems of the Fire Brigade from the one originally presented to us. The problem had been presented as a shortage of recruits and the need for a more effective recruitment campaign, but we saw it otherwise: as a problem of the internal organization of the Brigade in relation to its tasks. This led to substantial labour turnover in the Brigade, which necessitated considerable recruitment of new men on the one hand and on the other led to the projection of such a poor image of the Brigade and its members as to depress the number of new applicants and their quality. It followed that we did not believe that a recruitment campaign would solve even the recruitment problem of the Brigade, let alone the others. The directions in which we felt action might be helpful have been indicated in the text.

I still have fair confidence in our diagnosis, but the Fire Brigade itself neither accepted it nor acted on it, except in limited ways. There have been some improvements which might well have come anyway: in pay, in conditions of service, and in raising the firemen's status. These are welcome, but seemed to leave the focal problem – that is, restructuring the system – more or less untouched. Business went on as usual. We were not asked to go on to consider the implications of the report with the Brigade, nor to help in implementing it.

There were probably a number of reasons why our report and recommendations had so little effect. There was the nature of the organization we were working with. It was too big and, particularly, we reported to a local-authority committee far, far away from the focus of the problem and the people really involved in it. We were not able to do what we would have wished and had done in other organizations: to discuss the findings with the people directly concerned and to help them to start thinking about their meaning and begin to think about what could be done for themselves. Just sending a report 'cold' to a committee so far away from the scene of the operations, and so unfamiliar with what was really going on, could only provoke puzzlement and rejection. There would certainly have been difficulties with the trade union, which might also have found it hard to understand how our suggestions would actually benefit their members.

Be all these things as they may, I find myself full of regret that I did not manage to help an organization which I came to care about and a body of men whom I respect and became very fond of during the study.

NOTES

1. Geraldine Gwynne (now Eynstone) and myself. I am grateful to her for her help and companionship in the field work and her insightful contributions to understanding the data.

2. The 'watch' is a duty period and also the group of men who share it.

3. They had two weekend days off together once in six weeks.

8 The interaction between Epsom and the five mental hospitals adjoining it*

THIS STUDY was carried out in early summer 1968 at the request of the South West Metropolitan Regional Hospital Board, within whose region Epsom and its five mental hospitals fell.[1] The precipitant for the request was the rape of the adolescent daughter of a professional family in the town by a mental patient and the town's reaction. However, that incident, serious as it was in itself, sparked off an unexpectedly powerful reaction in the town since it seemed to channel anxiety and resentment about other incidents, including a murder by another patient, and about the town's situation in general, feelings which had been accumulating over the years, probably at least since the passing of the 1959 Mental Health Act. This Act, among other things, basically opened the doors of the mental hospitals and gave the majority of patients the freedom to come and go at will. At that time, the new policy of freedom for patients was warmly welcomed by the professional staffs in the mental hospitals and high hopes were entertained about the potential benefit to patients of being able to mix freely with the community.

At the time of the study the population of Epsom was some 70,000–75,000 and the number of patients in the five hospitals was about 7,000, a proportion of patients to residents of approximately 1:10. That proportion gives a somewhat misleading

---

*Revised version of 'A study of the interaction between Epsom and the five mental hospitals adjoining it: second verbal report of the findings given at a meeting held at the South West Metropolitan Regional Hospital Board, 10th September 1968'.

picture of the situation. The five mental hospitals were located all together on one edge of the town. (They would have been in the country when they were built, but the town had grown outwards.) The town was effectively split in two by the High Street, which was the main shopping centre and was also a busy trunk road, the A24. Patients rarely ventured farther than the High Street and were effectively concentrated in one part of the town with a population of about 30,000 people, a patient:resident proportion of about 1:4 or 5, potentially at least, although not all patients actually went into the community. This was an extremely high proportion and immediately raises questions about the absorption of so high an alien population, a topic to which I will return later (pp. 200–1).

The patients were not only 'alien' in the psychiatric sense of the term: they were also alien in the geographical sense. The catchment areas of the hospitals were basically London boroughs, although some patients might originally have come from even further afield. Residents of Epsom who needed hospitalization for psychiatric illness went to other hospitals in Surrey, the county in which Epsom is situated. Epsom was thus being asked to accommodate a very large number of psychiatrically disturbed strangers. From the patients' point of view, the community to which they had direct access was not their own community, which they knew and where they might find family and friends, but a strange place where they probably knew no one but other patients and hospital staff, and where there was no one to go out to or with.

Looking back on it now – and it is easy to be wise after the event – the situation in Epsom seemed little but a recipe for trouble. The situation was, of course, a hangover from previous mental health policy when psychiatrically ill patients were 'put away': locked up in hospitals far away from their homes, usually in the country where land and buildings were cheap. Patients were often expected never to leave the hospital and access for visiting was not considered very important. Such hospitals could be found all round Greater London and other conurbations, but as far as the author knows, no other locality had such a concentration of hospitals and patients as Epsom.

A team from the Tavistock Institute of Human Relations went into Epsom to try to find out more about the situation.[2] We spent a lot of time in and around the town during our three months' exploration and interviewed local residents individually and in groups, local-authority officials, police, officers of voluntary bodies, staff and pupils from local schools, publicans, restaurateurs and hoteliers, shopkeepers and members of a borough's Ward Committee, which was actively engaged in the protest and to which the raped girl's father belonged.[3] Professional, administrative and domestic staff of four hospitals were interviewed and patients from two hospitals. Observational studies were made in the town, especially but not only of places where residents thought it undesirable or unsafe to go such as Epsom Common or Woolworth's, to see what they actually felt like.

FINDINGS

1. The townspeople

Perhaps the most striking feature that emerged was how difficult it was to get hard evidence about what went on and who actually were the perpetrators of incidents. The fact that there had been a rape and a murder, both carried out by patients, was firmly established. The police had records of some incidents, criminal and other, but were firmly convinced that these were only 'the tip of the iceberg' of even the type of incidents that might come to their attention.

There were various reasons why the police were not called in when they might have been. Residents showed a good deal of tolerance and understanding for the patients in their plight and did not want to get them into trouble. Some incidents, especially sexual incidents, were not reported because family and friends of the victim wanted to protect him or her from further stress. In any case, the victim did not always tell. People felt discouraged about the prospects of a positive result from reporting an incident; for example, they said: 'You could never find the assailant anyway.' They were often unwilling to incur the cost in time, effort and money of following up incidents; for instance, local shopkeepers said they could not afford their own or their assistants' time to take a case of shoplifting to court.

There could be no reasonable doubt that no action was taken in a significant number of potentially indictable offences – how many, there was no way of telling. Some of the offences not reported may well have been serious: for example other cases of rape, an offence at that time particularly likely not to be reported. Respondents hinted broadly that there had been other rapes, which seemed quite possible. We could not sort out for ourselves whether cases people talked about were all the same incident, duly elaborated and distorted in the repetitive telling by townspeople, or whether they were different cases. The level of petty pilfering in local shops was certainly unusually high, though how high we could not tell.

In addition to those offences there was a good deal of disturbing behaviour. A particular form of disturbance was suicide and attempted suicide. We were told of a patient who made three suicide attempts in the High Street and succeeded on a fourth attempt. Or patients were reported as frequently throwing themselves in the duckpond near a local public house; whether to drown or just to go for a swim was not clear. There was obscene language, threats of a more or less serious kind, litter described in a way that meant not only such things as paper and cans but things not usually mentioned in polite conversation: excrement and vomit, the aftermath of drinking, not necessarily drunkenness; the performance of other acts like urinating in public places before witnesses, including children; bizarre behaviour or posture of a harmless kind like a patient who would stand for a long time with his hands on the crown of his head, just looking, or the woman who, in the High Street, pulled up her skirt, apparently without embarrassment, pulled up her knickers more firmly, dropped her skirt and went on walking. Or another who sat on the pavement sorting out sweets into two dirty handkerchiefs: 'That's for you: that's for me'; strange sounds and looks, especially from the mentally subnormal; patients who were improperly dressed – for example, flies undone: not the same thing as indecent exposure, but arousing some of the same fears and revulsion. Patients also begged and importuned local residents for money, cigarettes and other things. It is possible for the population of a community to accept a certain amount of such behaviour with equanimity; indeed, no community is free from it. But how much is too much? And how much was it reasonable to expect a community to accept from aliens in its midst?

Another factor that contributed to the uncertainties of the situation was how far it was correct to attribute the incidents, criminal or other, to patients. As we said above, such incidents happen in every community. How far, however, were patients being scapegoated and blamed for incidents perpetrated by others, including their own visitors? After all, Epsom had its racecourse, which might well at certain times have attracted other disturbed people to the area and contributed to excessive drinking and its sequelae. Or the very presence of the patients in the town might have encouraged disturbed behaviour by others who, without this disturbing stimulus, would not have behaved that way. What added to the general feeling of disturbance was the feeling of 'There but for the grace of God go I.'

In other words, the pressure of so much psychiatric disturbance in the community raised anxieties about oneself. It could be difficult to sustain the feeling of the unbridgeable gap between the mad, 'they', and the sane, 'me'. One's own primitive, mad understructure is too easily evoked by the presence of the mad other. One may feel one is clinging rather desperately to one's own sanity. Sexual acting out by others can evoke unwanted sexual feelings in oneself. The urge to act out such feelings oneself may be a threat to control. This was particularly a problem for the already disturbed members of the local community and for adolescents, in whom such problems and reactions are all too easily evoked.

The reactions of the townspeople to the situation were strong, especially following the rape: they were very frightened and very angry, and felt that something had to be done. They felt that the town could not or should not be expected to stand much more – 'One more rape . . .' 'One more murder . . .'. Apart from a possible major incident, they felt that things in general were getting worse.

Individually and communally the town had developed ways of dealing with the disturbance: how far these would hold in the

THE DYNAMICS OF THE SOCIAL

face of one more major incident or the cumulative effects of small ones seemed open to doubt. The town had learned to live with the situation, but for how long?

Psychological and psychosocial defences had developed to help people manage the situation: denial was prominent, linked with repression and motivated forgetting. A woman who said: 'I always read the local paper cover to cover' denied all knowledge of the rape, adding that she was glad she had not known because she would have worried about her own daughter. People often talked as though incidents did not matter so long as no actual assault took place. Challenged on that point, however, they were often able to admit the extent of the emotional upset caused by minor incidents, physically harmless. Manic defences were much used. It could be, and was, told as a funny joke that a patient entered a house, sat down on the stairs, took off his shoes and socks and settled down to cut his toenails. People could laugh at the lady who pulled up her knickers, the lady who divided out her sweets, or the patient who took off his clothes and went swimming in the duckpond, but . . .

Confusion and contradiction were rife, people not seeming to realize the significance of what they were saying, or how often they contradicted themselves. For example, one woman claimed that schoolgirls did not really worry about incidents they observed or were involved in; the next moment she was talking about the irreparable damage such incidents caused and how some marriages never recovered if the wife was involved. Defences appeared in the elaboration of incidents: for example, it appeared that the man who committed the rape was about forty years old and a monster – in other words, no woman would have been likely to get involved with him. Nurses who knew him well described him as a boy of eighteen and not unattractive – that is to say, a girl might have been tempted to be kind and sympathetic and so expose herself to danger.

There was also what seemed to be a kind of motivated ignorance about the very existence of the patients and the hospitals: 'Turn a blind eye and they won't be there.' This could be well sustained until some incident shocked people out of it. The hospitals themselves complained about being ignored.

When they had open days only the patients and their friends and relatives came, not the townspeople. One could, of course, ask why the townspeople should be expected to attend, since the patients were not 'their people' and the hospitals were somewhat alien excrescences on the side of Epsom. But all the same, our impression was that the ignorance was more blind than this would have justified: more deliberate. The degree of ignorance varied in different parts of the town: on the side of the town across the A24 from the hospitals it was extensive and little challenged by events. On the hospital side of the A24 it was more difficult to sustain in face of the evidence. There were exceptions, of course, people who mobilized generalized sympathy for mental patients and tried to help, especially with the mentally subnormal. But they were a small minority in the town.

Alarm and anger about incidents and the general strain of mixing with so many patients would be subdued by attitudes of sympathy, tolerance and sentimentality: 'Poor souls, they are ill.' 'They can't help being like they are.' These feelings were to some extent genuine and reflected some real change in attitude, but that did not wholly negate their defensive function. Combined with this, there was some splitting-off of the alarm and anger into the Ward Committee, which was the most active protest body in the town, fighting the battle for the whole town, full of the projections of the apparently milder citizens. We felt strongly that failing that Committee, some other group would have had to appear in the town to act on the widespread alarm and anger.

Another way the residents tried to deal with the general disturbance was by splitting the patient population into the harmless and the dangerous to an unrealistic extent: 'We are not bothered about the ESNs; it's the psychiatric patients that are the trouble.' Or: 'It's not the ill patients, it's the criminals.' 'It's just the psychopaths.' 'If they were locked up it would be all right.' It was probably true that the mentally subnormal patients were less disturbing and also continued to be more carefully monitored by staff than the psychiatric patients. It was also true that there were known criminals and psychopaths among the psychiatric patients. It might have been helpful and reassuring if the different kinds of patients could have been distinguished and treated differently, but it is doubtful how much this would have been possible.

The behaviour of such patients is relatively unpredictable: impulsive, subject to provocation by unforeseeable situations and in strange ways; who could have predicted the rape or the murder accurately? Probably not even the hospital staff, who knew the patients better than anyone. What was quite impressive about this was that people were genuinely trying to cope and to sustain tolerance, understanding and sympathy with the mentally ill, while at the same time having to deal with the fear and anger evoked by the pressure of so much disturbance in their community. They were trying to do this by falsely discriminating between the 'good' – that is, safe and deserving – patient and the 'bad' patient deserving only restraint or even punishment. Few people were wholly for or against all patients.

In addition to these psychosocial defences against the impact of the situation, Epsom residents had developed behavioural methods of coping to minimize the likelihood of disturbance and danger. These were considerably more in evidence on the hospital side of the A24/High Street than on the other side. There were certain things residents did not do, or did not do if they could help it. Very little use was made of Epsom Common, an attractive open space on the hospital side of town. The team walked on the Common on a Saturday and met almost no one, not even patients. The paths were overgrown. Men said they would not allow their wives and children to use the recreation ground. There was a rather eerie feeling about these areas, rather like the impression made by *Last Year in Marienbad*. There was almost no one there; five seats at the end were each occupied by one man who looked like a patient; a couple of children were playing in the middle distance; two old men were walking their dogs. An escorted party arrived, probably from one of the hospitals for the mentally subnormal. On a return visit on the afternoon of the same day, the recreation ground was still almost deserted except for some activity round the bowling green. Epsom Downs, on the other side of town, provided a startling contrast. There were lots of people, children playing freely, picnics, no identifiable patients, a happy relaxed atmosphere.

Probably rather stricter limits were placed on the movement of women and children than would otherwise have been: children were warned not to go to the recreation ground and certainly not to use the public lavatories there. Women walking their dogs made arrangements to do this in pairs or groups. (One would not, however, want to exaggerate the significance of this. They might have done it anyway for companionship.) Men said they were uneasy about going out alone because they might be thought to be a patient about to commit an assault. We could sympathize with this point of view since we had found ourselves looking at men on their own and wondering . . . Residents felt they had to take extra security precautions to guard their homes: better locks, door chains, dogs.

It seemed likely that residents also restricted their use of local shopping facilities, particularly in the High Street and on Saturday afternoons, which appeared to be the time when most patients were about. Few people seemed to shop on Saturday afternoons compared with adjacent towns such as Croydon, and many of those who were shopping were clearly patients. Not only were residents absent but so also, it seemed, were people from surrounding towns and villages who might have come into Epsom. Residents also restricted their use of certain roads and lanes and might make considerable detours to avoid those nearest the hospitals. (As I write this in 1988 these measures now sound all too familiar, a part of life in many towns, but they were much less commonplace in 1968.)

Residents also tried to prepare themselves for handling difficult situations they might encounter: how to talk to patients who might be awkward, perhaps in one's own house or garden, what help could be expected from the police or the hospitals, and how it could be summoned. A related problem not explored thoroughly was how much expense Epsom residents might be incurring through higher cost of community services like the police and social services.

We were also left with another open question: how far did Epsom residents move house across the High Street to get away from the hospitals? There was some evidence of this kind of movement. How many residents left Epsom altogether? The annual turnover of residents was about 6,000. How did this compare with other similar towns? How did the price of houses compare on the two sides of the town?

All in all, however, it did seem that the resident population of Epsom was being subjected to the impact of a considerable amount of disturbing behaviour and had some cause for complaint. There were strong feelings of fear, anger and puzzlement. Why did it have to be Epsom that had to put up with all this? Why did Epsom have to have all these hospitals and patients? Why indeed? One might have said that Epsom was being used as a kind of extended rehabilitation unit for the hospitals with unpaid, untrained, non-volunteer staff.

2. The patients

Our interviews with patients and hospital staff left us with considerable doubts about how far the patients' freedom to come and go in Epsom was really beneficial to them. Did it really give them a rewarding experience of being part of a meaningful community? Would it contribute significantly to their ability to return to living outside the hospital and lead a satisfactory life integrated into the community?

We have already said enough, perhaps, to answer the first question in the negative, but there are a number of other relevant considerations. These concern the situation patients were in when they came to hospitals in Epsom. A curious feeling of *déjà vu* drew my attention to other similar experiences which might help in understanding some of what was happening to patients.

First, there were the children evacuated from the large cities in World War II. Foster parents and the reception communities told terrible tales about these children: how awful they were. They wet their beds, had no manners, were delinquent, ungrateful and regressed. They were assumed to be like that always and their parents were blamed. There was at the time little understanding that their behaviour was largely a function of their circumstances: away from home, away from their parents, anxious about their parents in the dangerous cities, feeling rejected, lost, confused, frightened, angry. How much of the behaviour of the patients came from a similar experience? Were they also 'evacuated' – rejected, lost, frightened, angry in their strange surroundings?

Secondly, in a small town in World War II there were large contingents of foreign troops separated from their countries of origin, highly anxious about what was happening there, puzzled, alienated and tending to act these feelings out in the reception communities in sexual and other ways, behaving as they probably would not have done in their home communities. The local population talked a bit like the Epsom residents: women could not go out alone after dark; apart from sexual assault there was always the possibility of falling over a drunk soldier in the gutter in the blackout, and so on.

Thirdly, I was reminded of returning British prisoners of war, who were very estranged from their home communities, often bitter about being rejected and neglected, guilty about 'allowing' themselves to be captured, not certain at all of being acceptable to families and former friends in work situations. They too were likely to express their feelings against what they felt now was a somewhat alien community by sexual acting out, excessive drinking, and so on.

In tracing the parallel between the Epsom patients and those other groups, one could begin to think of the Epsom patients as suffering from, among other things, a displaced-person syndrome. They did not belong where they had been put and could be seen as expressing resentment against the reception population for the predicament in which they found themselves, even if it was not Epsom's fault. Some of the patients would have had a grudge against society anyway, but more than that seemed to be involved. Such 'aliens' tend to lack a sense of responsibility to the reception community. They neither carry over the ethics of their community of origin, nor do they explore and accept the ethics of the reception community. They are, as it were, conscienceless.

The patients coming into Epsom were aliens in more senses than one. In addition to the psychiatric illness and geographical alienation already discussed, they were often aliens also class-wise. Many came from a poor, working-class East London background into a typically middle-class, rather affluent Epsom. This was a natural setting for the expression of envy. They were in strange and alien surroundings – even the country itself being a strange and threatening experience for some of these town-bred patients. Indeed, the patients might well have felt and acted as though they were engaged in a war with society, Epsom bearing the brunt.

In other words, being placed in hospitals in Epsom and having the freedom of Epsom might actually have exacerbated the degree of disturbance in some patients, the more so since contact with the town would have confronted them very forcibly with their circumstances. From the viewpoint of Epsom, the alienation of the patients from their own community might well have increased the amount of acting out, and particularly the aggression to which they subjected the community. And basically again from the viewpoint of the patients and their treatment, such alienation and its sequelae are unlikely to be therapeutic.

Since, in fact, a comparatively small proportion of the patients took advantage of their freedom at any one time, the question inevitably arose of self- or other-selection to go out. Were the patients who went out really those most capable of using community facilities and getting therapeutic benefit from them? Were they, by contrast, patients who could best express the patient population's grudge against society and were most likely to be antisocial and aggressive? Were they on a mission for the others? We are not suggesting that the patients who went out were a uniform group, simply considering whether they included a significant number who were 'guaranteed' to cause trouble.

Apart from the above situation, we had other grave doubts about how far their freedom really benefited patients or, by contrast, how far it might actually constitute a risk for them. Many of the patients really did seem to be in need of care and protection. They were in hospital because they really could not manage life on their own; therefore, to give them too much unsupervised freedom might be to deprive them of what they needed for ease of mind or even safety. For example, patients who had been long in mental hospitals had lost the ordinary skills needed for living life outside and might need help in mobilizing them – something as apparently simple as learning again to cross a road safely. Young women patients might be just as much – or more – at risk of sexual assault from other patients or outsiders as the young women of Epsom. Patients were sometimes aware of their vulnerability and frightened by it.

A young woman patient approached Geraldine Gwynne and myself when we were observing and having lunch in the garden of a public house. She had been wandering around, taking drinks from anyone who offered them to her. We were the only women there without male companions. She seemed to feel some sense of security with us and tried to build a close relationship. First, she said to Geraldine that she was her sister. Then she said she was Snow White. I said: 'So where are your dwarfs?' She replied sadly and anxiously: 'No dwarfs today'. It is hard to describe the effect of these short interchanges: the lost quality of the girl, her need to be contained, her need for help and protection, her own psychotic awareness of the situation. It was intolerable to do nothing but talk to her. Incidentally, we overheard two nurses from another hospital, also lunching in the pub, debating whether they should take her back to her hospital. They had got the message too and were professionally and humanely concerned about it. The young woman patient was very vulnerable: her chances of being sexually assaulted or raped were quite high. How could it be good for her?

Patients were anxious about crossing the boundaries to the extent that some of them did not actually do so. Apart from their difficulties in coping with the practicalities of life, they were often afraid of people. To send them out on their own to face unknown people seemed little less than cruel. They were especially afraid of patients from the other hospitals. Unsupported crossing of boundaries might well have raised anxiety to an intolerable level and so increased the danger of acting out.

The question arose, in other words, of how far the 'bad' behaviour of patients was a function of their difficulty in managing their anxieties about being sent out into an alien community without the support and protection of hospital staff. It would have been interesting, for example, to do something we were not able to do: study the timing of incidents in relation to the time when patients crossed the hospital boundaries. Were significantly more incidents located near the hospitals? Were significantly more just after leaving or just before getting back? We were told that the murder was committed by a patient on his way back to his hospital, who knocked at a door – or rang the door bell – and killed the person who answered. Was it just too much for him to contain himself until he got inside again and could he have had more help in containing his anxiety and aggression?

In addition, there was the real danger of suicide. I am not suggesting that it is ever easy to protect a patient who is determined to commit suicide; but there may be other suicides, more 'casual' or opportunistic, which could be prevented by more protection or supervision. In other cases, it may be less suicide than 'accident' arising from diminished capacity to look after oneself: the suicide in the High Street, or going swimming in the duckpond. Further, suicide risks may be increased when patients are frightened or persecuted. Study of suicide attempts or threats suggests that in phantasy they may be less suicide than murder: the patient's phantasy is that he is killing phantasy enemies, people who are getting at him, or trying to stop visual or auditory hallucinations. He will survive and will be blessed with new idealized relationships. The problem is that he may succeed in killing himself and will certainly cause a lot of trouble even if he survives.

Patients were by no means always made to feel welcome when they went out into the town. The townspeople were afraid of them and angry, and however much they might try – as they did – to be understanding and helpful, they by no means always succeeded. Shopkeepers, publicans, caterers would, on the whole, rather not have had patients as customers because they always potentially meant trouble. They would, therefore, at best probably be somewhat restrained in their welcome. And for the protection of themselves, their premises and their other clients, they did at times have to be pretty firm and controlling or actually put patients out or call the police. It is hard to see how such experiences could have helped a patient get on better terms with his community, expect good experiences from it or learn to live in it more effectively. One feared that the opposite could happen.

Added to this problem was the patients' fear of the country – an additional reason, perhaps, why they tended to use the town rather than rural areas like the Common. Open spaces did not offer them the physical (and emotional) containment of the city, like Bethnal Green, with close buildings and lots of people. Their fear of other patients, both from their own and other hospitals, was exacerbated when they went out without their 'natural protectors', notably the nursing staff in the hospitals.

It was often difficult for a patient who was out to get help when he needed it – as reciprocally it was difficult for the townspeople to get help with a patient when they needed it. It was, of course, always possible to call the police or the mental welfare officer, but that would not necessarily have been the most appropriate move and a patient might not in any case have been capable of initiating the procedure. A difficulty here was in getting help from the hospitals or their professional staff. Before this could be done, someone had to establish to which hospital the patient belonged – not easy if the patient could not or would not tell. This often meant that the townspeople or the police could be left for a long time dealing with a difficult crisis for which they were not particularly well equipped and for which they were not really responsible, while the patient was left without professional psychiatric help.

We also questioned an assumption that seemed to lie behind the whole operation of giving patients the freedom to go out into the community: that just doing this would of itself be beneficial. I question this on theoretical grounds. In addition, the evidence from Epsom was that it was not a particularly therapeutic experience. Two essential elements seemed to be missing, or relatively so. The first was the preparation of patients who were about to go out – information-giving, for example, but more importantly, working over a patient's anxieties and phantasies about going out so that he would be more prepared for what he would find. Or, indeed, even arranging preliminary sorties to be carried out with an escort. The second was the reception of the patient when he returned and the opportunity to talk over and digest his experiences so that he could learn from them and change in himself. I am reminded again at this point of returning prisoners of war after World War II. They were not in the ordinary sense psychiatrically disturbed but had had traumatic experiences, had often been away for many years and were alienated from their community. We did not reckon it was enough just to send them back to their families and into jobs: they benefited from help, preparation before they went out into the community, and the chance to work through their experiences when they returned to their units.

I well remember painful group discussions on Monday mornings with men who had gone home for the weekend full of eager anticipation on Friday: hopes partly realized, partly disappointed – the only too common theme of the child who had not previously met his father and who said something like: 'I don't like that man, Mummy. Send him away.' These prisoners of war would on the whole have been better equipped than the Epsom patients to handle the situation themselves, but still benefited from help. So I return to the main point: that just doing something is not enough; provision needs to be made for preparation before the event and for digesting it afterwards. However much the hospital staffs recognized these needs and tried to meet them, resources did not make adequate provision possible.

This is not a criticism of the professional staff in the hospitals who, like the patients, were caught in a new and strange situation. They had on the whole been orientated to custodial care and it must indeed have been difficult for them to reorientate themselves to new roles and functions, especially since there seems to have been little general appreciation of what the changes really meant or of the change in the care patients would need. The nurses, in particular, did not seem to feel they had much support from the doctors in developing new aspects of their roles and functions.

To conclude this section, I would repeat the question: how much benefit did patients gain at so much cost to the people of Epsom? Was it worth it? It is difficult to answer these questions, but they deserve to be asked.

3. The hospitals and their staffs

One cannot overestimate the difficulty of the task the mental hospitals were dealing with, the most basic and intractable medical problem of our day. At the time of the study there had been some change in the objectives of the relevant professions. They were no longer content with providing custodial care, keeping the patient safe and, ideally, well looked after and protecting the community from the effects of his illness. They had become more therapeutically ambitious. This change was welcome, but brought difficulties in its train. The available resources were and were likely to remain inadequate to set up appropriate treatment for so many patients, some of them very ill indeed and having been ill and in custody for so many years. Comparatively little was known about treatment although there was excitement about possibilities: about the use of drugs, therapeutic communities, group psychotherapy, sorties into the community. But it was a confusing situation and many of the professionals themselves had little experience of the new possibilities and how to use them.

The very fact that they wanted to do more for their patients than before and that resources and knowledge were so limited tended to have certain effects on the staffs in the hospitals in Epsom. It was hard for them to believe in the efficacy of treatment, yet they wanted to. It was also hard for them to experience the anxiety and depression they would have experienced if they had admitted how little they had been able to do or might be able to do in the future. Hospital staffs, especially the nurses, seemed also to feel that they had rather low status: this appeared to be partly a result of the intractable nature of their task, partly that they seemed to feel that their own status somehow reflected that of their patients: 'People think we are loony as well.' Their own self-image, projected and felt as other people's image of them, reflected the feelings of helplessness and discouragement about their efforts to perform their task. Part of the problem seemed to be that, understandably, they tended to set their objectives too high, and so doomed themselves to disappointment. They could not but feel depressed if they compared their successes with those of general medicine and surgery, or

207

their own status with staff in general hospitals. They were, in other words, good and ready for hope to be held out to them of something better: more effective treatment, more success, such as they might feel had been offered to them by the 1959 Act.

The hospital staffs seemed to be tending to idealize the new situation; the newly given freedom to patients, combined with the improvement in drugs, offered hope of improvements or cures such as they had never had before. These hopes brought relief and encouragement; the danger was that this new situation would go too far and become a panacea, its limitations and dangers and the need for supportive measures to ensure its efficacy not being realized. People were a bit carried away. The new methods might be instituted without proper judgement and too adventurously. (Dr David Clark, formerly of Fulbourne Hospital, Cambridge, drew my attention to the fact that this was the second time the mental hospitals had been thrown open. The first was in the nineteenth century. It had not produced the hoped-for results. Subsequently, the hospitals had been closed again.)

Some of these problems appeared to some extent in Epsom. I discussed above how patients went out without much pre-paration by staff and came back to no work-through, as though the going out alone would be enough. Nor was there apparently much concern about when freedom might become licence in the hands of patients who might not be able to manage freedom, and lead to antisocial acting out. In the grip of their enthusiasm it was easy for hospital staff to forget how difficult they found these patients sometimes and so what their freedom might mean to the people of Epsom. It would probably be fair to say that the hospital staffs, particularly the nurses, also felt themselves somewhat alienated, identified with their patients, and felt their responsibilities to their patients more keenly than their responsi-bilities to their fellow-citizens of Epsom.

There were also, perhaps, some less acceptable ulterior motives encouraging sending patients out. It must have been a relief to get rid of them sometimes because they could be so trying and the nurses needed a break. Getting rid of the more difficult patients could give more time and opportunity to work with others who stayed in. 'Freedom' could become an excuse to neglect patients who were especially difficult to manage, so it was not really freedom but neglect or rejection. Some patients might be allowed to go out who should really have stayed in for their own and Epsom's sakes. A curious paradox could and did arise: that the hospitals were trying to treat their patients by sending them out of the hospitals.

There was indeed very little control over the physical boundaries of the hospitals. The gates were manned, but the person on duty did not control passage. The hospitals said that did not matter anyway because patients could easily get over walls and fences. I have discussed above the inadequacy of psychosocial boundary-keeping, the relative absence of work with patients about going out. It was difficult to tell how much influence was exerted by nurses as to whether they would go out or not. There was certainly some influence exerted on patients whom nurses did not think could manage outside, like a group of old ladies who had been hospitalized for years. The nurses actually took them on a supervised coach outing. Again, other patients might be encouraged to go out when it would have been better if they had not, at least without an escort. There seemed to be other reasons for this besides the idealization and enthusiasm for the policy.

There were times when nurses seemed to use this option as a means of expressing their own bitterness and anger against the community which gave them such difficult work to do and so little recognition for doing it. There seemed to be implicit messages around when we talked with nurses: 'You gave us these difficult and dangerous people to look after. Have them back and see how *you* like it.' Or: 'You cope: we can't.' Their own sense of inadequacy was projected into the community, so that they could feel superior: 'See how you can't manage, but we can.' In so far as people were acting on these feelings, one could say that the town was to some extent under attack. Particularly difficult or dangerous patients might be encouraged to go out so as to carry the attack. I am, of course, talking of unconscious feelings and impulses, not conscious ones. Wise judgements were therefore less likely to be made about which patients would really benefit from going out, and at what cost to Epsom.

These views also represented some disowning or denial of the nurses' own expertise, as though the people of Epsom could be expected to cope as well as they could and should cope. In so far as the hospital staffs did this, they further diminished their status in their own eyes and felt more degraded than ever. This view also probably affected their willingness to help in a crisis. The townspeople certainly sometimes felt that they were unwilling; for example, if they would not help unless they were sure it was one of their patients. After all, there would be no reason why they should help, anyway, if the townspeople were as good at it as they were.

Out of the policy that the patients would benefit from being out in the community, and the view that the community should have tolerant, sympathetic attitudes towards them, there sometimes developed a quite rigid, harsh, moral attitude among the professionals: 'They [the public] should look after the patients because they are ill.' This sometimes made it difficult for the professionals to understand and sympathize with just how difficult and frightening this might be for the public. I found similar attitudes in another mental hospital outside Epsom about patients going back to live with their families. Only the patient's good was considered and if it was reckoned that it would do the patient good to live with his family, that was that. What this might do to other members of the family or the need for them to have support were minimally considered. It becomes quite shocking when one realizes that the nurses knew very well how hard these patients were to live with, how frightening and sometimes dangerous they could be.

It would also be fair to say that there was a good deal of ambivalence about the provisions of the new Act. Hospital staffs felt some loss of control and were therefore anxious about having less control over patients than they had possessed. It had become quite difficult for medical and nursing staff to obtain the power to keep a patient in the hospital if they thought he should stay in. They were often angry about that and felt the situation might be unnecessarily dangerous. This anger sometimes made them almost caricature the Act: 'We have no power to keep patients in – so let them all go out.' Less restriction and fewer security precautions were exercised than could have been. The ambivalence was also related to some genuine uneasiness about the new situation, a wish not to go too far and beyond the patient's competence. There was a tendency to disclaim responsibility for doing something one was not quite sure one approved of.

Nurses who felt uneasy about giving patients too much freedom projected the responsibility into the doctors. They said they had tried to discourage patients from going out, but the doctors insisted. There was some failure to differentiate between legal and professional/moral responsibility and to project responsibility into the former, the Act: 'We cannot legally keep patients in.' So they sometimes disclaimed professional and moral responsibility for helping patients to behave appropriately about going out. In fact, quite a number of staff, particularly the nurses, did not go fully along with the Act and would have liked to retain fuller legal powers.

To conclude these comments on the hospitals: it would seem that they had had, and indeed were still having, difficulty in working out their reactions to the 1959 Act and its implications for how they managed their patients and the relationship between the patients and the hospitals on the one hand and the residents of Epsom on the other. This was a very difficult task and one could not have expected a quick adjustment. How far the problems the changes raised were really addressed it is hard to tell: for example, the development of a clear policy and guidelines for managing – not legally controlling – a patient's movement through the hospital boundaries into and out of the community.

CONCLUSIONS

All things considered, it seemed that the residents of Epsom had a case: that they were subjected to an unreasonably great burden arising from both the indictable offences committed by patients and from more general nuisance, including just the impact of too many alien people behaving oddly. The Regional Board seemed to accept this view and the responsibility for doing something about it. Thinking what to do about it was, however, no easy task. One certain thing was that in spite of the general wish to close mental institutions, there was no likelihood of Epsom's situation being relieved in the short term by the closure of one or more of its hospitals.

One point to which attention was given was the problems arising from the fact that the hospitals were absolutely independent of each other, each with its own management committee, so that each was free to pursue its own policies regardless of the others. So there was no formal co-ordination of the relationship of all five hospitals to Epsom. One result of this has already been discussed: no hospital would help in a crisis caused by a patient of another hospital, or unless it was established that it was one of their patients, so that the local people and services could be left coping for quite a long time without professional help. Another problem was that there was no over-all assessment of what might have been a reasonable number of patients to be about in Epsom at any one time, and no responsibility in the hospitals for informal 'rationing'.

There seemed good reason, therefore, to consider whether the five hospitals or the Regional Board should set up some co-ordinating body which could integrate policy and action for the five hospitals. One derivative of such a body could have been a mobile squad of nurses and other professional staff from all the hospitals which could act immediately when there was trouble without first identifying the patient's own hospital. They could liaise with the local services, particularly the police, to ensure that action was taken quickly and the burden taken off Epsom, and could perhaps have been a visible presence in the town to anticipate and prevent trouble.

The 1959 Act was not absolutely dictatorial; it gave some flexibility to the professions about how they might behave – for example how much use could be made of Section 25 to keep difficult and dangerous patients within the hospital; how medical and other responsibility could be operated to influence the number of patients who actually went out, bearing in mind the needs and rights of Epsom as well as of the patients. It is only too easy for professional people to develop a too narrow focus in caring for their own particular clients, and unfairly to neglect other people who also have rights and needs. For example, could more have been done in the hospitals to restrain known criminals and psychopaths or send them off to more secure accommodation elsewhere?

Some of these actions would have involved considerable changes in staff attitudes and a careful review of policy and how changes could be implemented. This would not have been easy and, as far as I know, did not take place.

Twenty years later, where have we got to, not only in Epsom but elsewhere, regarding Epsom not as unique but as just the most extreme example of a general situation? Disappointingly, not very far, I think. Mental health problems are still the most intractable in the health service; prospects of cure for patients or even significant improvement are little better, at least for the large number of still often chronic patients in mental hospitals. Definition of objectives is still rather vague and still, I think, tends to be overambitious. It is very hard to admit defeat or to accept that possibly a policy of 'maintenance' may be the most realistic and also the most hopeful – do as much as can be done, as well as possible, and be content.

I have recently had an encouraging experience where the staff of a unit worked hard and painfully on objectives and policy, with the result that they became less therapeutically ambitious and more realistic about the future prognosis of their patients, who were all or almost all chronic and sometimes quite deteriorated. The surprising and rewarding thing was that having established more modest objectives, staff began to feel more successful; their morale went up. They had the rewards of achieving their more modest and realistic objectives, and the most exciting thing of all was that the patients improved considerably when a more realistic assessment was made of their capacities and needs. Most of them could probably never live outside the hospital, but the quality of their life inside was immeasurably improved. Staff could feel proud of their achievement.

POSTSCRIPT (1988)
by A.J. Kember, Regional General Manager,
South West Thames Regional Authority

I am pleased that Mrs Menzies Lyth has decided to publish the findings of her research on public attitudes to the large hospitals at Epsom. I think it is encouraging to read this work and realize how much attitudes to people with mental illness and/or mental handicap have changed in twenty years. They are now being increasingly accepted back as full members of society as old prejudices die out. Partly as a result of this, and partly due to substantial planned investment in new local NHS services, the Epsom hospitals are being reduced in size, prior to eventual closure. It is especially encouraging how much today's residents of Epsom and Ewell and their representatives are involved in this process.

NOTES

1. Strictly, three psychiatric hospitals and two hospitals for the mentally handicapped.

2. Geraldine Gwynne, Miriam Lesser and the author.

3. A Ward is an administrative sub-division of a city. The Ward Committee is a voluntary committee of residents.

9 Day care of children under five: an action research study

A general view of day care

THIS STUDY was carried out in 1970–1 and attempted to establish a picture of day care for the under-fives, sufficiently detailed and accurate to make it possible to evaluate the way the day-care system worked and to suggest possible ways in which it might be developed or improved. We decided to work initially only in Greater London boroughs.

This paper attempts to give a general view of the day-care system as it then seemed to us. The other members of the team prepared detailed accounts about specific aspects of the system, the main conclusions of which are incorporated into this paper.[1] The research team's explorations into the day-care system made us feel very uneasy about the quality of care provided. We found similar feelings of uneasiness among the staffs of the Medical Officers of Health, including the staffs of day nurseries and within the nursery-nurse training colleges. A great deal of devoted work was being done by the staff of local authorities, both centrally and in the nurseries, and by childminders, but the system of day care had evolved in such a way as to be detrimental in certain respects to the welfare of the children who entered it or, at best, to make little contribution to the solution of the problems which often brought them into the system.

GENERAL FINDINGS
In what follows, I concentrate particularly on difficulties in the day-care system.

1. *The client population*

The clientele of the day-care system was not, of course, a cross-section of the population as a whole. Almost by definition, the clientele was in trouble. This arose not only because the nursery intake system gave priority to children from families in trouble, but also because normal healthy families, well integrated in their communities, were much less likely to put their children into the day-care system. The younger the child, the truer this was. In other words, children who came into this kind of care were likely to be the precipitates of family problems and to represent some kind of breakdown in the quality and amount of mothering available to the child.

The adults behind the children in day care were often themselves disturbed. Not only did they have realistic problems such as being single mothers, or occasionally fathers, but they tended also to have personality problems that intensified the impact of these problems, often the result of their own disturbed upbringing. Not every unmarried mother's child went into day care, for example. The child most likely to do so was the child of a mother whose capacity for making relationships was impaired, who could not mobilize the help of friends and relations in her plight and who also suffered from an underdeveloped or impaired capacity for mothering. These children were consequently at risk emotionally from the impact on them of troubled adults and their circumstances. Although not all the children were actually disturbed on entry, they were to a high degree in need of help and protection.

The situation described immediately raised issues about 'the unit of care'. It is probably a fair comment that the day-care system interpreted its function as caring for children who, for whatever reason, were not or could not be adequately cared for in their families. It had this in common with most institutions that care for children, such as children's hospitals and residential institutions. We questioned seriously whether the child alone was the appropriate unit of care or whether it was not desirable to give more help and support to the mothers and families from whom they came, to whom they returned and from whom they were likely to suffer unless help was given on a broader basis. This seemed desirable from the narrow perspective of organizing effective care for the child, as well as for the sake of the adults themselves.

The question of the appropriate unit of care was raised for another reason. A major factor in the psychological and social development of a child is the amount and quality of mothering available. The capacity for mothering is not a fully developed, natural instinct; it develops and is sustained through the constant interaction and mutual responsiveness between mother and child that gives immediate rewards in the relationship for both (Bowlby, 1969). Separation of the child from the mother for much of its waking day, five days a week, seemed likely to impair or further impair the quality and amount of mothering available during the remaining time.

This expectation was confirmed by observations. A significant number of nursery mothers did not seem very interested in their children: they appeared to lack a sense of responsibility for their care and did not seem to enjoy the limited time they had with them. Indeed, only too many contrived to find other places to dump their children when day nurseries or regular minders were not available, a situation that put the children even more at risk.

In fact, one could only conclude that a day-care system that separates mother and child for almost the whole of the working day, at least five days of each week, is potentially a threat to the maintenance of the mother–child relationship which is so crucial to the child's development. The day-care system would have to be quite exceptionally good to compensate for that. It would appear that the most effective contribution to the growth of children in the population which at present uses the day-care system would be the provision of services to support their families, facilitate longer contacts between mother and child, and foster the mother's capacity for mothering.

2. The output of the day-care system

There was little doubt that the day-care system did not, on the whole, turn out psychologically healthy children, able to function well in society and cope realistically with the demands of life; at least, such children are not its typical products (Bain and

Barnett, 1986). How much the day-care system fails to cope with problems already there, how far it creates or adds to problems, it is difficult to say. We came to believe that day nurseries needed to be therapeutic communities if they were to cope effectively with the kinds of children who were in them. They are certainly not, at present, designed to be that, nor are the staff trained or expected to run that kind of institution (Menzies Lyth, 1985; vol. 1, pp. 236–58).

The population of the day-care system appeared both to come from, and then contribute more than its fair share to, problem areas in society such as mental illness and delinquency. Many of the children emerged from the system with personality disorders. For example, they easily became desocialized, showed a lack of concern for others, ineffective and fragile relationships, apathy, 'laziness', reduced capacity to initiate contacts. They were precociously rather than genuinely independent, they showed little real attachment behaviour, some were aggressive, demanding, seductive and exploiting (Bain and Barnett, 1986). Consequently, they were likely to claim an undue share of the care provided by society for people in trouble, both currently and in later life. Too many of them seemed to be heading for services provided for the sick, the inadequate and the delinquent.

We had the impression from contact, for example with accident hospitals and approved schools, that day-care children appeared there unexpectedly often. They also provided more children for the day-care system in the future, as the day-care children of one generation tend to become the inadequate parents of the next. A more effective helping system for the present day-care population, both adults and children, would therefore not only reduce their distress but would also help to keep them out of other sorts of trouble, painful to themselves and expensive to the community.

3. The day-care age range
In terms of differential stages of development, needs and capacities, the age range infancy to five years is vast. Babies under six months need a totally different kind of provision from four-and-

a-half to five-year-olds if both are to develop well. The baby's capacity to tolerate separation and frustration is very limited. He really needs to be with his mother, or at least to have her available, all – or almost all – the time. Failing the mother herself, another reliably present, concerned woman is essential if this capacity is not to be overstretched, with permanent personality damage. The small baby does not relate easily to his peers, or find much sustenance in them. In reality they are only likely to compete for insufficient adult care in the nurseries. By contrast, the four-year-old can tolerate or benefit from quite long spells away from his mother in the daytime and needs and enjoys interaction with his peers. The number of care-takers necessary also varies very much with age. It is not possible for one person to look after many babies effectively; possibly only one or two. The possible size of group increases with the age of the child and changes in the appropriate type of care.

The nurseries as they were then organized did scant justice to the task of providing appropriate variations in care to suit the needs of this vast age range. Instead, the day-care system appeared to have been set up as an emergency measure to care for young children not old enough to enter the educational system whose families could not, or would not, cope. They seemed to have been set up in circumstances that did not permit enough consideration for the kind of problems raised above. In fact, the day-nursery system largely originated during World War II to facilitate the return of mothers to the labour force.

Finally, while we had no doubt that the nursery hours were too long for all the children in this age range, they were grossly excessive for small children up to the age of three. They were much longer than the hours of infant schools, let alone nursery schools. They suited working mothers better than children.

4. Pressures operating to bring children into the day-care system
Since we considered it important to keep as many children as possible out of the day-care system, we tried to find out what circumstances tended to bring them into it. Pressures were strong, most often the need or wish of the mother to work to provide or supplement the family income. Unmarried, separated

or divorced mothers made up most of this category. Social and psychological factors interacted with financial pressures. Some of the mothers' incomes from social security would have been nearly as high as their net earnings, less what they paid for day care. They were certainly not working only for the money. A few felt it vaguely wrong to accept social security when they were young and healthy. More important, perhaps, were the social and psychological needs of the mothers themselves. It would probably take a very robust and healthy mother to sustain and enjoy a relationship with a baby twenty-four hours a day without herself being sustained by the relationship with the baby's father, or another concerned adult. The mothers in the day-care population were often not healthy and robust; they were more likely to be lonely and dependent, with a limited capacity to develop and sustain relationships with other adults who could help and support them. They often relied on the ready-made relationships of the work situation for the adult company they needed, separated as they frequently seemed to be from their families of origin and displaced in their communities.

In two-parent families, the mother often went out to work not because the husband's income was totally inadequate to support the family but because the family wanted, or felt it needed, a high income to sustain a high standard of living, to feel it had established itself securely by buying a house and having a lot of material possessions, to save to go back to its country of origin. Such factors seem to operate particularly among immigrant families, whose need to feel established drove them to a high standard of living. They had often been accustomed to both parents going out to work in their countries of origin, but there an extended family would have taken over the baby-minding. They seemed unable, or unwilling, to differentiate between the effects of familial baby-minding and the effects of day nurseries or childminders. Inadequate living conditions tended to drive women out of the home to deal with loneliness and depression or even despair about being able to bring up a family well under such conditions.

Some of the social and psychological needs of those mothers and the need for supplementing family incomes might be met by part-time jobs. It was, however, difficult for mothers to find part-time jobs, either because of a dearth of them or because there was no effective organization for helping mothers to get in touch with them. Nor was there any obvious way of creating part-time jobs, such as by two mothers sharing a job which might have been linked with a private, mutual, baby-minding system. The situation was complicated by the fact that so many of the mothers with whom we were concerned lacked the initiative to make such arrangements themselves or to sustain the necessary relationships with employers, babies and other mothers. Private arrangements of this kind were known to exist among more socially and psychologically adequate mothers and were said to work well. However, no services seemed to exist which could help less adequate mothers to develop a similar mode of living and working for themselves and their young children.

In addition, income from a part-time job would not usually be enough on its own to support a mother and one or more children. Some supplement would still be necessary, making the mother once again dependent on social security, since there was no insurance system to cover this situation.

One should perhaps note too that the policy operated by many local authorities whereby mothers must work a minimum number of hours – in effect, full-time – to qualify for a nursery place exacerbated the situation. Although there was a certain amount of judicious blind-eye-turning, and not all local authorities did operate this policy, by and large a mother who wanted to work part-time would not get a nursery place, and would be forced into the childminding system or another private arrangement.

Society put a great deal of pressure on women, even the mothers of young children, to go out to work. Mothering as a source of satisfaction, and a valuable and difficult job, was denigrated and only lip service paid to its importance. The non-employed housewife was often regarded as a bit of a slacker even if she had young children. The needs of industry, teaching, nursing and the social services for women workers were constantly stressed, these needs being discussed in terms of their having priority and often in such a way as to make women feel guilty if they did not respond.

Would-be employers of these mothers did not always show much regard for their children. One Principal Nursing Officer said she had been shocked to find that her own nursing contemporaries, now hospital matrons, made no inquiry when employing married nurses about what provision they were making for their children. It can be very difficult for women to withstand pressures from friends, neighbours, former colleagues, potential employers and mass media. A childminder with young children of her own was under constant pressure from neighbours: they told her she was mad to stay at home and should put her own young child into a nursery and get a job.

The comparative isolation of the family in large conurbations also encouraged women to go back to work. The kind of woman particularly prone to feel this isolation was one who found it difficult to establish satisfying relationships with neighbours and other local contacts, to use local facilities and to make friends with the parents of her children's friends. A high proportion of them would probably be among the excessively mobile part of the population, people who never really put down roots. They were the kind of people who would drift back to work in order to achieve relationships of a sort without having to take initiative and responsibility themselves. A related problem was that living in a scattered and fragmented community meant that many married women did not get the reflected status from husbands' positions they would have in a more integrated community and might be driven to seek status in their own right by finding themselves a job.

The day-care system had to relate itself to these pressures and work with their effects on children, mothers and families. This was by no means an easy task and there was some danger that the local-authority staff who decided on priorities, and the nursery staff, might themselves be caught in the pressures and make inappropriate decisions. For example, they might act out of respect for parents who worked hard to earn a lot and establish themselves securely and on a high standard of living. They would give such parents a nursery place when it might have been better to give more attention to the deprivation of the child and to possible alternatives. Or again, the authorities sometimes acted out of mistaken kindness. Pressure was put on the young, devoted and unmarried parents of Z, aged eleven months, to take a nursery place on the grounds that they were exceedingly poor and mother needed to contribute some income. The young couple would probably have been willing to go on as they were for longer. The pressure was sympathetic but perhaps unthinking. Z was a healthy, happy child, developing normally and much loved by her parents. She reacted badly to the separation from her mother and did not sustain her good development under nursery conditions.

THE DAY-CARE SYSTEM

1. *Day nurseries*

Although we worked in only four nurseries, the findings were so consistent as to give us some confidence that they could be generalized and, indeed, they were supported by the comments of local-authority public health staff from their experience, and by other research (Bain and Barnett, 1986; Hopkins, 1988). We found in all four nurseries much similarity in the way staff worked with children which we attributed to the effects of training and, even more, to a common professional attitude which the nursery nurse seemed to develop during training and her early years of work. As in other professions, nurses who were unable to accept the general culture and attitudes tended to leave the profession, or to find their way to fringe parts of the system where they found the professional culture less oppressive.

Nursery nurses might go into private work where they had a closer relationship with fewer children and their mothers, or perhaps into hospitals. We observed, for example, that the nursery nurses in the children's ward at the Royal National Orthopaedic Hospital behaved in certain significant ways very differently from day-nursery nurses, notably in the extent to which they saw their function as supporting the mother–child unit and helping the mother to care for her sick child herself rather than taking the child over (Menzies Lyth, 1982; vol. 1, pp. 153–207).

In the day nursery the staff wished to deploy their skill and concern for the children in their care but had to do so under conditions which made it essential for them to erect personal and communal barriers against the pain of real awareness of the situations they were working with: of the tragedies in many of the families, the needs and disturbance of the children and the damage that day-nursery care itself might do. The fact that these barriers had to be erected unfortunately increased the likelihood that care would be defective.

I will now try to describe in more detail some of the problems we observed in day nurseies. Many nursery staff themselves came from deprived or disturbed backgrounds. Some had parents who were divorced or separated when they were very young; others had themselves been in institutions from an early age. One nurse had been in a boarding school from the age of three and 'loved every minute of it'. Their own experiences had too often led to overidentification with deprived children, to a forlorn hope of overcoming their own deprivation by caring for others, and to an unfortunate tendency not really to understand their own experiences. They had failed to gain insight from them to deploy effectively in relation to other children like themselves. It was only too common for staff like the three-year-old school boarder to deny that they themselves had suffered from their early experiences or not to recognize suffering in other children.

Closely linked with this point is the idea that by doing nursery-nurse training one can learn to be a good mother. Too often this is a counsel of despair. The girl's experiences with her own mother have resulted in her having an inadequate model of mothering which she wishes to modify, an inadequate basis therefore for relating as an adult in a truly motherly way to real children and being intuitively in touch with them. Nor was the training or experience of working in a nursery likely to help her achieve her ambition of learning how to be a really good mother. She was doomed to disappointment and the nursery children she cared for would not have a good mother-substitute.

Because of their early experiences, too many nurses were themselves inadequate people who could not easily cope with the demands of life. They often seemed to have drifted into the work because they had not done well at school, could not think what to do next, and somebody suggested they might take up work with children. They tend to rely unduly on the notion that if one is female one must by definition be good with children, a notion that is only too often incorrect.

In fact, nursery staff tended to relate to children in ways that deprived the children of real understanding and concern. Staff, particularly young student nurses, often said they chose this job because they loved children, or had always wanted to look after children, sometimes particularly mentioning deprived children. The 'love' was genuine, but it was indiscriminate; it was not based on a real relationship with real children, not all of whom are lovable, and none of whom is lovable all the time. It gave no place to the hatred children can arouse, which must be coped with by everyone who looks after them. It allowed for no confrontation with the child's or their own hatred, an important maturational experience for both. This rather unreal sentimental love is a very different thing from the professional concern for children which enables one to understand and relate individually to them, including the child whose problems make him difficult to love.

Nursery-nurse training appeared to do little to change indiscriminate love into mature professional concern. The student nurses lived and worked in a setting where indiscriminate care was the rule, where stability of relationship between nurse and child was continually disrupted by staff changes including the in-and-out movements of students between college and nursery, and where attachment between nurse and child was often discouraged on the mistaken grounds that it was bad for a child to become attached to another woman when he would return to his mother in the evening.

The shock of contact with real children in nurseries, children who were often distressed and difficult, usually meant that students themselves went through a period of pain and distress in the early stages of their training. At this point they were often able to make some intuitive contact with the distress of the children which evoked painful, though possibly unconscious, memories of their own early problems. This intuitive awareness, if effectively handled during their training, could have been an important growing point for the students. However, there seemed to be no situation where students could bring their observations and the distress they aroused and work them over with people who understood both the students and the children and communicated their understanding to the students in a way which would facilitate their emotional development, increase their intuitive understanding of the children, and so help them towards mature professional concern (Hopkins, 1988).

In the nurseries there seemed to be no group situation where this quiet, contemplative, digestive kind of teaching could be done; teaching was entirely on the job. The student was taught by the staff in the room where she worked, 'teaching' being very much centred around doing what the student was told to do for children. In the colleges one found considerable concern about the students' distress and disturbance; staff made it known that they were available to students who felt they needed help. However, in our opinion this is not the most effective way of maximizing the learning from the students' observation and experience and their shock and distress about them. It twisted a potential and necessary learning opportunity for all students into a somewhat irrelevant counselling relationship for the very distressed few who had to admit weakness and seek help from usually overpressed staff.

Lacking teaching of this kind, students had to develop defences against realizing the real meaning of the behaviour of the children they worked with; defences which were detrimental both to their own development and to the care of the children. They did not develop a real understanding and knowledge of children. They denied the significance of the children's behaviour and failed to understand and respond to it adequately. For example, a member of the team spent a couple of hours cuddling and talking to a severely distressed three-year-old spending his second day in a nursery; the staff nurse, who had neglected this child all day, remarked to another team member: 'That lady seems to have taken a fancy to that boy.' Nothing could have been further from the truth. He was an unattractive child but he was desperate, having just been separated, 'rejected' by the mother who had always looked after him. He was reacting quite normally to his situation, but the staff nurse regarded him as rather silly and a nuisance; no special care was being given to the special needs of this new child.

This raises another very crucial point. The nursery nurses seemed no longer able to distinguish between the normal and the abnormal and to respond appropriately. Normal distress reactions were often treated as a nuisance and the child as difficult; calm and detachment, indiscriminate relationships with staff, were regarded as normal and helpful. In particular, nurses often did not understand distress signals and respond appropriately; aggressively disturbed children got attention because they were a nuisance and had to be controlled; quiet, withdrawn, isolated, disturbed children were neglected because they were not a nuisance although often their need was greater. These defences also led to failure to understand the significance of social and psychological handicaps in children, like slow speech development or lack of concentration, to which no special attention was given. At the same time a great deal of care and concern were likely to be given to the physically handicapped child.

Another massive defence against confronting the real impact of the children was escape into activity. This took two main forms, both of them depriving and detrimental to the children. First there was the escape into chores. Staff frequently retreated wholly away from the children into other rooms where they occupied themselves with things like washing or ironing while a totally inadequate number of staff continued to cope with the children. This was in marked contrast to a good ordinary home situation where the mother is likely to take a baby or young child, if awake, with her and maintain a relationship with him while she gets on with her chores, giving up the chores when he needs her care. We respected the staff's need to escape from a very distressing situation for them which they had not learned better ways of coping with, but it was not good for the children.

Secondly, there was overactivity with children. Staff seemed to need always to be doing things and making the children do things. 'Play with a purpose' seemed to be a key concept and, in

227

our opinion, was vastly overdone. There was considerable infilt-ration of ideas from nursery schools and a failure to understand crucial differences between the nursery school and the day nursery. Nursery-school children spend much less time there and it can, therefore, appropriately satisfy their needs for pur-poseful play in relationships with peers, while the need for a quiet time in a more contemplative relationship with an under-standing adult can, ideally, be satisfied during the rest of the day. Purposeful play much of the day, relieved only by the rather restrictive routine meal, washing and rest time in the day nurseries is too much for the under-fives.

It was striking in the nurseries how, when members of the team sat still in a room with or without a notebook, there would be a drift of children towards them – notably the quiet, disturbed children who would gradually initiate contact, often first by touching, then perhaps by climbing onto a lap and perhaps, finally, starting to talk. There was an obvious need here for quiet contact that nursery staff were usually too busy and too anxious to meet. The need was painful to the adult who did try to meet it. The distress of these children was not easy to bear. We had little doubt that the overactivity initiated by staff, and induced in children, was an unconscious device used by staff to avoid painful confrontation.

Staff also seemed to develop defences against recognizing that many of the problems they must try to cope with were insoluble, although they might be ameliorated to some extent. It is not comfortable to work in an atmosphere where one may feel condemned ultimately to be relatively ineffective. Certain problems were, therefore, not admitted to exist, and little attempt was made to deal with them. As described above, social and psychological handicaps were usually not recognized and were little helped. There tended to be a fairly narrow concentration on physical care, though even that was not always well done, and on activities that kept those children who participated entertained and apparently content, while children not participating were often not noticed. The need to feel one is coping when really one cannot leads to a narrowing of

the objectives one thinks one should meet, which is likely to have a detrimental effect on the children.

Another example was a tendency to set up the wrong developmental objectives for the children, since these might be easier to achieve than appropriate objectives and gave a more rewarding sense of success. Staff tended to regard as successes those children who became what they described as independent: who required little attention, co-operated well with the routines imposed on them by staff and in other ways were precocious and conforming. In fact, such children tend to develop false personalities, insecurely based independence, restricted capacity for creativity and for making really satisfying relationships with others.

In conclusion, one can only say again that while staff in nurseries worked hard and often devotedly to care for the children, the attitudes which they had developed over time to their work and to children did in fact only too often interfere with the real effectiveness of the care they gave in terms of the children's psychological and social development.

Several features of the relationship between nursery staff and parents diminished the value of the service given to both children and parents. As we commented above, the unit of care was perceived to be the child, whereas we regarded the appropriate unit as being the family. Matrons showed much concern about mothers' ineptitude to cope with life and gave them a great deal of help. This included anything from reminding a mother to take her contraceptive pill each day to making dental and doctors' appointments for mothers. However, most of the help was given to the mother incidentally and individually and not as a part of total family care by nursery staff with the object of optimizing the overall care of the child.

The amount of knowledge that nursery staff had of a child's family and home circumstances was, with few exceptions, quite inadequate to permit effective help with family problems. Such information as there was seemed to be lodged in the matron or possibly her deputy. Indeed, there seemed to be some kind of ethic that it was a breach of confidence to divulge information to the staff who actually cared for the child. Staff, especially student nurses, complained that the dearth of information about mother and family interfered with their care for the child. On the other hand, there was little evidence that the staff sought opportunities to get to know the parents or helped the child, if he was verbal, to tell them his own version of his family circumstances. A major breakdown in communication was that nursery staff did not usually seek to find out from a mother how exactly she herself brought up the child so that they could match their care to hers, or possibly help her to improve hers. On the whole, one suspected that the staff were really not too eager to know and thereby to add to the burden of problems of which they were aware, but which they could do little to solve.

This staff attitude was matched on the parents' side by an apparent unwillingness to get involved with the child and those who cared for him in the nursery. Parents usually did little to initiate relationships with staff. Partings from the child in the morning tended to be swift and abrupt and often lacked affection as the parent rushed off to work. Parents obviously did not plan to have time available to exchange views and information about what went on with the child and how to care for him. Reunions in the evening usually took place fairly rapidly and not very affectionately when a tired and perhaps irritable parent met a tired child who might well have spent the last hour or so aimlessly waiting to be picked up. The setting was not good for parent–staff interaction in which information might usefully be exchanged about the child or family circumstances. In this one sees examples of the breakdown of the parents' concern for the child.

One is struck by the contrast here with the more healthy, often middle-class families, delivering or collecting children from nursery schools and play groups. This is a much more leisurely and friendly affair where mothers, staff and children relate to each other to exchange information and hear about each other's satisfactions and problems and parents take an interest in the general affairs of the school. Further, whereas entry into nursery school seems to develop friendships between children and between parents and strengthens the bonds of a family with its community, nothing of the kind seems to happen among day-nursery families. Their need for such community links is much greater, but the development of these links is inhibited by ineptitude in forming them. Nurseries seemed to do little to foster these mutually helpful bonds between families.

Nursery staff often had, at a conscious level, sympathy for mothers and families and a relative absence of moral strictures of the conventional kind against the sort of behaviour which brought them and their children into the day-care orbit. Unfortunately, this was often matched by subtle negative attitudes which militated against the staff's being helpful to the mothers personally, to the mother–child relationship or even to the child in the nursery. There was, for example, considerable rivalry with mothers and a need to outdo them in the care of the child; this included disrespect for the way the mother reared the child and replacement of the mother's methods when they differed from those of the nursery. Whether mother's or nursery's method was better was in a sense irrelevant; it was more important that the child might often suffer unnecessarily through the nursery's enforcing a different routine from the mother's and through lack of co-ordination between mother and nursery. This is particularly true of babies. Babies sometimes went hungry because the nursery would not give them the bottle they were accustomed to at home. Potting was forced early on babies who had no experience of it with their mothers.

Parents were often only too willing to collude with seeing the nursery as knowing best. They alleviated their own guilt about abandoning their child by a strong, irrational conviction that the nurses were experts and must know more about children than they did. So they did not complain or even ask for things. They did not investigate the reality of the nurseries and were sometimes afraid to complain, as they said, in case the nurses reacted angrily and took it out on their child. They were in general too easily satisfied with the care given and tended to make unrealistic judgements about its quality. They said that the children learned such good manners; that they had become so independent and that their speech was so much improved. They seemed to be unaware that these very things might in themselves imply problems – that the child had become precociously independent of his mother when he should still be dependent; that his capacity for spontaneous response had diminished; that idiosyncratic modes of communication, so important to mother and child, were being eroded.

The lack of involvement of a mother in the care of her child was particularly acute when the child first entered the nursery. The nurses believed the child's entry was more likely to be successful if they made a clean break. Even those mothers who could have stayed in the nursery with the child were not encouraged or invited to stay. The mother of the 'new' boy described above was at home waiting for admission to hospital, and could have stayed with him in the nursery, but no one suggested that she should. We had no doubt that entry and settling into a nursery would have had a less traumatic effect on children and on the mother–child relationship if mothers had been present a good deal at first.

In the Royal National Orthopaedic Hospital we were able to contrast the settling in of children accompanied by mothers and of children who came alone. The difference was dramatic. The child's fears about the new situation were allayed by exploring it with his mother and having her to turn to when he got into trouble. His relations to the staff developed more easily when he could turn to his mother rather than the staff when he wanted to, and when he could observe his mother in a friendly and co-operative relationship with the nurses about his care. He was still distressed when his mother finally left, but his distress was mitigated by the effects of the mutual exploration with his mother, by his memories of her there, by a better relationship with the staff, by a greater certainty that his mother would come back to him in a place where he has already had experience of her caring for him. His distress was infinitely less than that of a child who went through the whole process alone and because he had not been there with his mother, had less trust in her coming back to reunite with him (Menzies Lyth, 1982; vol. 1, pp. 153–207).

Two other features made for particular difficulty in relationships with parents. First, the training made no provision for preparing nursery staff to relate to parents or to the parent and child together, and orientated them only to the children.

Secondly, the staff themselves were so young, often students, and had so little experience of life themselves, particularly of motherhood, which would have helped them relate more intuitively to the parents and to the parent–child unit.

There were a number of problems in the operating system, some of which have already been discussed: for example, the inadequate support for both student nursery nurses and staff in their difficult and painful task. The level of fatigue and stress was high and there was little provision within the system for handling them. Labour turnover and sickness leave were both high, problems which were also met by Bain and Barnett in another nursery in 1975–6, where labour turnover in the first six months of their work was at the rate of 438 per cent per annum, while sickness absenteeism was on average fifty-three days per staff member per annum. These are startling figures and describe a situation which was disastrous for the children's making and sustaining relationships. As the remodelling of that nursery proceeded the figures fell to 159 per cent and 5.7 days respectively.

Matrons relied considerably for support on local-authority nursing staff and appreciated the help they gave, but it was not possible for the local-authority staffs to give enough time or detailed support. Matrons worried about losing that support later when the nurseries were to be taken into the social service departments. They were also concerned about the problems of their staff and spent quite a lot of time helping individuals in distress, but this did not contribute the kind of support system that would have been given, for example, by a case conference once or twice a week; nor did nurseries seem to make use of other local facilities which might provide expert help with problems in the care of these disturbed children and so reduce the strain. For example, only one Principal Nursing Officer reported a formal contact with a local Child Guidance Clinic where the psychiatrist held regular meetings with her nursery matrons. Some nurseries did not even know where their nearest Child Guidance Clinic was.

Nor were the Child Guidance Clinics often brought in to help children and parents and indirectly to relieve staff. This was striking in view of the number of disturbed children and families in the nurseries. One could not help feeling that this was all of a piece with the denial of the importance of social and psychological handicaps and the need to feel that the staff could cope adequately with rather intractable problems. Visiting medical officers seemed to go along with the staff in concentrating mainly on physical well-being.

A difficult problem was the child:staff ratio. There seemed no doubt that even when a nursery was fully staffed the number of children each staff member had to care for was too great to make it possible to develop the intimacy and consistency of contact that is necessary for the healthy emotional development of a child. Only too often the staff was not up to strength because of illness, leave, courses, vacancies. The cost of providing adequate numbers of staff would be formidable, leaving aside the cost of raising salaries to a level that might attract staff of a more adequate quality than some of the present staff and students.

The way the staff:child ratio militated against intimate and stable contact between nurses and children was exacerbated by the frequent changes in staff. It seemed comparatively rare for anyone except the matron, deputy matron, warden and possibly domestic staff to stay for any appreciable time; many staff nurses and students stayed less than a year, few more than two. While some nurses left for reasons common to their age group – such as marriage, pregnancy or the wish to broaden their experience through foreign travel – it seemed to us that an appreciable amount of the movement could be attributed to the conditions of their job, notably the high level of stress and fatigue and the low level of reward. In addition, the indiscriminate care and low level of attachment gave them little sense of responsibility for the children, which might have encouraged them to stay, instead of giving up the work altogether or moving off to care for other children elsewhere.

Another staffing problem was the lack of male contact for the children, many of whom lacked fathers in their own homes. We were particularly struck by this in one nursery which had very decrepit buildings needing almost constant repair, so that the children had become quite familiar with council workmen and obviously much enjoyed the relationship with them. Another matron reported how important it was that senior boys as well as girls from a local school came into the nursery to help.

For various reasons – such as inadequate staffing, escape into activity, and so on – nurseries often developed a system of operating based on a rather inflexible routine, this being all the worse because the routine was related more to the need of the staff to get their work done and sustain their own timetables than to the needs of the children. Children might be washed and sitting at table doing nothing half an hour before a meal could possibly be served; afternoon rests seemed more related to staff need for a break than to children's needs. Getting children ready to be collected reflected staff's need to get away on time rather than children's and parents' needs. We saw children sitting around in outdoor clothes doing nothing for up to an hour before their parents were expected.

There seemed to be several problems in the grouping of the children in nurseries. In particular we have found ourselves questioning the validity of the 'family grouping' system,[2] especially if it is sustained for the whole day. The vast difference in the interests and capacities of children between infancy and five made it difficult for them to join well in activities together. The smaller children were often knocked about by an aggressive older child or by an older child just rushing about carelessly. Nursery children did not seem particularly likely to develop the kind of concern and care for younger children that one finds among siblings in healthy families; older children might also get an unfair share of staff attention simply because they are more able to sustain the kind of activities staff thought good for children. Unless the total group was very large, say sixteen to twenty, the children had little choice of companions at their own level of development and might be forced into activities at the wrong level.

Few schools would attempt to integrate such a range of development in the same class or occupy them with the same activities. A group of sixteen to twenty is too large for such small children, generating too much activity, noise and fuss and reducing the direct contact between adult and child. The advantages of family grouping were said to be giving children the experience of mixed age groups as they would have in an ordinary family, and keeping siblings together. But what family has twelve to twenty children under five? On the whole we would probably prefer a smaller age range in each group with different sizes of groups and different child:staff ratios according to age. This would enable older groups to model themselves more appropriately on nursery schools, while the younger groups develop a different model of care more appropriate to their developmental level. This is not an easy problem to solve and probably needed further exploration, but it would become easier if there were appreciable numbers of part-time children in the nurseries. For a shorter day we would feel that grouping according to age would be the best method.

2. Childminders[3]

The problems in this area of day care seemed in many ways even greater and were certainly a focus of anxiety among local-authority staffs. A central problem was controlling the quality of care even among registered childminders. Health visitors who monitored the system felt they could do little more than ensure adequate physical conditions of care, and were usually unable to control, or even effectively influence, the social and psychological conditions. Some local authorities were giving consideration to training registered minders, but training was optional, where it existed. The risk was that the better and more concerned minders might attend training and the less good, who needed training more, would not.

In our experience, registered childminders varied enormously in quality. The best undoubtedly provided a much higher standard of care than the nurseries. We visited one who was a trained nursery nurse who had gone into private work and then married. She had a stepson and a baby of her own and was registered to mind three children. We observed her giving a very high standard of care, relating easily to the children, mediating well between conflicting demands from them, relating them well to each other. She described her relationship with the mother of the children and gave an impression of helping the mother to understand her children's needs and of being in close communication with her.

At its best the childminding situation can provide something much more like the ordinary family situation and can engage the child in ordinary family circumstances which provide so much for his development: outings, participation in chores, shopping, coping with sibling rivalry, and so on. At the other extreme, the worst minders give much less adequate care than the nurseries: neither psychologically nor always physically adequate.

One minder on the day of our visit had gastroenteritis, as did two of her own children. The minded children were there as usual, one at least with the full knowledge of his mother. This boy was described by the minder as being very backward and never speaking. When the interviewer had been there about half an hour, talking to the minder and playing quietly with the boy at the same time, the boy handed her a toy bus and said 'Bus', a comment met with cries of astonishment from the minder and her older child, who had never heard him talk like that before. We could only wonder what kind of attention the minder usually gave this child.

According to health visitors, other local-authority nursing staff and the more aware childminders, parents exercised little more effective control over the quality of minders than the local authorities could. They were reported as not seeming to care, often never crossing the doorstep of the minders' premises to see what they are like, being only too glad to dump their children anywhere. This view was confirmed by interviews with parents. Relationships between parents and minders often seemed to be difficult. Parents begrudged the fees, especially since they might well pay less for better service in a day nursery. Minders, on the other hand, often felt badly paid for the service they provided, and indeed it seemed that often the minder had little payment for her work when the cost of meals and other materials was deducted. Parents and minders were often in conflict about the amount of service to be provided – for example, the number and content of meals – and there were difficulties over keeping up payments. Such difficulties often led to disturbance in the care of the child through the development of negative attitudes in the minder, who might become careless and begrudge the child both physical and psychological care.

Money was a contributory factor to one of the most serious problems, the instability of the relationship between child and minder. Children were moved with disturbing frequency between minders, and nobody seemed able to control this. Parents and minder fall out, and the child is moved. Parents get behind in paying minders' fees, and one Monday morning the child 'disappears'. The mother loses her job and looks after the child at home while she seeks another one; then she finds another minder. Minders give up work, and the child has to move. There is absolutely no guarantee of continuity of relationship between the child and the mother-substitute: a disastrous situation for development.

In the time at our disposal we did not try to contact unregistered minders, which would, for obvious reasons, have been very difficult. Local-authority and nursery staffs, however, assured us that the situation was even worse here. Not only did the fact that they were unregistered imply that they were unsatisfactory in some way, although this might be only because of some deficiency in physical conditions – it also meant that they were uncontrolled. Certainly some of them minded too many children in quite unsatisfactory, or even dangerous, physical conditions. Certainly some of them were exploiting children and parents in an unconcerned way for gain. Lack of registration tended to impose secrecy so that children might be deprived of freedom, shut in, kept undesirably quiet. Local-authority nursing staffs were very alarmed about this situation but felt there was little they could do about it.

Finally one should, however, record the amount of concerned and excellent care that was given by another type of unregistered minder, often a member of the mother's family who lived in the home and cared for the child, in particular the devoted grandmothers of illegitimate children.

Interplay between nurseries and childminders may adversely affect children and their parents. A particularly disturbing feature is that parents may use childminders to defeat good principles being operated by local authorities through health visitors and nurseries. One could only approve the policy of not usually taking babies into nurseries before they were six months old, but parents defeated this by taking their babies to minders, or even putting them into residential foster care. By the time the baby came into the nursery at six months it might have been with several minders, be estranged from its mother and quite disturbed.

These parents were also likely to be the least concerned about their children and least careful about the quality of minding. The thirty-five-hour rule for working mothers also drove mothers who would have preferred nurseries to minders because not all mothers who wanted to have their children in day care wanted to work such long hours; a few did not work at all. Some mothers used both systems: nurseries in the daytime Monday to Friday, and minders who took over the babies from them in the evenings or weekends to free the mother to follow her own interests, in which her baby often had a relatively unimportant part.

Of the two systems, the nurseries certainly seem preferable in spite of the excellent care given by good minders, since nurseries are subject to control or influence and one can hope more easily to improve the quality of care in them.

TRAINING OF NURSERY NURSES

There appear to be problems in both the recruitment and the selection of student nursery nurses. Nursery-nurse training seemed to be attracting too high a proportion of young girls with personal problems who found it hard to cope not only with the work, but with the problems of life outside their work. The latter was especially difficult for provincial girls who were uprooted from familiar surroundings and often felt displaced and strange in London. This was a major source of concern for staff in training colleges. The students were coping with the personal and social problems of late adolescence with little in the way of a holding situation, since apparently no residential facilities were provided in the colleges.

Not enough seemed to be done to attract more mature women, particularly those who have reared children of their own and have warmth and experience to give other children. The few we met in the nurseries seemed to be able to give more appropriate care to the children on the whole than did the young girls. Attention would need to be given to their salaries and conditions of work, including allowing for part-time work. The possible detrimental effect of part-time staff on children would be eased if more of the children could themselves be part-time.

Students themselves were often dissatisfied with the content of the courses and felt that much of it was unhelpful or even irrelevant to the practical tasks and problems of the nurseries. This was true also of staff who were on refresher courses. They tended to be somewhat discontented and depressed about their work and wanted help with everyday problems and with their feeling that they were not giving adequate care to the children. They did not feel they got this help from the courses. Some of this discontent might, however, have been unfairly directed at the courses; it might more properly belong to conditions in the nurseries which did not provide effective on-the-job teaching for students, nor support for either students or staff.

Our own impression of the courses was that they were often ahead of nursery practice, but were still deficient in some ways. Only about 50 per cent of the course was given to child care, the rest to general education, some of which at least seemed of doubtful relevance for the work and not very interesting to the students. Of the 50 per cent time allotted to child care, most went to physical care and comparatively little to understanding the emotional life of the child, the significance for his development of his relationships or the meaning and handling of behavioural difficulties. No attention seemed to be given to the need to work with parents and try to sustain and develop the mother–child relationship.

Training also seemed to be based on some misunderstanding of the needs of the child, particularly the under-threes but also the three-to-fives in whole-day care. The orientation seemed to owe too much to the nursery school and consequently to place too much emphasis on play and creative activities as a means to keep the child busy and help him be (precociously) independent. Young children cannot do this all the time. They need time for quiet, unorganized interactions with adults, and staff need to be trained to manage this. Children need time for just messing about in activities that may be of great significance to them although not necessarily very comprehensible to adults. Nowhere in the course do students appear to be taught about the importance of such play and of respecting and understanding its meaning to the child. In other words, students are not taught how to understand and respond to the child's deeper needs – indeed, one might say they are taught how best to protect themselves against these needs.

This serves to introduce another point: that their training, in common with that of others, is too much based on conveying facts and does not give nearly enough opportunity for them to consider and explore their own observations and experiences with the help of teachers skilled in understanding both the students and the children. This has already been discussed earlier and we would like now to link it with the lack of effective liaison between colleges and nurseries that worried the staff of both, was detrimental to the students' learning and caused them great stress.

There was a gap between what was taught in the colleges and the usually more backward practice in the nurseries, which meant that the students could not practise what they were taught, inadequate as that might be. They might indeed have to negotiate between contradictory teaching and instructions from college and nursery staff and experienced considerable conflict and distress. Too much of the teaching seemed to be left to the colleges and not enough was done in the nurseries, where 'teaching' seemed to be almost entirely orders, instructions or suggestions about ongoing situations, with no time for relaxed, thoughtful explorations away from immediate practical tasks and problems.

Implicit in this situation was the fact discussed above: that students' shock and distress when confronting the nursery situation were neither adequately dealt with from the point of view of alleviating them, nor adequately mobilized in the teaching situation to increase their sensitivity and intuitive contact with children. The students thus too often became hard and insensitive, defended against awareness of children's needs.

We also had the feeling that the nursery-nurse training had, in common with other forms of nursing training, some imbalance between practical and theoretical work so that students spent too much time in practical work and had too little time and opportunity to withdraw and learn effectively from it. They made up too high a proportion of nursery staff and this precipitated them too quickly into too much responsibility, tending to make them recoil from it and not, in the long run, helping them to accept responsibility well. The students we saw were too often forced into an unreal split between themselves as students in college and themselves as nursery nurses coping pretty fully with difficult situations and with little immediately available teaching or support. Training also probably stopped too abruptly when the student was qualified. This is another way of repeating the point made above: that some support system is desirable for nursery nurses, and especially for recently qualified students.

To conclude: it was our impression that there was a good deal of discontent about the training within the system itself: uncertainty about the adequacy of its content; uneasiness about the stresses and strains of students; anxiety about the level of effective liaison between colleges and nurseries. This discontent was available to be mobilized to make changes if help were given about the direction of change and how to bring it about.

CONCLUSIONS

The main conclusions that emerged from this preliminary study were:

1. That separating the child under five from his mother (or mother-substitute) and putting him into all-day care, either in a day nursery or with a childminder, is to put him at considerable risk with regard to his social and psychological development.

For babies and very young children, any regular and lengthy separation from the mother is undesirable. Three-to-five-year-old children are still too young to be put in all-day care five days a week, but are able to tolerate more separation from their mothers and can benefit from up to a regular half-day in nursery or nursery school and from the activities there with other children.

2. That the present day-care system is defective in many ways in relation to the care of children under five. This is true both of local-authority nurseries and of the private sector, nurseries and childminders.

These conclusions suggest two main directions of action to reduce the developmental risk and to improve the prospects for the kinds of children most likely to use the day-care system:

(a) To try to reduce the numbers of children who actually enter the day-care system and the amount of time spent there by those who do.

(b) To improve the quality of day care for those who remain in the system.

Basically, reducing the numbers of children in the system and the length of time they spend there seems to resolve itself into the problem of how their mothers and families can be helped to become more able and willing to keep these children at home and care for them themselves. What community resources, therefore, could be mobilized in support of this operation? Since financial problems were a factor in sending mothers prematurely back to work, it seemed important to explore in more detail the possibilities of modifying the financial support system.

For example, one could raise the question of whether maternity benefit is sufficient or lasts long enough and what would be the possibility of modifying it. Or again, one might consider the payment of additional family allowances to mothers of children under five, or even under three, who stay out of employment in order to care for their children at home. In other words, we are proposing a search for some kind of non-degrading way of giving financial support to mothers to stay at home to look after their children.

It would also be important to review the way the authorities operate their financial policies: for example, should they help the mothers of young children to go out to work by giving them day-nursery places when, if a family income is genuinely too low, there are other means of supplementing it? It may also be mistaken kindness to be generous over day-nursery fees, since low fees may increase the propensity of a parent to put her children into day care. The methods of paying childminders and the fees paid to them would be included in such financial exploration.

Many potential day-care families need psychosocial support. One should, therefore, consider how all the services likely to be involved with these families should co-operate to support them, particularly the mothers, and help them to sustain and enjoy their relationship with their children – full-time if possible, certainly for part of every day until the child is five. Such action would need to start when the mother is pregnant and be continued as necessary in the years that follow. The services likely to be involved would include maternity and child welfare clinics, health visitors, local-authority social services and, very importantly, the day nurseries themselves.

The local employment situation also needs exploration to get information on the possibilities of part-time jobs for young mothers. Local employers and staff in local offices of the Department of Employment would be key people here.

Any action taken as above would need support from appropriate changes in attitudes to the relative importance of women looking after their own young children or going out to work and putting the children into day care. It would be important to explore not only how the attitude of the general public can be modified but – perhaps more importantly – how attitudes in professional people who work with these mothers could be modified where necessary so that they appreciate the hazards of day care and the importance of keeping very young children with their mothers as far as possible.

Whatever the success of measures taken to reduce the number of children in day care, many children will remain there, at least part-time. One must also consider, therefore, how day care itself can be improved. A reduction in the number of children in day care would of itself facilitate an improvement by making it possible to concentrate the children in the more effective parts of the system such as local-authority nurseries and the better-registered minders and by lessening pressures on parents to place children with unregistered minders.

The improvement of the day-care system falls into two parts: improvements in day nurseries, and improvements in the child-minding system.

We would suggest, as an approach to improving day nurseries, working with one or two nurseries to build a different model of how a nursery might operate. This would involve, for example, working with staff and students to modify their attitudes and skills, exploring how they can help the mother to sustain a relationship with her child, how they could more effectively help mothers themselves, optimum nursery hours for children, types of grouping, types of activity, and so on. These could be related also to considering nursery-nurse training, probably in collaboration with the college which trains the students for the nurseries in which work is being done. Finally, one should also consider the use by the nurseries of specialist services, both for the children and for staff support.

Regarding childminders, the main areas for further investigation seem to be selection, training and control. The question of control is closely linked to the method of employment and remuneration. There is also the question of how the childminder relates herself to other services for the benefit of the children and their parents.

To implement the kind of action-orientated investigation discussed above, it would seem that the most appropriate unit for work would be the local authority, since this is the smallest authority within which one could co-ordinate the activities of most of the services involved. The assistance of certain central government departments would also be necessary to ensure the co-operation of their local offices. The training college working with that authority would also need to be involved. Ideally, therefore, one would wish to seek the collaboration of a local authority in developing an improved and holistic approach within its area to the care of the under-fives.

However, it may be difficult to involve a local authority on such a scale, especially in view of the present situation regarding the reorganization of the social and medical services. If a smaller operation only were envisaged, then we would think it advisable to concentrate on the improvement of day care, working on the building of the nursery model and the modification of the childminding system.

POSTSCRIPT (1988)

Later, in 1975–9, another team from the Tavistock Institute, Alastair Bain and Lynn Barnett – a team to which I acted as consultant – picked up the findings of this report and explored the possibility of developing a new model of care. They successfully collaborated with a nursery and local authority to design a revised model of nursery care, more effective in meeting the children's needs, more effective in staff training and support and with better liaison with mothers and families. Later, Lynn Barnett worked in her local area in Devon to develop an even more advanced model of care, where a day nursery became a family centre. These studies are reported in *The Design of a Day Care System in a Nursery Setting for Children under Five* (Bain and Barnett, 1986).

A major problem remains, however. These developments show that on a small scale and with consultants working in an institution it is possible to change the model of care with benefit to staff and client alike. Note also the author's work in the Royal National Orthopaedic Hospital (Menzies Lyth, 1982; vol. 1, pp. 153–207). The painful and yet little-tackled issue is how one can transfer the successful model to the hundreds of other institutions of the same general kind: all day nurseries, all children's hospitals. There must be a way: we have not yet found it.

NOTES

1. 'A first report on the children', by Joyce Robertson; 'A working note on mothers of children in day nurseries', by Sheila M. Scott; and 'A working note on day-nursery staff', by Geraldine V. Gwynne (Menzies, Robertson, Scott and Gwynne, 1971).

2. The system of having the children in mixed age groups, infancy to five years.

3. Women who care for children during the day in their own homes and are paid by parents.

10 The aftermath of disaster: survival and loss*

ONE CANNOT DRAW a rigid distinction between the survivor and the bereaved. The bereaved feel themselves to be survivors of whatever caused the death of their loved one, even if they were never threatened by what killed him. The survivor of a disaster is also bereaved. Even if he has not lost known and loved people, he has been in the presence of the dead and dying, which cannot but affect him. Finally, he must mourn for something he has lost of himself: 'I am not the person I was: I will never be the same again.' The question, however, is whether in the end the survivor will be less of a person than before, a more disturbed person, or whether he can become more of a person, the disaster becoming a focus for growth. The outcome will depend on a number of factors: his own pre-disaster resources and those of his natural environment; family, colleagues and friends; the availability of professional help, if needed; and the nature and severity of the disaster.

When a disaster strikes, bereaved survivors include many different categories of people at varying distances from it. Some have been involved in the disaster and escape; some have narrowly escaped being there, such as staff who changed their shift and were not but 'should have been' on the *Herald of Free Enterprise* the day she sank; children who missed the Aberfan disaster because they were not at school that day.[1] There are people who feel responsible for 'sending others to their deaths',

*This paper is a slightly extended version of a paper with the same title given at a conference organized by the Tavistock Clinic, 13 June 1987.

such as staff responsible for duty rosters on the *Herald of Free Enterprise* or senior officers who order troops into battle. To some extent we tend to feel we are survivors when we hear of such disasters, suffering shock, horror and grief while yet finding reassurance and triumph from not actually being there, the more intense if we might have been there – almost – 'disasters I just missed': 'I was on that train the day before'; 'I had a friend who was there!'

What strikes one most about survivors really close to a major disaster is how complicated their reactions are. Their own and other people's views of them are fraught with apparent contradictions. The survivor is a victim – as much, though differently, as those who perish. I stress the 'victim' since people have a tendency to prefer the easier but less realistic view that the survivor is all right, he is lucky, he must be strong and competent to have survived when others perished, and so on. Bereavement gets more sympathy than survival.

The most frequently discussed aspect of the survivor is probably survivor guilt. This has many facets. The survivor feels guilty about being alive when others have perished. This is the more intense if the survivor feels he has, or actually has, done less than he might have done to help others, worse still if he has actually saved himself at their expense, pushed them out of the way of escape or manipulated selection for the gas chambers. Others perished instead of him, or even because of him. He feels guilty about abandoning people for whom he should have cared even if he could not really help, and about abandoning principles and attitudes that he formerly cherished and tried to live by.

Where there was warning of the disaster before it happened, survivors suffer terribly from guilt about not having taken more active steps to prevent it. It was known, and there had been complaints, that the Aberfan coal-tip was dangerous. It was known, and there had been complaints, that the method of operating the *Herald of Free Enterprise* was dangerous. It is all too human to turn a blind eye and hope it will never really happen, especially if one has tried to get something done and failed. However, one may have to pay the price in guilt afterwards.

The survivor suffers less from these reactions if he has been brave and self-sacrificing, has taken risks to help others, or is injured. Even then he may feel unworthy, cowardly and despicable. If he had been really brave, he would have died still fighting the disaster. He feels guilty that others died for him, even if they did not: 'There but for the grace of God go I.' He feels guilty about being lucky, about his triumph over the less lucky dead. Survivors may feel contaminated by death and the dead. Their close contact with death makes them awesome. They worry that people will not want to mix with them because of this. And there is evidence that people do really avoid mixing with bereaved survivors: for example, the multiply bereaved in the Bradford football fire complained that acquaintances did not even wave to them from across the street.

The survivor may feel he has been punished for some sin, usually consciously unknown but assuredly linked with primitive unconscious wishes and fantasies. For example, primitive world-destroying fantasies are easily connected with the truly devastating destruction at Hiroshima. Survivors indeed described the destruction in time and spatial terms which were exaggerated even beyond the truly awful destruction: annihilation of the whole world, of the whole of humanity, for generations to come, perhaps for ever. Deaths of close family in the Holocaust resonated with early death-wishes against parents and siblings.

The realization of these primitive wishes by methods resembling those in the primitive phantasies must have been horrific and terrifying – that is, by gas and burning which would symbolize the child's phantasy weapons, his anal and urethral attacks on people close to him. Such feelings were exacerbated by identification with the aggressors even if the survivors were not actually collaborators. By contrast with these people, the survivor may feel specially selected to be saved. Therefore he is privileged, one of 'God's chosen people'. He triumphs in this but at the same time has to justify his position by being especially good, moral, responsible, humanitarian.

Survivors are likely to experience an identity crisis: 'I am not the person I was, but who am I?' In the most severe disasters, few survivors are likely to escape a complete shattering of their pre-disaster personalities and identity. Notable are Hiroshima and the Holocaust, but something similar must happen to people near the epicentre of a severe earthquake. This effect stems from the shattering of the usually moderately safe, supportive and familiar external world, identified with a safe, supportive and familiar idea of a world inside oneself, the internal image of a mother safely nurturing the survivor and others. The experience is more devastating, it seems, when the disaster is the result of human action deliberately intended to destroy human beings, as at Hiroshima and in the Holocaust. Any view of humanity as relatively benign and trustworthy is destroyed as one experiences the 'inhuman' act of aggression, which, however, is also 'human' . . . What of oneself – can one be like the human/inhuman aggressor too? The survivor's view of himself is further shattered as he contemplates the aggressor's view of him as the 'subhuman' object of his aggression: valueless, bestial, dispensable in the aggressor's universe.

The shattering of the familiar external world shatters the internal world that gives identity. The survivor feels there is no containment, no functioning part of himself or others that can help him put himself together again. There is no source of safety and comfort, no source on which he can draw to help himself and others. He has lost his identification with nurturing internal images from whom he could derive the capacity to help others. It was apparently notable after the Holocaust that women survivors who had children were for the most part inadequate mothers.

Loss of identity is exacerbated by the loss – or temporary loss – of role, especially of roles linked with nurturing or being nurtured. It was extraordinarily difficult to maintain these roles in concentration camps. Hiroshima survivors were further devastated by being unable to sustain a traditional nurturing role by giving water to dying victims, water being a more than usually powerful symbol for life-giving in Japan (Lifton, 1968; Krystal, 1971). Returning British prisoners of war after World War II also illustrated this point. Prisoners returning from the Far East camps were anxiously awaited, since one supposed that because of the terrible conditions in these camps they would be in a dreadful state and hard to help. They were in fact in a better state than expected and in some ways in a better state than prisoners from the European camps. There were a number of reasons for this, one of which is relevant to our theme. In the European camps, officers and men were separated; they lost their roles and relationships to each other. The only official authority was the enemy. They came back with an understandable hostility to authority that was hard to modify so that authority and associated roles and role-relationships could once again be seen as potentially benign and nurturing. In the Far East camps, officers and men stayed together in their familiar relationship, nurturing and being nurtured, commanding and being commanded in a relatively benign authority which could confront the sadistic and destructive authority of the enemy.

Again on the theme of relationships: BBC television showed a moving account of a woman in the Bradford football fire and her role and relationship to her young son. She had left him to get herself a cup of tea when the fire broke out between them. She behaved realistically and sensibly when she heard her son call out to her. She in turn called out to her son not to try to come to her, which he could not have done, but to save himself by going out of the front of the stand away from her. Then the mother *forgot about her son* while she made her own escape. Once again it was realistic to do that while she concentrated on saving herself – the best thing she could then do for her son was to ensure her own survival. Both did survive, although the mother did suffer severe emotional after-effects through having temporarily abandoned her role as his mother and her normal relationship with him.

While working in the Royal National Orthopaedic Hospital (RNOH) to help improve the psychosocial care of the very young children there, we found, as others had found before us (Bowlby, 1969; Robertson, 1970), that an important safeguard was the presence of the mother. As far as hospital conditions allowed, she had to continue to carry on her normal role as his mother for the maximum benefit to accrue from her presence. For example, she must be the main authority over what happened to him, the person who did the main child-care tasks even when this meant she might have to learn new ways of doing things, like how to change nappies for a child in traction. She should continue to be a source of fun and joy, his first resource when in distress. It emerged that not only did the child benefit from this attempt to sustain the mother in her natural role, but so also did the mother. Mothers became more attached to their children, more confident and assured in their mothering. This contrasts dramatically with the distress of mothers who cannot be with their children in hospital and cannot sustain their role, which has a permanent damaging effect on their mothering (Menzies Lyth, 1982; vol. 1, pp. 153–207).

When identity is thus shattered and roles and role-relationships are disrupted, the survivor is faced with the need to provide himself with a new identity, since to be without an identity may leave him feeling too lost and confused. The danger is obvious – and is substantiated by studies of survivors – that an inappropriate, pathological identity may be adopted and become fixed. Lifton, discussing survivors of Hiroshima, describes how their immersion in the dead and dying, and the overwhelming effect of that, led to a powerful identification with the dead and to the development of a personality and lifestyle which could best be described as death-in-life (Lifton, 1968). Victims of the Holocaust show similar features, although the underlying dynamic is not identical. Years of lying low, not opposing the camp authorities openly, led to a similar death-in-life identity, feigning a kind of death in order to survive. On a different scale, a group of Maudsley Hospital and Tavistock Clinic psychotherapists, working with traumatic cases who had sought psychotherapy, found a similar dynamic. Clinical evidence suggested that the pre-traumatic identity had been rather shaky and the trauma was a final blow. The result was similar, however, to that for disaster survivors: the development of an inappropriate identity that failed as a container and inhibited really working through the trauma – an identity such as 'I am the girl who was raped'.

Identity as a survivor/victim is often reinforced by association and identification with others who have had similar experiences. This may give a sense of belongingness that they might not easily find in any group which did not share their experience – 'how could anyone else understand us?' They may feel unable to establish a belongingness to ordinary humanity again. But membership of such a group may in itself be quite a dead thing, lacking liveliness and meaning, death-in-life. Such mutual identity may also give survivors a feeling of being special and superior, of belonging to a unique group, an attempt to cope with awful feelings of emptiness and to justify demands on society for special care.

A feature that contributes to the death-in-life syndrome but has been less noticed in the literature is another kind of relationship with the dead. Guilt is much discussed. Less is said about fear of the dead, a more paranoid reaction: for even when the real situation justifies intense anxiety, paranoid fears remain. Particularly intense paranoid fears are aroused when the dead have died violently, when they have disappeared completely as at Hiroshima, in the Holocaust, and in the case of the 'disappeared' in Argentina; when their bodies and souls have not been put to rest by culturally appropriate methods and ritual. They are the 'homeless dead' who continue to walk the earth and haunt the living. In the primitive unconscious, the dead are not really dead; they remain aware of their state and continue to have ordinary human feelings: in particular to be envious and resentful, possibly vengeful, towards the living. Placation and appeasement are the order of the day: death-in-life will not provoke the dead as living a full life would.

A final point about the survivor syndrome: it feels as though the disaster makes a complete break with all one has known before; one's previous experience, one's proven ways of coping both practically and emotionally. New ways of coping may be developed which are useful in the immediate situation – for example, what Lifton describes as a 'psychic closing off' which may help the victim to develop a state of numbness which enables him to hold total shock, terror and panic at bay (Lifton, 1968). This makes it possible to cope with the situation in some way and facilitates survival. The victim can be unaware of the profound threat to his sense of invulnerability, immortality and faith in the structure of human existence. Particularly notable in concentration-camp victims is what one might call constructive paranoia: a highly developed awareness and alertness, a view of the world as highly dangerous and of people, especially authority, as hostile – indeed, murderous. This was evident to a lesser degree in the prisoners of war returning from Europe. If this is not too powerful it can indeed support a degree of fighting back which sustains life and self-respect.

The danger is obvious. These defences, constructive and possibly life-saving in the disaster situation, become pathological if they continue to function when the survivor is back in ordinary life. They lead to inappropriate roles and relationships with others, particularly authorities and helpers who, they feel, cannot be trusted. This was the case with prisoners of war returning from Europe. Above all, the continued use of such primitive defences inhibits or prevents the working through of the disaster experience and the building of a more healthy new personality and way of life. The disaster literature highlights those difficulties in working through the experiences: for example, the vividness of memories of the disaster experience and the continuation over years of vivid and unchanging nightmares. Memories are ready to be re-evoked in all their original power by current events that literally or symbolically resemble them. Records of Holocaust victims show that breakdown may occur after years of apparently healthy, if restricted life, when some such event occurs – for example, a small domestic fire may revive the full horror of the gas chambers.

The survivor, then, has a difficult and complicated task to accomplish in working through those complex feelings and relating to others who also have complex feelings about his situation. I would like now to consider what resources may be available to help him should he need or want them.

Suggestions have been made that a National Disaster Centre should be established such as already exists in other countries. This would have some obvious benefits – particularly, I think, in making available people experienced in the massive organizational problems involved in coping with major disasters and in backing up local services. However, a National Disaster Centre would have some dangers, notably a danger common in our society that the problem is 'split off' from society in general and lodged in a 'special' institution along with a considerable part of the responsibility for dealing with it. This allows other people to opt out and 'forget' about it. These institutions have been described as 'limbo institutions' (Miller and Gwynne, 1972): hospitals for the insane or homes for the old or the chronically disabled. An NDC risks becoming such a limbo institution; everything might be left to it, including things it could not really do such as providing enough local helpers quickly. If such people do not already exist, they cannot be produced quickly. I will discuss this point below.

Features of such opting out and forgetting are only too obvious in relation to disasters and survivors. How long do we actually remember disasters as against suffering immediate acute shock and horror and perhaps making a quick contribution to the disaster fund? Then we forget! Alternatively, how many of the severe disasters of, say, the last ten years does the average person remember? The disaster, the victims and the survivors are forgotten long before physical or emotional recovery can possibly be achieved. Such forgetting must add to the pain of survivors and helpers alike when the world abandons them.

This is part and parcel of the way people ignore or at least inadequately recognize signs of imminent disaster and of our capacity to deny or ignore ongoing disasters in our midst – unless, that is, we happen to be involved in them as victims, survivors, police, helpers or even aggressors. We who were alive then knew about the beginnings of the Holocaust. Typically, we denied its existence or at least what it meant to the victims and what it might lead to. We are no different today. Large- and small-scale disasters are denied or our awareness of their meaning softened to the point where we can bear it and do not feel impelled to do anything about the disaster. Sometimes we could not do much about it anyway, which makes awareness even more unbearable or denial more powerful.

I do not propose to range over the whole gamut of ongoing world disasters, but only to contemplate those that are currently going on literally in our midst and are partly or completely ignored unless some scandal or crime brings them forcibly to our notice – as we saw in Cleveland in 1987 in relation to child sexual abuse. Afterwards we quickly forget again. Some of these disasters or disaster areas are institutional and fairly large in scale. We too have our ghettos and concentration camps where people who shock and distress us are shut up and forgotten. For example, many thousands of small children are cared for all day, every weekday, in day nurseries although there is evidence that day nurseries as they are usually run constitute a hazard to the psychosocial development of the children (Menzies, ch. 9 above; Menzies, Robertson, Scott and Gwynne, 1971; Bain and Barnett, 1986). Institutions that care for the aged often operate in such a way as to accelerate the psychosocial deterioration of the residents. One could make a long, long list of such institutions with their forgotten people. In addition, there are individual and family disasters which, however, are repeated hundreds or thousands of times: non-accidental injury, broken marriages, the unemployed.

And there is death. Sooner or later this affects us all, as bereaved and ultimately when we die ourselves. Death too is in a sense in limbo. To mention death or the dead is almost taboo. It is an uneasy joke that the Victorians could talk about death but not sex, while current society can talk about sex but not death. One could perhaps see the emphasis on sex now as a massive communal defence in a society where death or the threat of death – indeed, annihilation – is too much present. The dreadful thing is that this communal attitude to death makes society and individuals more vulnerable to its effects, since it inhibits the process of mourning and recovery.

The victims of these disasters are ubiquitous in our society, appearing in all kinds of institutions in addition to those specifically designed to deal with them. Thousands of children from disturbed homes, sexually or otherwise abused children, children from day nurseries, are in ordinary schools. They need help and may not get it except in their schools. How far could or should such institutions and those responsible for running them take on some of the burden of helping with the disasters that come within their boundaries, even if this may not be their primary task? They seem to do this to a very limited extent at present and accept little responsibility for the disasters within their boundaries. I recently heard of two schools whose heads had died in post. These deaths were dealt with – *not* dealt with – by a simple announcement to the pupils. Sometimes teachers have instructed children not to talk among themselves about distressing events like the death of another child. Hospitals are notoriously bad at dealing with the distress of patients and relatives, and especially with death. One need hardly elaborate. Such institutions also often follow the practice of splitting off problems to specialists like school counsellors or bereavement counsellors so that other people are freed of the responsibility for the painful task. This often means that help is restricted to the severely disturbed and others in less need get nothing.

My point in making these comments is not to criticize the inadequacies of these institutions in caring for clients involved in ongoing disasters. Nor is it only to draw attention to the need to pay more attention to the people involved in the disasters in our midst and help them more effectively. It is, rather, to draw attention to the fact that in such institutions there is a large reservoir of people with potentially good capacity to deal with disasters if only they could be helped to develop their skills and insights and to become more aware. In other words, I am postulating that if people were better able to cope with the chronic disasters in their midst, there would be many more people available and able to help with a major acute disaster should it occur. As things are, following a disaster such as the *Herald of Free Enterprise* or the Bradford football fire there is a terrible dearth of helpers and the burden on available helpers becomes well-nigh intolerable. The burden in theory and practice could be better spread.

I am not suggesting that it would be easy to achieve such a situation. It would mean a change in society's relation with death: an increased capacity to confront it, a recognition that talking about death, the dead and the dying is actually helpful in furthering mourning and recovery even if it is painful and distressing. It would also mean dealing with widespread views that it is bad to talk about such things, and the best thing is to hush them up, turn a blind eye – 'least said, soonest mended'. The recently bereaved do not at the time necessarily share that view and may feel ostracized, rejected and very lonely. But that does not necessarily stop them behaving like that in their turn with other mourners. Evidence that talking things out is therapeutic does not seem to have penetrated too far beyond the specialists.

Another area of attack on the problem is through change in the institutions – especially, but not only, those which in themselves are disaster areas. It is possible to achieve such changes although it is quite complex, especially if one needs to do it on a large scale. Central to the problem is the need for attitude change in staff, increased recognition of the problems in their clientele, increased understanding of the dynamics of the problems and increased ability and willingness to confront them. This may mean considerable change in institutions like hospitals and day nurseries, where a significant part of the basis for staff–client relations has been a set of defences protecting staff from the impact on them of clients and their problems (Menzies, 1970; vol. 1, pp. 43–85). It can, however, be done.

This was an essential feature of the work done by the Tavistock Institute in the RNOH. The relation between staff and patients and families changed significantly as staff became more able to be fully aware of the distress patients and families suffered and of the reverberations of this in themselves. Staff came to regard confronting these feelings and working openly with them as an essential part of their role. The relief and support this gave to patients and families cannot be exaggerated. The change was vividly demonstrated when two child patients died. The death of children is rare in orthopaedic hospitals – only these two died in the four years of our work there. But both died in the same week. The effect was devastating, but also very interesting. The staff working with the Tavistock Institute took it for granted that this was something to be discussed and worked with openly. They talked among themselves and with us to help deal with their own distress and consider how best to help others. Then they talked with the families of all the patients and with the verbal children. Other parts of the hospital behaved in a more conventional way: stiff upper lips, no crying, no talking, business as usual, competence and efficiency as a means of reassuring themselves and others. Feelings between the supporters of the two approaches became quite heated.

Bain and Barnett achieved similar results in the day nursery where they worked (Bain and Barnett, 1986): greater awareness among staff of the terribly distressing problems among children and parents, more intuitive appreciation of the children's needs, greater willingness and ability to confront them and work them through so that they could give more effective help to both parents and children. The results of a follow-up study of the children cared for under the changed system were encouraging in relation to the initial objective of providing a better setting for children's psychosocial development.

But central to our present theme is that these studies developed the capacity and willingness of staff to deal with disaster in miniature. There is no reason to doubt that their capacity to help in a major disaster would also have been increased. To achieve the result on a larger scale would probably require, among other things, a considerable change in the training of the professions concerned, help to develop new attitudes to confronting problems with clients, and a broadening of the concept of their professional roles to encompass a wider view of the care of clients – care which would include concern with problems beyond the narrower task of teaching, nursing, or whatever.

Such an increase in the number of helpers potentially available in a major disaster has advantages beyond numbers and the spreading of the load. These helpers would be local and know local circumstances and people. They would already be known to the local people and in touch with them in the normal course of their work. Being already known is of the greatest importance. In moments of great stress, including survival and bereavement, it is hard to make contact with and trust a stranger. It can require quite a lot of energy when people do not have much to spare. It can feel like an intrusion rather than help. Even more important, perhaps, is that people maintain contact with the helpers for 'normal' reasons: a child goes to a nursery or school as usual, a hospital patient is in contact with the nurses already, a patient goes to his doctor for a routine check-up, a parishioner 'bumps into' the vicar as though by chance. There is no 'thing' about going specially for help. Of course, it is essential that the helper should recognize the new dimension in the relationship and work with the reactions to the disaster. People do not come specially, but they do have special needs to be met.

In a disaster situation all survivors would benefit from help, though some need it more than others. It is important, therefore, that it should be available to all and easily accessible. It may, indeed, be important that an approach for help need not be openly made but can be disguised within another existing helping relationship. At the RNOH, the hospital initially suggested that families should be assessed before admission so that special help could be provided for the most disturbed. We did not agree, on the grounds that in such circumstances all families are disturbed – a normal reaction to abnormal circumstances. Singling out 'specially disturbed families' might lead to self-fulfilling prophecies and actually increase their disturbance. On the other hand, families suffering only 'normal' disturbance might be neglected when they too needed help. So help should be available informally to everyone in the ordinary course of the work with them. This meant it had to be provided by all, not only by specialists like social workers. It had to come especially from those people most constantly in contact with patients and families – that is the nurses, who could supply it while carrying out their ordinary nursing duties. The nurses learned and deployed increased insights and skills with all patients and families.

Locally based and fairly ubiquitous helpers also have the inestimable advantage that they can often make contact quickly and without special effort from the client – as soon, that is, as their normal relationship is taken up again. An early approach to working through the aftermath of the disaster has tremendous advantages, yet it cannot easily be made on purpose, as it were, without the dangers of people feeling they are abnormal, inadequate or psychiatrically ill. Helpers who can make contact early are in a good position to detect people who may in fact need more help than they themselves can provide and direct their clients to where they may find it. Such tactics may well alleviate the problems that are a feature of so many disasters: the long-drawn-out nature of the ensuing problems if help is not given.

People do not recover but continue for many years to have the kind of reaction described above.

It is too late to think of training such helpers after disaster has struck. However, the severe stresses and strains, the degree of horrors and grief are likely to give rise to a temporary need for support for them, someone with whom they in turn can share and work through their feelings, to relieve the awful burden of what they have to hear and what it arouses in them. The nursery nurses in the RNOH had this kind of back-up all the time from the ward sister, the social worker and the Tavistock team, and it is doubtful if they could have sustained their role without it. People from outside the disaster area can be of great help in this way, especially in having a little more distance from the horror.

CONCLUSION

This paper touches mainly on one aspect of a complex and difficult topic. From what I have said, however, there may be a glimmer of hope that the aftermath of disaster need not be all negative. It is possible for survivors to grow and mature from their experiences, however many do not succeed in doing so. With better and more immediate help, more of them could certainly recover. This was true for the children who were in the care system developed at the RNOH. They showed no signs of the disaster suffered under other systems of care as described by James Robertson (Robertson, 1970). Instead, they showed every sign of developing normally. As a bonus, their mothers often matured from the 'disaster' of having physically damaged or deformed children. They were more strongly attached, more assured and confident in their mothering. The complex and difficult task this paper suggests would be to develop more effective help with the disasters in our midst, which would in turn increase the effectiveness of community resources to help when a major disaster hits.

NOTE

1. A passenger ferry, *Herald of Free Enterprise*, sank outside Zeebrugge harbour, Belgium, in 1987. A coal-tip in the mining town of Aberfan, South Wales, collapsed in 1968, burying many schoolchildren alive. Bradford football stadium was engulfed in fire during a match in 1985.

The writings of Isabel Menzies Lyth

All works are published in London unless otherwise indicated.

I.M.L. vol. 1 = *Containing Anxiety in Institutions: Selected Essays*, volume 1, by Isabel Menzies Lyth, Free Association Books, 1988.

(1939) 'The authoritarian element in wage-distribution'. Unpublished MA thesis, St Andrews University.

(1947) (with J.D. Sutherland) 'Two industrial projects', *J. Social Issues* 3, 2: 51–8.

(1948) 'Psychological aspects of joint consultation', in *Industrial Welfare Society: Joint Consultation. A Symposium*. Industrial Welfare Society, pp. 13–19.

(1949) 'Factors affecting family breakdown in urban communities. A preliminary study leading to the establishment of two pilot Family Discussion Bureaux', *Human Relations* 2: 363–73; this vol. pp. oo–oo.

(1949) (with Enid Eichholz and A.T.M. Wilson) 'Report of the marriage welfare sub-committee of the family welfare association', *Social Work*, January.

(1950) 'The jute industry in Great Britain', in *Chambers's Encyclopaedia* (1959), vol. 8. George Newnes.

(1951) *Technical Report. World Health Organization: Working Conference for Public Health Nurses* (Noordwijk, The Netherlands, October 1950). Tavistock Institute of Human Relations.

(1951) (with E. Anstey) *Staff Reporting*. Allen & Unwin.

(1959) 'A case study in the functioning of social systems as a defence against anxiety: a report on a study of the nursing service of a general hospital', *Human Relations* 13: 95–121. Reprinted Tavistock, 1961. Later published as *The Functioning of Social Systems as a Defence against Anxiety*. Tavistock Institute of Human Relations Pamphlet, no. 3, 1970; *I.M.L.* vol. 1, pp. 43–85.

(1960) 'Nurses under stress', *International Nursing Review* 7, 6: 9–16. Also published in *Nursing Times*, 1961, 57: 141–2, 173–4, 206–7; *I.M.L.* vol.

1, pp. 100–14.

(1960) (with C. Sofer) 'Problems and opportunities in inferring attitudes', in Market Research Society: *Attitude Scaling*. (MRS Publication no. 4.) Oakwood, pp. 35–47.

(1963) *Mental Health Services at the Centre de Santé Publique at Soissons, France*. Report to the World Health Organization. Tavistock Institute of Human Relations.

(1963) 'Communication and counselling', *Occup. Health* 15, 3: 146–53.

(1965) 'Some mutual interactions between organizations and their members'. Paper read at the Sixth International Congress of Psychotherapy, London, 1964. *Psychotherapy and Psychosomatics* 13: 194–200.

(1965) 'A note on driving and road accidents (including a critical evaluation of the Ministry of Transport's Christmas 1964 poster campaign)'. British Safety Council. (See this vol., ch. 6, pp. 124–41: 'The driver's dilemma'.)

(1966) 'Drinking and driving. A note on drivers' reactions to the proposed Bill making it an offence to drive with a blood-alcohol concentration above a prescribed limit.' British Safety Council. (See this vol., ch. 6, pp. 124–41: 'The driver's dilemma'.)

(1967) 'Some social and psychological aspects of road safety'. Tavistock Institute of Human Relations. (See this vol., ch. 6, pp. 124–41: 'The driver's dilemma'.)

(1968) 'A study of the interaction between Epsom and the five mental hospitals adjoining it'. Report to the South West Metropolitan Hospital Board. Tavistock Institute of Human Relations (this vol., pp. 191–214).

(1969) 'The motorcycle: growing up on two wheels', in H.S. Klein, ed. *Sexuality and Aggression in Maturation*. Baillière, Tindall and Cassell, pp. 37–49; this vol., pp. 142–57.

(1969) 'Some methodological notes on a hospital study', in S.H. Foulkes and G.S. Prince, eds *Psychiatry in a Changing Society*. Tavistock, pp. 99–113; *I.M.L.* vol. 1, pp. 115–29.

(1970) 'Psychosocial aspects of eating'. Paper read at the 13th Annual Conference of the Society for Psychosomatic Research, London, 1969, *J. Psychosom. Res.* 14: 223–7; this vol., pp. 61–7.

(1971) (with Geraldine Gwynne, Joyce Robertson and Sheila Scott) 'An action research study of the day care of children under five'. Tavistock Institute of Human Relations; this vol., pp. 215–48.

(1975) 'Thoughts on the maternal role in contemporary society', *Journal of Child Psychotherapy* 4, 1: 5–14; *I.M.L.* vol. 1, pp. 208–21.

(1975) 'A case study in the functioning of social systems as a defence against anxiety', in A.D. Colman and W.H. Bexton, eds *Group Relations Readers*. Sausalito, CA: Grex, pp. 281–312.

(1976) 'Interactions between organizations and their members', *Architectural Design* 46: 88–9.

(1978) 'Young children in long-stay hospitals', *Midwife, Health Visitor and Community Nurse* 14: 308–10.

(1978) 'The emotional development of the child: attachment, dependency and independence'. Unpublished paper, privately circulated by the National Association for the Welfare of Children in Hospital.

(1979) 'Staff support systems: task and anti-task in adolescent institutions', in R.D. Hinshelwood and N.P. Manning, eds *Therapeutic Communities: Reflections and Progress*. Routledge & Kegan Paul, pp. 197–207; *I.M.L.* vol. 1, pp. 222–35.

(1980) 'Bion's contribution to thinking about groups'. Paper read at the memorial meeting for W.R. Bion, British Psycho-Analytical Society, 20 February 1980; *Int. Rev. Psycho-Anal.* 8, 3, 1981: 8–11; also in J.S. Grotstein, ed. *Do I Dare Disturb the Universe? A Memorial to Wilfred R. Bion*. Beverly Hills, CA: Caesura, 1981, pp. 661–5; this vol., pp. 19–25.

(1980) (with A. Bain) 'Some current attitudes towards the care of the young child'. Paper read at the Tavistock Clinic Diamond Jubilee.

(1982) 'The psychological welfare of children making long stays in hospital: an experience in the art of the possible'. Tavistock Institute of Human Relations Occasional Paper no. 3; *I.M.L.* vol. 1, pp. 153–207.

(1982) (with Tim Dartington and Gianna Henry) 'The psychological welfare of young children making long stays in hospital'. Final report to the Department of Health and Social Security. Tavistock Institute of Human Relations; vol. 1, pp. 153–207.

(1985) 'The development of the self in children in institutions', *Journal of Child Psychotherapy*, 11, 2: 49–64; *I.M.L.* vol. 1, pp. 236–58.

(1988) *Containing Anxiety in Institutions: Selected Essays*, vol. 1. Free Association Books:

1. Reflections on my work:
   Isabel Menzies Lyth in conversation with Ann Scott and Robert M. Young: pp. 1–42.

2. The functioning of social systems as a defence against anxiety (1959, 1961 [1961b], 1970)
   A report on a study of the nursing service of a general hospital: pp. 43–85.
   Responses to 'The functioning of social systems': Defence mechanisms in nursing: a review by a Registered Mental Nurse: pp. 89–94.
   Letter from Isabel E.P. Menzies to *Nursing Times*: pp. 95–7.
   Letter from 'Another RMN', *Nursing Times*: pp. 98–9.

3. Nurses under stress (1961 [1961a]):
   I *Nursing Times*, 3 February: pp. 100–4;

II *Nursing Times*, 10 February: pp. 105–8;

III *Nursing Times*, 17 February: pp. 109–14.

4. Some methodological notes on a hospital study (1969): pp. 115–29.

5. Action research in a long-stay hospital: Two papers (1973, 1982, revised 1987): pp. 130–2.

    I Action research in a long-stay hospital: pp. 133–52;

    II The psychological welfare of children making long stays in hospital: an experience in the art of the possible: pp. 153–207.

6. Thoughts on the maternal role in contemporary society (1975): pp. 208–21.

7. Staff support systems: task and anti-task in adolescent institutions (1979): pp. 222–35.

8. The development of the self in children in institutions (1985): pp. 236–58.

Bibliography

All works are published in London unless otherwise indicated.
I.M.L. vol. 1 = *Containing Anxiety in Institutions: Selected Essays*, volume 1, by Isabel Menzies Lyth, Free Association Books, 1988.

Almansi, R.J. (1986) 'Review of Edwin R. Wallace, *Freud and Anthropology*, Psychological Issues Monograph 55', *J. Amer. Psychoanal. Assn* 34: 725–8.

Bain, A. (1982) *The Baric Experiment: The Design of Jobs and Organization for the Expression and Growth of Human Capacity*. Tavistock Institute of Human Relations Occasional Paper no. 4.

Bain A. and Barnett, L. (1986) *The Design of a Day Care System in a Nursery Setting for Children under Five*. Tavistock Institute of Human Relations Occasional Paper no. 8.

Bernton, H.S. (1952) 'Food allergy with special reference to corn and refined corn derivatives', *Ann. Intern. Med.* 36: 177–85.

Bion, W.R. (1948–51) 'Experiences in groups', in *Human Relations*, vols I–IV.

—— (1952) 'Group dynamics: a re-view', *Int. J. Psycho-Anal.* 33. Also in Klein, Heimann and Money-Kyrle, eds (1955), pp. 440–77.

—— (1961) *Experiences in Groups, and Other Papers*. Tavistock and New York: Basic.

—— (1970) *Attention and Interpretation*. Tavistock.

—— (1979) *A Memoir of the Future*, book three, *The Dawn of Oblivion*. Perth: Clunie.

Bowlby, J. (1969) *Attachment and Loss*, vol. 1, *Attachment*. Hogarth.

Brosin, H.W. (1953) 'The psychology of overeating', *New Eng. J. Med.* 248: 974–5.

—— (1955) 'The psychology of appetite', in M.G. Wohl and R.S. Goodhart, *Modern Nutrition in Health and Disease*. Philadelphia, PA: Lea & Febiger, pp. 76–89.

Bruch, H. (1961) 'Transformation of oral impulses in eating disorders',

Psychiatric Quarterly 35: 458–81.

Fenichel, O. (1946) *The Psycho-Analytic Theory of Neurosis.* Routledge & Kegan Paul.

Foulkes, S.H. (1948) *Introduction to Group-Analytic Psychotherapy.* Heinemann.

—— (1964) *Therapeutic Group Analysis.* George Allen & Unwin.

Freud, S. (1911–15) *Papers on Technique.* in James Strachey, ed. *The Standard Edition of the Complete Psychological Works of Sigmund Freud,* 24 vols. Hogarth, 1953–73, vol. 12, pp. 85–173.

—— (1913) *Totem and Taboo. S.E.* 13.

HMSO (1956) *Domestic Food Consumption,* p. 2.

—— (1959) *The Mental Health Act.*

Hopkins, J. (1988) 'Facilitating the development of intimacy between nurses and infants in day nurseries', *Early Child Development and Care,* 33: 99–111.

Janis, I.L. (1958) *Psychological Stress: Psychoanalytic and Behavioural Studies of Surgical Patients.* Chapman & Hall.

Jaques, E. (1955) 'Social systems as a defence against persecutory and depressive anxiety', in Klein, Heimann and Money-Kyrle, eds (1955), pp. 478–98.

Klein, M. (1957) *Envy and Gratitude: A Study of Unconscious Sources.* Tavistock.

—— (1963) 'Our adult world and its roots in infancy', in M. Klein, ed. *Our Adult World and Other Essays.* Heinemann Medical.

Klein, M., Heimann, P. and Money-Kyrle, R. eds (1955) *New Directions in Psycho-Analysis.* Tavistock and New York: Basic.

Klein, S.H., ed. (1969) *Sexuality and Aggression in Maturation: New Facets.* Baillière Tindall and Cassell and The Institute of Psycho-Analysis.

Krystal, H., ed. (1971) *Massive Psychic Trauma.* New York: International Universities Press.

Lewin, K. (1935) *Dynamic Theory of Personality.* New York/London: McGraw-Hill.

—— (1943) 'Forces behind food habits and methods of change', in *The Problem of Changing Food Habits.* Committee on Food Habits, National Research Council, NRC Bull. 108. Washington DC.

Lifton, R.J. (1968) *Death in Life – Survivors of Hiroshima.* New York: Random.

Menzies, I.E.P. (1959, 1961, 1970a) 'The functioning of social systems as a defence against anxiety', *Human Relations* (1959) 13: 95–121. Also printed as Tavistock Institute of Human Relations Pamphlet, no. 3; *I.M.L.* vol. 1, pp. 43–85.

—— (1970b) 'Psychosocial aspects of eating', *J. of Psychosomatic Medicine*

14, 3: 223–7. This volume, pp. oo–oo.

—— (1971) 'A general view of the day care of children under five', this volume, pp. oo–oo.

Menzies, I.E.P., Robertson, Joyce, Scott, S.M. and Gwynne, G. (1971) 'An action research study of the day care of children under five'. Tavistock Institute of Human Relations, unpublished.

Menzies Lyth, I. (1982) 'The psychological welfare of children making long stays in hospital: an experience in the art of the possible'. Tavistock Institute of Human Relations Occasional Paper no. 3; *I.M.L.* vol. 1, pp. 153–207.

—— (1985) 'The development of the self in children in institutions', *J. of Ch. Psychother.* 2, 2; *I.M.L.* vol. 1, pp. 236–58.

Miller, E. and Gwynne, G. (1972) *A Life Apart*. Tavistock.

Pennington, A.W. (1953) 'A reorientation in obesity', *New Eng. J. Med.* 23.

Pyke, M. (1969) *Food and Society*. Murray.

Randolph, T.G. (1947) 'Masked food allergy in the development and persistence of obesity', *J. Lab. Clin. Med.* 32. Also in *Proc. Cent. Soc. Clin. Res.* 20: 85.

—— (1948) 'Food allergy', *Med. Clins. N. Am.* 32: 245–63.

—— (1956) 'The descriptive features of food addiction', *Quart. J. Stud. Alcohol* 17.

Rice, A.K. (1965) *Learning for Leadership*. Tavistock.

Robertson, James (1970) *Young Children in Hospital*. Tavistock.

Robertson, James and Robertson, Joyce (1969) Film: *Young Children in Brief Separation. John, 17 months: For Nine Days in a Residential Nursery*. 16 mm: sound: 45 mins. Concord Films Council and New York: New York University Film Library.

Rowe, A.H. (1928) 'Food allergy: its manifestations, diagnosis and treatment', *J. Am. Med. Ass.* 91: 1623–31.

Stack, Mary (1988) 'Very super saturated', *Guardian*, 14 May 1988.

Trist, E.L. and Bamforth, K. W. (1951) 'Some social and psychological consequences of the longwall method of coal-getting', *Human Relations* 4: 3–38.

Index